AUSTRALIA
A Nation of Immigrants

A colourful gathering of Australians in the national dress of their former home countries. (Australian Picture Library)

AUSTRALIA
A Nation of Immigrants

TIM DARE

CHILD & ASSOCIATES
AN ALL-AUSTRALIAN PUBLISHER

For Jolyon Dare

Originally published in 1985 as *Australians: Making a Great Nation,* by Child & Henry Publishing Pty Ltd and Western Plains Publishers

Published by
Child & Associates Publishing Pty Ltd,
5 Skyline Place, Frenchs Forest, NSW,
Australia, 2086
A wholly owned Australian publishing company
This book has been edited and designed in Australia by the Publisher
This edition, revised and reformatted, 1988
Text by Tim Dare
© Tim Dare 1985, 1988
Printed in Australia by The Griffin Press
Typeset by Deblaere Typesetting Pty Ltd

National Library of Australia Cataloguing-in-Publication Data

Dare, Tim.
  Australia, a nation of immigrants.

  Includes index.
  ISBN 086777 021 X.

  1. Pluralism (Social sciences) – Australia – History. 2. Minorities – Australia – History. 3. Social interaction – Australia – History. 4. Australia – Foreign population – History. 5. Australia – Emigration and immigration – History. I. Title. II. Title: Australians making a great nation.

305.8'00994

Unless otherwise credited, all illustrations have been supplied by courtesy of the National Library of Australia, Canberra, ACT.

Acknowledgements

The author wishes to thank those senior officers of the Department of Immigration and Ethnic Affairs, now retired, who gave invaluable assistance and direction during the preparation of this book. He also wishes to thank *Time* magazine for permission to reproduce material quoted on page 195.

  The author also wishes to record his appreciation of the invaluable assistance of B. C. Ducker (MA Cantab.) in evaluation of historical trends.

The publishers wish to acknowledge the inspiration and assistance given by Al Grassby during his time as Commissioner for Community Relations.

Contents

AUSTRALIAN NATIVES
PUBLISHED 1789.

CHAPTER 1

The First Australians

IN 1982 AN ARCHAEOLOGICAL consultant, Mr Bob Pearce, made an amazing discovery of broken stone implements in a claybed near the banks of the upper Swan River, north of Perth. The fragments were uncovered by accident, and sent, almost as a matter of routine, to Sydney University for carbon dating. As recently as the middle of this century archaeologists believed that man arrived in Australia 25 000 years ago, and this was enough to make him a very old citizen of planet Earth. He was thus a subject of curiosity. He had arrived in Australia when the last Ice Age was nearing its peak and the frozen wastes had sucked so much water out of the sea that the level of the oceans fell to the point where much of the shallower seabed was exposed. This would have made migration much easier than when the oceans had been high. The drop in sea-level had

An early engraving of Aboriginal tribesmen.

exposed hitherto submerged parts of the earth that could thus be used as stepping stones.

Archaeologists had long known that the first Australians arrived thousands of years ago, but where they had come from, and how, had been a mystery. It had been assumed that they could not have reached these shores in the flimsy bark canoes that early modern man used. Not unless they had the benefit of stepping stones.

For how long had the stepping stones been available to those early adventurers? The Ice Age began, slowly, 100 000 years ago: it was safe to assume that man arrived when the oceans were at or near their lowest level. But archaeologists have been obliged to alter their estimates since traces of habitation were dated at between 35 000 and 38 000 years, at Lake Mungo in New South Wales. As the first Australians had almost certainly arrived in the north and worked their way southwards, this meant the first landfall must

An early artist's impression of an Aboriginal tribal ceremony. European artists found it very difficult to portray Australian Aborigines accurately.

have been about 40 000 years ago. The early men would have moved slowly and only when they needed to. Migration to the south of Australia could have taken hundreds, or even thousands of years.

Furthermore, although there have been various theories about the directions in which the pioneer Australians spread, it was usually accepted that they reached the west coast last. The oldest traces of mankind there – before Bob Pearce's find – had been dated at 21 000 years BP (Before Present). They had been found in the Pilbara.

Bob Pearce's find, when carbon dated, turned in the remarkable age of 38 000 years BP. That shook existing theories so much that archaeologists have been forced to revise their thinking a great deal about the earliest Australians. As of late 1983, archaeologists were working on the theory that man first set foot on Austra-

lian soil somewhere between 50 000 and 53 000 years ago. In the space of a few years, the estimated span of the occupation of Australia has therefore doubled. Fifty thousand years, in terms of human life, is a mind-boggling figure, and does not mean much to the average person accustomed to thinking back no further than the period of white settlement of the continent. To put the span in its full perspective, it means that Aborigines have inhabited Australia for 250 times longer than whites. The Aborigines have been here for more than 2000 generations, compared with 8 generations of whites. Put another way, the white man has been part of Australia for only 0.4 per cent of the entire period of human occupation of the continent. The proportion will diminish, of course, if older finds are made. It now seems possible that man may have arrived much earlier even than

50 000 years BP. (One estimate, not generally accepted, is 120 000 years BP, made by Gurdip Singh, a palynologist or pollen analyst of Canberra.)

The discovery by Pearce came at a time when Australians of European extraction were showing a marked revival of interest in their black compatriots – not least because of the land rights debate and sporadic, but continuing, exertions by black leaders to gain greater respect from whites for Aboriginal customs and folklore while simultaneously attempting to prise a greater share of the national wealth from the whites' grip. It seems certain that the old European Australian attitude ('We don't care who had the land before us, we're the ones who developed it') will change to one of wonderment that the Aborigine could survive for 2000 generations *without* the benefits of what the white man terms 'development' of resources. The modern white could not have done that. The early white explorers perished because they could not cope with the extremes of the vast, arid land. It was a killing pan. Few thought to learn from the Aborigine, whose entire lifestyle was devoted to co-existing with the land and whose rituals, customs – some too

Another rather inaccurate picture of a native inhabitant: R. M. Westmacott's impression of an Aboriginal woman of the Murray region. (Mitchell Library)

would say religion – were rooted in the stony wastes as well as in the lush coastal strips.

The other point to be made is that the Aborigines existed and to a degree prospered for about 1992 of those 2000 generations; no extreme in the oldest continent, not the Ice Age, nor vast changes in the landscape over that enormous period of 50 000 years, was too much for them to endure. Even though the changes occurred over many generations, there was always much to fear and much that could have finished them. They survived it all. Yet in the space of a few short years their entire existence was imperilled by the white men, who shot them, poisoned them, hounded them and – perhaps most significant of all – plagued them with exotic diseases that quickly took a terrible toll. In a few generations the black population was drastically reduced on the mainland. In Tasmania, where about 3000 to 4000 blacks lived when the white man arrived, the Aborigines were wiped out in a period so short that, in terms of the span of their occupation of the island, it could be described as an eye-blink.

The Aborigines had gone to Tasmania long ago when there was no passage to be made. They walked across the 15 million-hectare Bassian Plain, a huge land bridge, now, of course, submerged by Bass Strait. There, huddled in caves for warmth, they had survived the worst of the Ice Age. Far back in prehistory, they had hunted wallabies and gathered shellfish while great hunks of ice floated down the coasts and glaciers glinted on their slow path down the mountainsides. Of all human races, they were the southern-most inhabitants of Earth.

When the ice melted, about 10 000 to 12 000 years ago, the Aborigine had been cut off from the mainland. His numbers were small, but somehow he lasted. Then he was gone, the victim of the white man's ignorance, malice and stupidity. All that remains of him are the artefacts, paint-ings, carvings, food scraps, charcoal and his own bones, now the subject of careful scrutiny by the descendants of the people that extinguished him. It was one of the most shameful episodes in the history of the British race.

Man has inhabited Australia for much longer than he has lived in North America, for example. It was only in the last Ice Age that modern man (*Homo sapiens*) appeared, and it is only in the past 10 000 years, since the end of the Ice Age, that he has learned to weave cloth, harvest cereals and domesticate animals. Jericho, the oldest of towns, dates to 9 000 BP – 1000 years before Britain finally separated from what is now Continental Europe. It is only in the past 250 years that man has harnessed the world's power and mineral resources. Little wonder, then, that the first Australians did not develop the skills that peoples did elsewhere, notably in Europe: not only were the first Australians isolated, but their numbers – estimated at somewhere between 100 000 and one million by the first white settlers – were not large given the time they had been here. Moreover, they were spread out over more than 7.6 million square kilometres. (The area was much larger than at present, because when earlier generations roamed the continent the seawater drawn into the ice caps during the Ice Age left large areas exposed beyond the present coastline.) The climate changed, becoming much drier – the inland lakes became saltpans and the vegetation that the giant marsupials depended on all but disappeared. The giants of the animal kingdom in Australia became extinct, but the Aborigine adapted, and so lived on.

Co-existing with those giants must have been nerve-racking. The largest of the prehistoric kangaroos, for example, was frightening, a full three metres tall, dwarfing prehistoric man. The giant roo, Procoptodon, had a single toe on each hind foot. Its trunk was much thicker than

Diprotodon was almost 2 tonnes, had a head almost 1 metre long, ate plants, and was a marsupial parallel of the rhinoceros. (Peter Schouten)

that of the graceful teardrop-shaped Big Red which exists today, and its head was much broader at the jaw and neck. The tail joined the back like a tree trunk. And it was formidable. The hunter-gatherers threatened it – and it threatened them. A story handed down through thousands of years tells of the panic that ensued when an Aboriginal tribe in the western flat-lands of New South Wales sighted a mob of giant kangaroos. The roos were so tall that they stood out even in the endlessly distant heat-haze. In the Pleistocene, the age that extended from 2 000 000 BP to 10 000 BP, the balance of nature was often very different from that which exists now; when the roos advanced, man retreated, but not quickly enough on this occasion. The giant roos tore the Aboriginals to pieces with their massive legs.

Today we group animals like these under the term 'megafauna'. They included the tank-like Diprotodon, which had a head almost a metre long, was a plant-eater, and would have weighed almost 2 tonnes when fully grown. It was a marsupial parallel of the rhinoceros. Thylacoleo, a marsupial that resembled a lion, was the size of a leopard and was a man-eater. The largest wombat was *Phascolonus gigas*, not to be trifled with. The Aborigine co-existed with these outsized creatures 20 000 years ago, and mega-fauna may have survived until 6000 BP, according to the latest evidence.

The early white settlers would no doubt have dismissed the Aborigine's stories of his ancestors being killed by giant kangaroos in the Dreamtime as tall tales. The whites could see no evidence that there

The giant wombat, or Phascolonus gigas *roamed Australia 20 000 years ago. (Peter Schouten)*

had ever been giant kangaroos. That the Aborigine's forebears had existed in an earlier age was conceivable, but that stories could be handed down through countless generations, with fidelity as well as great care and feeling, was unthinkable. (Most white settlers were illiterate, and few would have been able to put names to their forebears beyond their grandparents: how could ignorant savages, who had no written language, claim to know the history of their tribes when they could not accurately keep count of the passing years?) The notion that the Aborigine had an entirely different approach to life, and one that was valid even though it was different from the white man's approach, does not appear to have dawned on the early white settlers. The white man would walk among the Aborigines for almost two hundred years before archaeologists, painstakingly piecing together the minutiae that had survived long-dead generations of blacks, would begin to spread the word that the white man's science could substantiate those tall tales. The black man's vivid history was one of erupting volcanoes, rising seas, and lush vegetation in an inland that turned to semi-desert way-back-when. The vulgar creatures had a history, after all. It only remained for the white man to acknowledge it, and to date it.

What the white man has been able to discern about the arrival of the first Australians, how they lived and where they came from, has become more fascinating by the decade. Some long-established theories are being ash-canned. Among the most important of these was that the Aborigine came from regions of India or Japan. It is currently accepted that he came from the land mass directly north of Australia and that he has survived at least two climatic changes in Australia. Vast areas of the continent once

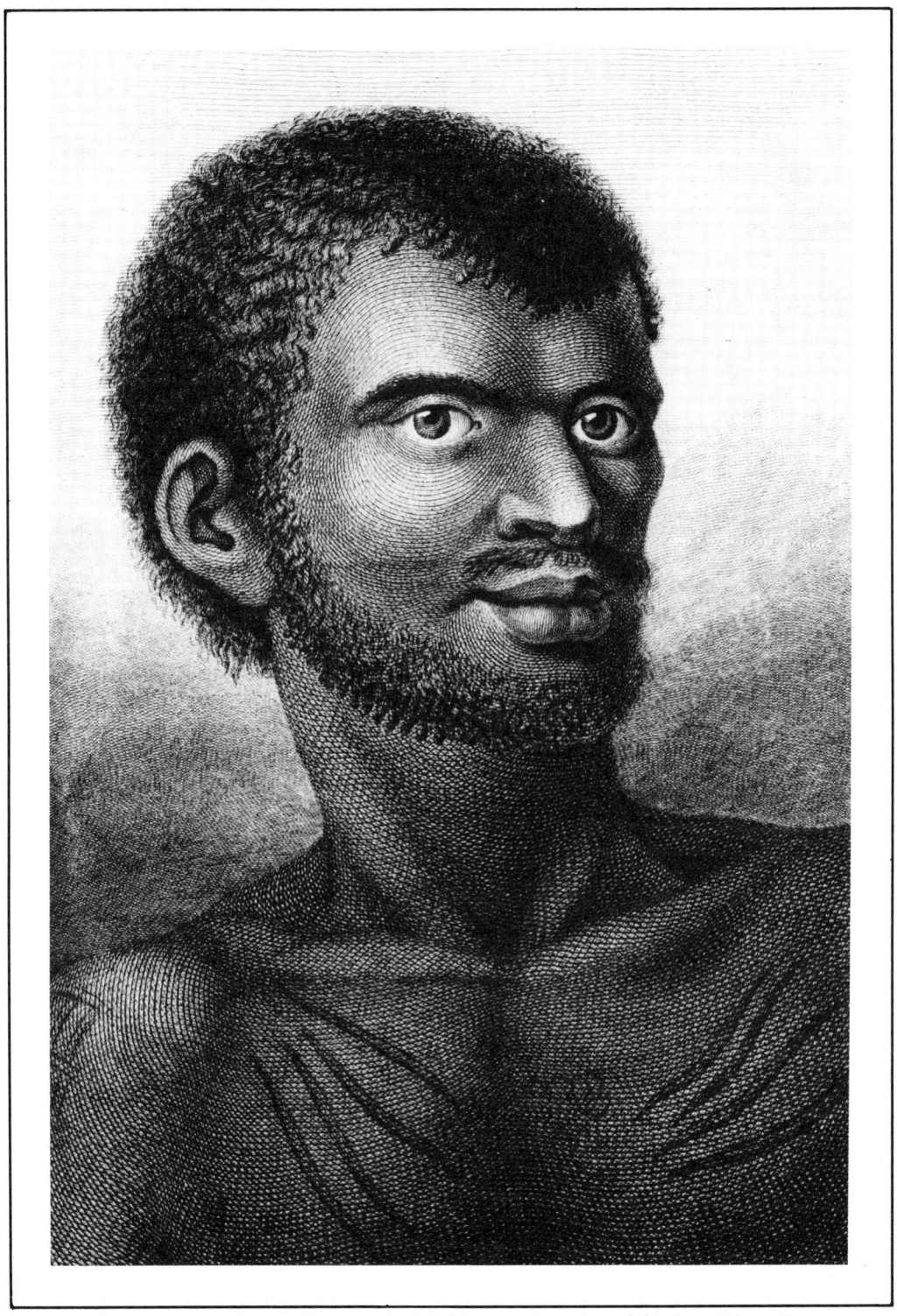

Un Homme de la Terre de Van Dieman is the plain stated caption of this late eighteenth century French work of a Tasmanian Aborigine.

resembled the tundra sweeps of modern Alaska and the Yukon. Later, Aboriginal firing – a hunting technique – denuded the landscape of rainforests in the tropics, and in Tasmania and other areas of the south-east mainland the savanna grasslands were replaced by dense scrub in a few decades.

There was a certain fascination among the first white settlers – mixed with a rather disproportionate revulsion – when it became clear to them that the Aborigine lacked many of the characteristics that whites took to be the mark of civilised man. This conception of the black man as uncivilised was based, of course, on the European's conception of himself as the epitome of civilised man: all other breeds were lesser breeds. The revulsion had much to do with the appearance of the Aborigine. He was unkempt, and as cleanliness was next to godliness, he was not viewed favourably. He was feared because he was different and because he could retaliate with marked effect when his people were subjected to atrocities. He had survived in the wide brown land, but that was about all – at least as far as the white man could see.

The black man seems to have made a very unfavourable impression on the white man at the outset. That was long before Cook arrived, and it was in the west. Given that European navigators had dreamed of discovering *terra australis incognita* for so long, the wonder of it is that discovery of the black man by the white occurred relatively recently. The idea that a great land mass existed somewhere south of the Asian latitudes dated back to pre-Christian times.

Pedro Fernandez de Quiros, a Portuguese religious fanatic born in 1565, was determined to establish a civilisation dedicated to the Holy Spirit on *terra australis*. Sailing from South America in the service of the Spanish, he came to what he imagined was *australis* in 1606, and named it 'Austrialia [*sic*] del Espiritu Santo', but he had missed East Coast Australia by a few thousand kilometres. Espiritu Santo still exists, as one of the outer islands of the Vanuatu (New Hebrides) chain. The late prehistory of Australia is full of chance misses like Quiros' for in late 1606 Luis Vaez de Torres, also Portuguese, sailed from Austrialia del Espiritu Santo to the east coast of New Guinea on a voyage to Manila. Torres sailed through the strait that now bears his name, and gave the name Cape Keerweer to what is now Cape York.

Dirk Hartog, a Dutchman, is known to generations of Australian schoolchildren because on 25 October 1616, while sailing from Cape Town to Macassar in the *Eendracht*, he reached Shark Bay, Western Australia, and stopped on an island long enough to leave lasting evidence of his visit – a tin plate. The Dutch named the land he discovered Eendrachtsland, or Landt van d'Eendracht. (In 1697 Willem de Vlamingh or Vlaming, captain of the *Geelvink,* also sailed into Shark Bay. He found Hartog's plate, replaced it with his own, and in time evidence of Hartog's visit found its way to Holland. In 1902 the plate, most significant in establishing the early history of Australia, was found by J. F. L. de Balbion at the Rijksmuseum in Amsterdam.)

William Dampier, discoverer of the west coast of Australia.

Captain James Cook as portrayed by Nathaniel Dance.

Wrecks have been recorded in Australian waters since the latter two-thirds of the seventeenth century. An English ship was wrecked on the coast in 1622, and the crew found their way to Batavia. Between 1642 and 1644 Abel Tasman undertook epic voyages to the South Seas in attempts to penetrate *terra australis incognita*. Finally, in 1688, William Dampier, an English buccaneer in the full sense of the word, landed near Dirk Hartog Sound (now King Sound) at Shark Bay, before continuing north close to the coast.

Dampier is remembered elsewhere as the man who, in 1704, marooned Alexander Selkirk on the island of Juan Fernandez, leaving him to his own devices there for four years. Out of that heroic adventure came the novel *Robinson Crusoe* which has delighted generations of European schoolchildren as a monument to the ingenuity and fortitude of the white man isolated in an alien environment. But what is of more interest to us is that Dampier and his men made the first recorded sighting by whites of the inhabitants of the great south land. 'The miserablest people in the world ... differ but little from brutes ... of a very unpleasing aspect ... no sort of clothes, no housing, their only food is a small sort of raw fish,' Dampier wrote in 1688.

Almost a century passed before Captain James Cook 'discovered' the east coast of Australia. Cook, the son of an agricultural labourer, had spent time in a haberdasher's shop before gaining an apprenticeship to shipowners in Whitby, Yorkshire, his native county. Most of the credit for his epic voyage in the *Endeavour* went to Sir Joseph Banks, who had been educated at Harrow, Eton and at Christ Church College, Oxford University, and thus had far more social clout than Cook.

But Cook is the one we revere now, and he is considered the greatest mariner of them all, surpassing Magellan, Drake, Columbus and the rest. He was perhaps more perceptive than Dampier when it came to considering the lot of the black Australian. 'In reality they are far more happy than we Europeans ...they live in a tranquillity ... they covet not, they live in a warm and fine climate ... they think themselves provided with all the necessarys [sic] of life' was Cook's wistful appraisal. It was a popular romantic view of the eighteenth century of the noble savage, particularly, for example, the Tahitians, whose beauty and languid paradise instantly captivated sailors after a long and perilous voyage from Europe.

Australia, however, was not Tahiti: life was difficult, and sometimes harsh, for the Aborigine. Cook, whose voyage paved the way for white settlement, had looked beyond the unfamiliar visage of the black Australian. The extreme conflict between the Dampier view and the Cook view would surface again and again in white settlers' judgments of the Aborigine, and still does. Mostly whites have agreed with Dampier. That, among other things, must have made the task of divesting the Aborigine of his land easier to stomach. The whites had superior numbers and force, and the Aborigines yielded, often meekly. Now that whites have begun to

'Snake feast in my camp', from the book Among Cannibals *by Carl Lumholtz, 1890. Lumholtz was a Norwegian naturalist who worked in the Herbert River region of North Queensland in the 1880s. His view of the Aborigines was typical of the period.*

An Aboriginal tribesman of Central Australia. (Ken Stepnell)

This illustration demonstrates the difficulty early artists found in coming to terms with the unfamiliar animals and surroundings of the Australian bush. This is a watercolour of 'an opossum' by John Webber painted sometime in the 1790s.

In this photograph, taken in the early part of this century, the Aboriginal king's adornments reflect his tribal status.

acknowledge past wrongs, there is a black backlash not unlike that of the Israelis whose parents went unprotestingly to the gas chambers.

In the story of Aboriginal-white contact, wrote R. M. & C. H. Berndt in their book *The World of the First Australians*, 'basic similarities are overlaid by such striking divergences that the total affect of the impact, through time, has been devastating. The Aborigines could hardly have been subjugated by a people more unlike themselves, and less in sympathy with their whole orientation toward living.' The Aborigines' world, the authors said, 'broke up around them, and they turned

for support to the newcomers who had brought this about, so their dependence in more than an economic sense increased.' What ensued reinforced the charges of inferiority, and so the Aborigine was caught in a vicious circle.

The Berndts describe the dilemma facing Aborigines in a few lines – the popular stereotypes that are pervasive and difficult to eradicate.

Active and alert in the traditional scene, since their survival rested on being so, in this new situation they were accused of being inherently lazy and prone to idleness. Settled in static

17

Captain Arthur Phillip, commander of the First Fleet and the first governor of the colony of New South Wales.

of attention, to lack the ability to concentrate. Because their rhythm of everyday living was based on a different time-perspective, dependent on natural sequences (sun and moon, the cycle of the seasons) rather than on a rigid pattern of chronological reckoning, they were accused of being shiftless, having no sense of time. Capable of sustained effort in hunting and ritual affairs, responsible in attending to their own economic and social obligations, they were censured now as undependable, unwilling to work, basically irresponsible.

The popular folklore which has grown up in Australia about the Aborigines rests only in small part on an informed understanding of their traditional life, say the Berndts. 'It is a patchwork of exaggerations, distortions, half-truths, compounded on the basis of emotional prejudice, and supported by evidence from contact situations in which Aborigines have made, from that point of view, a poor showing.'

True enough. A patchwork of exaggerations, distortions and half-truths, compounded by emotional prejudice and supported by evidence from contact situations would also imperil relations between the descendants of the earlier white settlers and non-Anglo-Saxons from disparate regions much later, during the great immigrations.

The first whites who came into contact with the descendants of the first Australians found it difficult to regard the Aborigine as a human – or, at least, as *Homo sapiens*. Much later – long after thousands of Aborigines had perished from white man's diseases, or been killed by whites – the white man began to take an academic interest in the origins of the first settlers.

By this time – a few decades into the twentieth century – the Aborigine had again become a curiosity, not least

camps, laden with cast-off clothing which they had no means of maintaining in good order and repair, they were reproached with dirtiness as an inherently Aboriginal attribute. Accustomed as they were, traditionally, to relying on memory for transmitting and reproducing detailed genealogies, myth and song material, and the minutiae of 'natural history' information necessary to everyday living, now they were claimed to have a short span because his numbers were dwindling and those of the whites were growing. It has been established that in Victoria the black population declined by between 2000 and 3000 from 1835 to 1839. There was brutality in parts of South Australia, Western Australia and the Northern Territory, right up to the early 1940s. There were killings in Queensland, by both races. Tasmania's Black Drive of 1830 is part of our history now.

Some of the early observations of the black man by the white blow-ins and johnnie-come-latelies were, however, surprisingly perceptive and admiring. The nineteenth-century white man was less inclined to tolerance of people of other races than the generations that followed him. Brabazon Harry Purcell, in a paper delivered to the Royal Geographical Society of Australasia in Melbourne in 1893, said Queensland and Northern Territory blacks had been regarded as ignorant and lazy, but stood very high in the esteem of all who had had anything to do with them or had had the opportunity to study their social laws and customs. They had a fixed code of morals which would not be a disgrace to any civilised community, Purcell noted, rather patronisingly. Many, if not most, white Australians would have found that difficult to believe in the social climate of the colonial period. Purcell said Aborigines were not endowed with an immense amount of brain power, but in physical prowess 'they excel their white brother'. He had known them to walk 144 kilometres in Queensland without a drink of water, and there was at least one recorded instance of a male Aborigine travelling 176 kilometres without a drop.

But white Australians, almost to a man, continued to regard such feats as further evidence that the 'Abo', as they called him, was, after all, a genetic odd-ball. ('Did you see old Jackie yesterday – got thrown off that brumby he was trying to break, landed flat on his back, but he got straight up, dusted himself off, and went

on with his work.' 'Yeah, ha ha ha.') The 'Abo' was good at stock work (while he remained on the job, as distinct from succumbing to the temptation to go 'walkabout') and he could take a solid punch to the head in a boxing match, or even walk for days in the waterless desert ... but that didn't make him a white.

That was how the white stockman and station hand viewed the Aborigine. But not all white Australians viewed the original Australians that way, even in the eighteenth and nineteenth centuries. Those with a scientific bent or background soon realised that the Aborigine was not like the natives of Polynesia, New Zealand or South-East Asia, and began to wonder. It was assumed, almost from the outset, that the Tasmanian was different from the mainland Australian, since his skin was a different shade and some features, such as his hair, were different. By the time whites had claimed all of Australia for themselves and white rulers had taken to appointing themselves as patrons of individual blacks (such as Bennelong) and even sending an Aboriginal cricket team to the playing fields of England, a healthy and not altogether ignorant curiosity had developed about the black man.

All the early records of English and French navigators showed that they regarded the Tasmanians as trusting, docile and childlike. They were polite, full of childish merriment, and were not a true Australian black, the theory went, but rather part-Negroid or Melanesian. Their population was guessed at about 8000 in 1804 – thirty years later their numbers were down to only 200, and 70 years further on the last of them passed away. She was Truganini. After Bennelong, she is the Aborigine best known to white Australians.

The blacks came to Australia when it was still part of Sahul, which is to say, New Guinea, the Australian mainland and Tasmania. As the last Ice Age, generally considered to have begun about 100 000 years ago, advanced like a gigantic prehistoric outgrowth, it sucked up the seas in such huge quantities that the ocean level descended, increasing the size of the land masses. Sahul, or Greater Australia, was about one-quarter larger than the combined area of its three components today. At the peak of the Ice Age icebergs floated past the frosty caves where the Tasmanians huddled.

Sixteen thousand years ago the ice began to melt. It was not until 12 000 BP that the seas rose high enough to swallow

Captain Arthur Phillip's official journal relates some of the events of 26 January 1788 when white settlement began.

CHAP.
VII.
bered with underwood than in many other ~~other~~ places, yet their magnitude was such as to render not only the felling, but the removal of them afterwards, a task of no small difficulty. By the habitual indolence of the convicts, and the want of proper overseers to keep them to their duty, their labour was January 26th, rendered less efficient than it might have been. In the evening
1788.
of the 26th the colours were displayed on shore, and the Governor, with several of his principal officers and others, assembled round the flag-staff, drank the king's health, and success to the settlement, with all that display of form which on such occasions is esteemed propitious, because it enlivens the spirits, and fills the imagination with pleasing presages. From this time to the end of the first week in February all was hurry and exertion. They who gave orders and they who received them were equally occupied; nor is it easy to conceive a busier scene than this part of the coast exhibited during the continuance of these first efforts towards establishment. The plan of the encampment was quickly formed, and places were marked out for every different purpose, so as to introduce, as much as possible, strict order and regularity. The materials and frame work to construct a slight temporary habitation for the Governor, had been brought out from England ready formed : these were landed and put together with as much expedition as the circumstances would allow. Hospital tents were also without delay erected, for which there was soon but too much occasion. In the passage from the Cape there had been but little sickness, nor had many died even among the convicts; but soon after landing, a dysentery prevailed, which in several instances proved fatal, and the

9   scurvy

the Bassian Plain, and the Tasmanians were once more cut off from mainland Australia. A further 4000 years passed before the isthmus between the mainland and New Guinea disappeared beneath the waves, and it took another 2000 years for the sea to rise to its present level. Even so, a drop of only 30 metres would join Australia and New Guinea again.

The Aborigines lived through it all. When the water receded all those generations ago to create a new coastline, they advanced; when the waters returned, they retreated, but gradually, over many lifespans. The big animals which had roamed the continent, the frightening megafauna, were all long gone – or so it has been assumed until recently. We do know that the whole dimension and face of the continent changed during the black man's tenure. He was still there, and he knew a lot about the changes that had occurred and about the history of his people, even though it had never been written.

As a matter of fact, he knew a lot more about the history of his forebears, tens of thousands of years dead, than did the whites who set foot in Botany Bay in 1770; men such as Banks and Cook, and in Farm Cove eighteen years later, Phillip and others. Their knowledge went back only as far as recorded history; the convicts, most of whom were illiterate, didn't know much more about their history than had been handed down verbally in their families, and that would probably extend back, therefore, only two or three generations. That a beetle-browed savage, observing the white man's arrival from the safety of a clump of gum trees, his hair lank, his skin dirty, his whole appearance and demeanour the very antithesis of the traits of the white man's civilisation, might know much that the intruders had no way of knowing, was, well, unthinkable. So nobody thought about it. The intruders, as they struggled through those first few generations of white settle-

'Start for an Expedition'. An engraving from 1888.

ment to establish a foothold on the dry, alien continent, so different from the British Isles, thought little for the most part of the blacks except in fear or curious, halting fraternisation. The more adventurous whites who set forth into the interior to make their names as explorers scarcely paused to consider that the clue to their survival in the desert, when all food and water was gone, might lie in the boundless knowledge and ageless instincts of the people they regarded as sub-human.

In time, after the white man felt secure enough about his occupancy of the continent to indulge his mild interest in the original settlers, several theories were developed about their origins. Central to the most credible of these was a belief that the Aborigine was a hybrid, because his features varied so much in different areas of Australia, and there were specially noticeable distinctions between Tasmanians and mainlanders.

One version of the multi-origin theory was put forth in a paper entitled 'Ethnology of the Blacks', printed in April 1898, in the *Journal of the Royal Anthropological Society of Australasia*. It was edited by 'Dr Alan Carroll, M.A., D.Lit., Ph.D., D.Sc. &c, &c,' who was regarded as one of the greatest ethnologists in the world. The paper claimed that the Tasmanian was a cross between Negrito and Papuan because he possessed all the essential features and characteristics of those races. 'The present black people belong to the Neolithic or polished stone-age and culture, and those of previous and older blacks who were in Australia in the palaeolithic age and culture,' it said. The Papuans had crossed into Australia with the Negritos, and had discovered this continent, then made their way to Tasmania before the present wide water of Bass Strait existed. 'They did not have Dravidian implements or culture, and were when first found, very different in all ways to the Australian blacks; their weapons

and tools were ruder and more like palaeolithic implements, and they had not yet received their Australian dog.' The Papuans had reached and occupied all the islands of Micronesia, Melanesia and Polynesia, and in many of these islands the Papuans had found the Negritos were there before them, and they killed the men and married the women, the paper went on, in biblical cadences. The Negritos were the earliest inhabitants of all the islands throughout Australasia, and used palaeolithic implements. Less than six years earlier, Dr Carroll had written that 'although Australasia has been occupied by Europeans for over a century, very little has yet been done scientifically to learn anything satisfactorily about the origin of its black natives, and nothing about the length of time they have been on the island-continent, or where they came from before they migrated here.' It was known that there were more than two hundred and fifty dialects (the number known would swell dramatically in the following decades). 'The Australian blacks are rapidly being cleared off, the Tasmanian blacks have all disappeared, and therefore no time should be lost in commencing and undertaking this important work, so necessary if we are to learn all that remains about the tribes still living …' Carroll believed that the Aborigine was not a primitive man, but a decadent one.

The work he spoke of consisted of collecting Aboriginal myths, legends, songs; investigating the traditions; making physical examinations of the dead as well as the living; scientifically examining Aboriginal shell heaps and cooking mounds, the swamps they inhabited, water holes and springs where they congregated, and their wells. Caves were searched, the dust lining their floors carefully sifted for evidence of previous generations; riverbeds and watercourses were explored, as well as old burial places. Carroll erroneously held that the Aborigine

Low as he was on the social scale, the convict knew he wasn't on the bottom. This 1841 illustration shows convicts slaughtering Aborigines, who aroused both fear and suspicion.

had come from the highlands of India, a cradle of nations, because he'd traced a similarity in some common words, including that for 'water', used by races there and in Australia.

There are many theories about the origins of the Aborigine, often markedly different from the latest thinking. According to Joseph Birdsell's 'trihybrid' theory, expounded in 1949, there was an initial wave of Oceanic Negritos. They had been rolled back by a second wave, the Murrayans, and there followed a third wave,

the Carpentarians, the last of the Pleistocene migrants to reach Greater Australia. All three waves had reached Australia during the last glaciation, two of them more than 25 000 years ago. The first arrivals were believed to have formed the basis of the populations in New Guinea, Tasmania and some small areas of Queensland rainforest, while the second group settled most of eastern and southern Australia. Some of the experts believed – after the theory of Carpentarian man was discarded – that two sepa-

Four of the last of the Tasmanian Aborigines. Truganini, the last to die (1876), is at right; William Lanney, her fifth husband is also shown in this group, which posed in 1866.

rate populations had come to Australia in prehistory. A prime reason for this view was the anthropological studies which showed great differences in the thickness of Aboriginal skulls. Some were very thick (robust) and some much thinner (gracile); they could therefore not be of the same derivation.

In an attempt to explain just who the Aborigine was, scientists began looking as far afield as the dwarf or Negrito or Negrillo peoples of the Andamans of India, the Philippines, Micronesia, Melanesia, and those of Central Africa – just about any old group with black skin. It was postulated that the Papuan came originally from the hills and forests of India, or those of Asonesia, or Melanesia,

or the interior of New Guinea, or the New Hebrides (now Vanuatu) and other islands. In other words there was no end of theories which indicated that the Aborigine might have come from almost anywhere.

But gradually theories of origins that stretched the imagination to geographically remote regions were allowed to lapse, including the alleged connection with the Ainu of Japan or the Dravidians (the non-Aryan races of southern India) and the Veddahs of Sri Lanka. Twentieth-century biochemical and anthropometric data indicated that the Australians and New Guineans were closer to one another than to any other group, and suggestions that the New Guineans were more closely related to Africans were dropped for want of sufficient evidence. So, too, was a basic assumption that had been held ever since the eighteenth century; that Tasmanians were of different stock from mainlanders because they had different features. They had not used the boomerang, had no dingo, but it gradually became obvious that the differences between the two were no more clearly marked than the differences that existed between Aborigines in different parts of the mainland, and these were often pronounced.

The white man was, however, always ambivalent in his assessment of the Aborigine, who was simultaneously derided for his backwardness and admired for characteristics that he possessed in stronger measure than the more sedentary whites, or for abilities that the white man lacked, such as tracking, finding food and water where none apparently existed, and generally managing to survive no matter how harsh the deprivations of the inland. John Hutt, the second Governor of Western Australia, who took office in 1839, commissioned a report on the conditions of the Aborigines in the colony, including a summary of their character. The job fell to the Advocate-General, George Fletcher Moore, and is worth recalling as a reminder to bigots.

What a singular race of beings! Shrewd and intelligent, not yet possessing even the rudiments of civilisation; ignorant of art or science, yet able to obtain a ready livelihood where civilised beings might be starved; knowing nothing about any metal, yet able to fashion weapons ... having neither house nor home; domesticating neither beast nor bird; for their imperfect taming of the wild dog can scarcely be called an exception; cultivating neither grain nor fruit; naked yet unwilling to bear the trammels of clothing; looked down upon as the lowest in the scale of beings, yet proudly bearing them-

Truganini, also known as Lallah Rookh, was 65 when she posed for this portrait.

selves, and condemning the drudgery of the man who despises them; cheerful, confiding, kindly of disposition, yet treacherous, implacable in revenge and glorifying in massacre; enjoying the most unrestricted state of liberty, yet in daily danger of death; living, in short, in a state of society resolved into its very first elements; having no worship and little superstition – revering no God – dreading no devils – without a rule of conduct in this life, without hope of reward or fear of punishment in the next. Here is a people as truly singular as their own vegetable productions – unique as their own animals; and in a condition in the world as rare as their own swans. They are a race worthy of the study of the philosopher.

It became obvious that the Aborigine had a 'purer' blood line than many Europeans, in the sense that, no matter how many waves of black immigration there had been to Australia, they had come from the lands directly to the north; the Europeans were already the product of a mixing pot of Celts, Latins, Slavs,

Teutons. The Celts, without counting several minor divisions, showed a marked diversity of bloodstreams. Purity of bloodstream probably meant more to people who disapproved of the Aborigines than it meant to anybody else.

The Aborigine was variously regarded as gentle and barbaric: he would cause no trouble if unprovoked, but would kill if sufficiently aroused. The whites regarded it as their right to take his land, since he was primitive and did not have a recognisable system of land 'ownership'. In the loneliness of the bush, half-a-world away from the civilisation that bred them, the whites, who were suspicious of one another because of the basic divisions of convict and free settler, did not need much sometimes to lose their equilibrium.

An example of the tragedies that this strain could produce occurred at the Risdon convict deportation station on the Derwent, in Tasmania. Incorrigible convicts were sent there from as far afield as Sydney; Governor King regarded them as

Aborigines indulge their passions in a Sydney street, c. 1838. The whites saw them as violent and too savage to tame.

A photograph of Aborigines from Lake Tyers, Victoria, taken in about 1886.

pollutants unfit even for the infant convict colony. There were only a few free white settlers at Risdon, and relations between blacks and whites had been consistently friendly. An Aboriginal hunting group speeding after kangaroos and wallabies came over the crest of a hill near the white settlement on 3 May 1804. A white settler hoeing in a field took no notice of the blacks, nor they of him, as they sped past after the quarry, but a soldier panicked, apparently believing the Aborigines were attacking. The company was ordered to fire, and half of the blacks were slaughtered. The white labourer, named White, was shocked. News of the massacre swept through the tribes, and their confidence in the white man was destroyed. As Sir Joseph Carruthers noted, the convicts stole Aboriginal women, stole and sold black children, and the blacks retaliated by stealing cattle.

It has been recorded that one group of black women were chained to trees after they were stolen; when their husbands came to release them, the black men were shot by whites lying in ambush. A convict bushranger awaiting execution admitted that he had habitually shot natives for food for his dogs. A party of soldiers and constables shot seventy blacks in the crevices of two big rocks in 1827. Seventeen blacks were shot down while bathing. In the Black Drive of 1830, during Governor Arthur's administration, 5000 men were armed with 1000 muskets, 30 000 cartridges and 300 pairs of handcuffs. The cordon they formed spread across Tasmania. The result was the discovery of a party of blacks sleeping around their fires. Two blacks were shot; one man and a boy were captured. The financial cost of the debacle was £30 000, but that was the least of it. That same year, Lord Stanley introduced in the House of Commons his Bill for the emancipation of slaves, for which William Wilberforce and Zachary Macaulay, among others, had struggled so long – Wilberforce as early as 1788, the year Australia was settled by whites. 'This Bill marked the entrance of man into the human family,' Ralph Waldo Emerson, American poet and essayist, remarked. But that year also marked the virtual exit of a race from the island of Tasmania, and thence from the globe. A Methodist brickmaker in Hobart organised most of the remaining Tasmanian blacks – fewer than two hundred souls – for removal to Flinders Island, where they died off rapidly.

The Australian Aborigines were worse off than the American Indians: they lacked the numbers to fight back against their oppressors, and their tribes were much smaller, making cohesion and organised opposition by large numbers of Aborigines difficult if not impossible. They did not have the horse, nor the beneficial intrusion of friendly 'foreign' whites to give them arms as did the Indians. The Indians died, just the same, and in alarming numbers, like the Aborigines, from the white man's diseases as well as his brutality.

The debate on the benefit or otherwise of the mission stations to which so many Aborigines retreated after the whites consolidated their grip on Australia will likely continue as long as historians continue to take up their pens. Of more immediate importance is the outcome of their demands, in the 1970s and 1980s, for land rights. It is not too much to say that the vociferousness of these demands came about in no small way as a measure of white protest movements, which began during the Vietnam War, and continued in support of other causes when the conclusion of that war left a 'protest vacuum'. The quest for black rights arouses a lot of passion in white Australians, many of whom cannot understand why such largesse is necessary, or what it will solve. The gap between black and white living standards is greater by far in the 1980s than it had been in the 1880s. There is strong feeling among Australian whites in the 1980s that if blacks are to gain control of lands that are potentially valuable to whites, then the blacks must justify control of that land. Other whites feel that land rights are an extravagant expression of white guilt, a sop, an atonement for the excesses of colonial whites who were, after all, of another generation, and hardly Australian anyway. None of this surmounts an indisputable fact, however: that an entire people and their way of life had been uprooted and imperilled, and a new generation of Aborigines, led by educated, articulate and angry men and women, with ample support from white sympathisers, is going to get redress, and a lot of it. Today, it seems that the bulk of the white population is not sufficiently opposed to the proposals for land rights to prevent the Aborigines getting a substantial measure of what they are demanding. It has taken the potential loss to whites of something tangible and valuable, as implied by land rights, to start the public thinking about the Aboriginal issue. The average Australian has yet to really consider the psychological and cultural damage that has been done, but at

Aborigines on Wonnaminta Homestead, New South Wales, 1892, when their numbers were fast dwindling.

other levels there is growing consideration and concern about that, and a feeling
that the process must be reversed.

The white man, who uncovered enough
of nature's mysteries to create the atomic
age – and thus the key to the destruction
of all life – should thus be bright enough
to understand the modern Aborigine's
predicament; or at least the irony of it.
The Aborigine sitting under the gum
trees beside a riverbed at the Alice does
not have to possess the abilities of an
atomic physicist or an astronaut to know
that his ancestors coped well enough until
the advent of the white man. He is worlds
apart from the whites, but if that were a
fact instead of a metaphor, it is one
hundred to one on that his world would
survive longer than that of the whites in
the atomic age. Whites, of course, do not
wish to live in the black man's world, but
that does not mean that they have nothing
to learn from it – and perhaps they will
learn, if enough of it survives. The blacks,
in turn, could do a lot more to learn from

the white man, and their unmitigated
obstinacy has been to their own dis-
advantage.

Meanwhile, the race to discover the
approximate length of the black man's
long life in this country continues, and as
white archaeologists push that date
further back into prehistory, the fascination grows. There have been people in
South-East Asia for more than one million years. There has been no complete
land bridge between Asia and Australia at
any time during the past three million
years.

The first real archaeological excavation
in Australia was not made until 1929; the
first university post in Australian
archaeology was not created until the
1960s. Sydney University got an
anthropology department in 1925, but it
was the only one in Australia for nearly
three decades. Yet we now know that
Aboriginal society has the longest continuous cultural history of any people in
the world. We know that this society has

'Civilised Girls from the vicinity of Townsville' from Among Cannibals *by Carl Lumholtz, 1890.*

its roots in the Pleistocene. The study of prehistory is in its infancy: there are more known sites to yield secrets than there are archaeologists to search them. Who knows what they will reveal? Joseph Birdsell's 'trihybrid' theory is under fire: genetic mutation was held by Josephine Flood, in her 1983 work, *Archaeology of the Dreamtime,* to be the reason why the Tasmanians were small, with spirally, curly hair – so different from mainlanders. The three-wave theory has gone under: current thinking is that the Carpentarians are the result of relatively recent contact between Aborigines and non-Aborigines along the north coast of Australia. It is known that Aborigines generally are not of blood groups A2 and B1, but research is unable to provide clues, so far, to the biological origin of the first Australians.

The chief racial groups of mankind, as they exist now, go back about 100 000 years, to the African, Caucasian and Oriental-Australian. Studies of the mitochondrial DNA clock suggest that the Aborigines are a mixed and varied population, deriving from the hybridisation of two distinct lineages, *Homo sapiens* and *Homo erectus*, if the timing on the mitochondrial DNA chart is correct. The split and mixing of the two lineages could have occurred in Asia, and the human who resulted may have come to Australia much later. We do know that there are two distinct lineages in the mitochondrial DNA of Aborigines, and this may explain the existence of robust and gracile skeletons. An American researcher, Rebecca Cann, has suggested that Australia is the cradle of the modern human race – that the first modern man evolved here, 40 000 years ago, from *Homo erectus*, and that he spread throughout the world.

To put *Homo erectus* in his proper perspective, he was not the last human before *Homo sapiens*. One Australian anthropologist has suggested that the early humans of Java belong to *Homo erectus*, who spread out from Africa to Asia between 1.5 and 2 million years, ago. *Homo erectus* was almost, or completely, upright in stance, unlike his forebears. It is worth noting, perhaps, that he had a cranial capacity that varied between 775 cubic centimetres and 1300 cubic centimetres. Modern man's brain averages 1300 cubic centimetres; earliest man had a brain capacity of less than half that of *Homo erectus*, had conspicuous brow ridges, a sloping forehead, a protruding face, thick skullbones, massive jaws and teeth, and stood about 153 centimetres tall. Peking Man, an example, lived 300 000 to 500 000 years ago.

Between *Homo erectus* and *Homo sapiens* there was, for example, *Homo soloensis*, but Flood believes that the first immigrants to Australia were among the earliest, most generalised, representatives of modern man, *Homo sapiens*; their ancestors appear to have evolved in Asia, over a period of almost 2 million years, and the earliest humans in Asia are all believed to belong to *Homo erectus*. The basic modern Aboriginal skeleton is robust, rather than gracile, and so are most Australian prehistoric remains. It is uncertain whether there were two main immigrations, when the sea level was low, or a continuous trickle of people. The gracile people were camped on the shores of Willandra Lakes more than 30 000 years ago, and they were preceded by robust people: the gracile people had to enter Australia when the sea level was very low, about 50 000, perhaps 55 000 years ago. 'The facts, figures and dates all support the Aboriginal oral traditions of how they have come to live in Australia,' says Flood, 'since before time could be counted, since the Dreamtime.'

The current theory is that the lusher areas on the coast and more permanent of the river systems were settled first; only in the last 10 000 to 15 000 years did Aborigines go to the drier regions. Either this, or big-game hunters rapidly settled throughout the continent. But some authorities, such as J. Peter White and James F. O'Connell (whose work, *A Prehistory of Australia, New Guinea and Sahul* appeared in 1983) do not believe that Sahul or Australia was rapidly populated, because they don't believe the inhabitants' habits would have changed from those of the Wallaceans who came here, who were hunter-gatherers; there is no evidence, they say, that the early arrivals were big-game hunters. The work of analysing the gradual changes in Aboriginal implements and art work goes on. It will be interesting, in the years ahead, to see whether that work brings closer understanding between white and black Australians. Perhaps whites will make the first move: black anger may not abate for some time, and it is a mark of the return of the black man's pride in his race.

A Joseph Lycett watercolour of Aborigines spearing fish, diving for crayfish, and cooking their catch, in the early years of the colony of New South Wales.

Kindling fire, as they had done for 2000 generations, was scarcely a problem in any conditions for Aborigines. This watercolour by William Romaine Govett was painted in about 1836.

CHAPTER 2

The Whites Settle

WHEN CAPTAIN ARTHUR PHILLIP and the First Fleet entered Port Jackson, his crews and their motley charges were greeted by a vista that must have induced conflicting emotions. They could have been nothing but impressed by the Heads, which are among the most striking sentinels at the entrance to any major harbour in the world, and the views on either side of the water which stretched, spectacularly, further west than most would dare to go for long after the party was ashore. Anxious to go ashore they were, after eight months and one day sailing half-way around the world. But among the total complement of the 11 ships – more than 1400, of whom more than 700 were convicts – not many were elated. Port Jackson was an open prison compared with the

Captain Cook taking possession of the Australian continent, 1770.

prison hulks they had left behind in the River Thames, but it would be a prison none the less. January in Sydney is hot and steamy, the foliage is drained to a pale khaki by a remorseless sun that turns skin pink in a few hours, and the insects are voracious.

The plan to send the First Fleet had its origins in 1786, and the actual decision was announced by King George III to Parliament less than four months before the ships left England. Virginia and Maryland had been the chief recipients of the 1000 convicts transported each year to the United States between 1750 and 1775, but the American Revolution had stopped the traffic, and British gaols were at bursting point when Botany Bay was selected. Some historians still regard that choice as puzzling. The use of Australia may have been decided by Britain's £250 000 a year bill for imported flax used for sailcloth,

The First Fleet sailing into Port Jackson on 26 January 1788. Phillip had recognised it as 'the finest harbour in the world' and decided it was a better site for the first settlement than Botany Bay.

canvas and ships' cables: Australian soil was deemed capable of providing superior quality flax. The cost of the choice was high: it took £190 000, a large sum in those days, to equip the fleet, which brought, among other things, 700 spades, 700 gimlets, 8000 fish hooks and, as far as we know from what was recorded, one bible only.

The thirteen colonies that had lately been accepted, even by King George (a monarch described as mad, with prolonged intervals of lucidity) as the independent United States of America, had come into existence over the previous century and a half in circumstances that were hardly more propitious than those in New South Wales. Winter in the northeast of the United States is harsher than the summer in Sydney, and the first white settlers who went to America were very different from the first white settlers in Australia: the white Americans regarded the bible as the premier item of their equipment. They were a stern, pious, energetic lot, and some of them were well educated.

Americans revere their origins; Australia has shown little enthusiasm for hers, preferring to gloss over it save for evincing some sympathy for the many convicts who were victims of poverty and a fierce rule of law which resulted in Draconian sentences. Victims the forgers and thieves and poachers and Irish rebels may have been: pious, even mildly energetic or well educated nearly every one of them was not. They had no sense of forging a new nation. Why would they? In the long run-up to Australia's Bicentennial celebrations newspapers outdid themselves in their attempts to publish every name and personal detail of the first convicts, but the odour still remains. Still, that period was long ago, we have come a long way and our origins can be viewed with some humour. An item that appeared in the *Irish Times* in late 1983 headed 'Correction', read 'A sentence from a story about the Australia-Ireland Bicentennial Conference in an early edition of yesterday's *Irish Times* said that it had been a revelation to discover that "Aussies were sheepstealers, convicts and prostitutes when they started out". This should have read "Aussies were *not* sheep-stealers, convicts and prostitutes when they started out".'

Anyway, Captain Phillip pronounced Sydney Harbour the 'finest in the world' and named the settlement in honour of the lord who had announced, on 18 August 1786, the plan to send convicts to the southern continent. Now they were here, almost as far from home as it was possible to go. Whites who had seen Australia from a distance, or set foot, fleetingly, on her soil, were filled with foreboding. As far as we know, only one of them had been here before with Cook: a simple grave at Laughtondale, near Wisemans Ferry, outside Sydney, bears the name of Peter Hibbs, who was a boy when he sailed with Cook, came back with Phillip, and lived to ninety. What stories he could have told us if anybody had bothered to record them.

When Phillip hoisted the flag, for all anybody knew the only mark whites had made on Australia consisted of the simple grave of Forby Sutherland, buried at Kurnell by Cook's men during their brief visit. It was not quite eighteen years since the April day when midshipman Isaac Smith of Cook's 373-tonne bark *Endeavour* had become the first white man (as far as is known) to set foot on the eastern side of the vast and mysterious continent. (Two murderers, an eighteen-year-old cabin servant and a twenty-four-year-old soldier, had been exiled on the coast of Western Australia after the Dutch ship *Batavia* ran aground on the Abrolhos Islands, about 50 kilometres offshore, in 1628: there is no record of their fate, but they surely had no future. Smith had a future; his feat of the first steps has not been immortalised in history but he went on to become an admiral in the British Navy.)

Cook had said that 'the country produces hardly anything fit for man to eat' and Joseph Banks, the botanist who had hogged the publicity back home in England had thought Nieuw Holland 'barren … in a very high degree'. Both were in effect echoing the sentiments of Dampier.

Unable to live off the land or to make it produce adequately, famine threatened the convicts and their keepers several times in the first years. Only public hangings of the culprits deterred others from thieving food.

Considering the land, climate and human resources, it is doubtful if British settlement of any land had ever been started in more pessimistic circumstances.

Of the land beyond the settlement, the First Fleeters could know nothing. Like most first settlers, they weren't too anxious to find out about it. Phillip and those closest to him in command regarded the exercise, naturally, as a great opportunity to serve King and Country and advance their own careers. The Aborigines who warily observed the arrival of the whites could have had no more reason for optimism about the outcome than the gloomiest of the convicts and overseers. King George III had instructed that there should be no wanton destruction of the people Cook had characterised as a timorous and inoffensive race; the monarch wanted 'no unnecessary interruption' of the natives 'in the exercise of their several occupations'. This was an ambiguous command, interpreted with extreme liberality by the new arrivals. The Aborigines' chief occupation, right back through the ages, deep into prehistory, had been to keep their race alive. The creation of a new way of life, in some ways unique in the world, was about to begin, and the destruction of one certainly unique, and at least 2000 generations old, was thus virtually inevitable.

And so the white takeover of Australia began, although the population increase was so slow that for most of the first half century the settlement was little more than a large gaol. Not all of the convicts were villains, and it is true that in the century leading up to Australia Day, 1788, the number of capital crimes on the English statute books had increased threefold to about one hundred and fifty: many of the convicts were transported for offences that today would warrant only a suspended sentence or a good behaviour

Convicts boarding a hulk or prisonship, HMS York in Portsmouth Harbour, England. Transportation to an alien land was a fearsome prospect.

bond. Nonetheless, it is fanciful to pretend that the bulk of the convicts were, at best, better than disreputable and lazy. They were good for little or nothing, and certainly were unsuited to nation-building.

About one hundred and sixty two thousand of them (figures vary) arrived over a period of eighty years, the vast majority before 1840, but it was not until 1868 that the last stepped ashore, at Fremantle. About one-third of them were Irish; if that seems disproportionate to the population of Ireland compared with England's, it should be remembered that the Irish were fractious when not rebellious, and would have been less inclined to uphold the law than if they had been running their own show. As a class, the convicts were almost uniformly from what the English referred to, unadmiringly, as the lower orders; in Ireland, that meant just about everybody.

The Cockney was prominent in the convict ranks, and he too was crude in many ways, but because of his big-city background and the nature of his previous existence he could live on his wits. His accent lingers in Australia to this day as Broad Australian (as distinct from Educated Australian, spoken by the middle classes, and Southern English, spoken by a few at the top rung of the social ladder), and his brashness is still evident, passed down through generations, particularly in Sydney, where he predominated.

The Irish, though numerous, were at the bottom of the pile, as they mostly have been in societies, both free and penal, wherever they were forced to co-exist with the English. Today, Australians of Irish ancestry have more in common with Australians of English, Scottish and Welsh ancestry than they do with Australians of non-British ancestry, regardless of religious affinity such as the Irish have with Italians. It is a disturbing feature of history that nations living side by side, as

the Irish do with the British, often simply cannot get along, and nationalism exacerbates the tensions between them. It is, however, unlikely that there are any two nations on earth existing side by side and speaking the same tongue, which are by nature less attuned to one another in terms of instinct and tradition than England and Ireland. The English, with some justification, regarded the Irish in the seventeenth and eighteenth centuries as pretty much a lost cause, incapable of reform and lacking the discipline necessary to modernise themselves as a progressive, self-supporting country. 'They'd still be scratching the fleas off themselves if it weren't for England' about sums up the British attitude at that time. The Irish, for their part, detested absentee landlords, loathed the armed invaders, bridled at the discrimination to which they were subjected and – quite rightly – regarded British treatment of Ireland and its people as the worst blot in all the long history of British empire-building. And ever since the first Irish convicts and free settlers decided to cast their lot in New South Wales rather than return to their bleak homeland, the basic conflict between them and the British – above and beyond all, between them and the English – has never been far below the surface in times of tension, particularly over religion, the abuses by English-descended authorities on the goldfields, and the use of Australian troops in British wars when Britain was at loggerheads, or undeclared war, with Ireland. Yet the Irish, always a minority in Australia, have managed to carve out for themselves and maintain in this country a remarkable stake.

Much that visitors to Australia today find distasteful in the Australian character and national make-up can be traced to the early convicts. The Cockney-Irish ethos, as we should term it, takes many forms, including lack of initiative, resistance to change, and obstinate refusal to stand up and be counted except in oppos-

Irish free settlers receive their priest's blessing on setting out for a new country. There has been a large and influential Irish element in Australia's population since 1788.

ition – all in all, an underdog mentality, an inferiority complex, what has become known as the 'national cringe'. The Irish and Cockneys saw themselves that way before they were thrown into the docks of courts in England and Ireland. It would take a massive infusion of people of different stocks, long after the six colonies had been established on Australian soil, to begin to change that outlook. But if we accept that a national ethos is firmly ingrained in the first decades of a nation's history by those whose influence sets the general tone, then it is not difficult to accept what Australia's was to be – or rather, especially, that of New South Wales. (There would be marked differences in non-convict States, South Aus-

tralia in particular, and Victoria, which had few convicts.)

The influence of the pilgrims is still part of the American Way, as well as American folklore and tradition, from breast-beating guilt to strictness of forms of religious worship (though the original model while still adhered to by many has also been diluted and in some cases abandoned). So it was in New Zealand, which still bears many of its early Scots-influenced traits. And in Australia, the model was unique. It is with us still, for good or ill.

What of the men who ruled over this motley collection of Cockneys and Celts? Very little of much meaning has been taught in Australian schools about them,

Captain Arthur Phillip and Margaret Charlott Phillip, his first wife.

and they emerge from the pages of most history books as one-dimensional people, imposing their will as they saw fit on the ill-bred masses beneath them. Australian history neglects the fact that Captain Arthur Phillip, the first Governor of New South Wales, was a second-generation Briton. He was half-German, something that has not been lost on historians in his father's native land: not a few of the accounts in the Mitchell Library in Sydney of Phillip's life and works are written in German.

Jacob Phillip emigrated to Britain from Frankfurt am Main, in the German Rhineland, where he had been a languages teacher. He married Elizabeth Breach, the widow of a Royal Navy captain, who was to have a great deal of influence on the career of their son Arthur, born in London on 11 October 1738, just ten years after James Cook. Young Arthur was educated at Greenwich School, where Britain's seafaring traditions washed over

him. After three years of tradition there, he was bound as an apprentice on the ship *Fortune,* trading with Greenland, but in 1753 or 1755 entered the Royal Navy. He retired on half-pay in 1763, after the Seven Years' War; in the same year he married Margaret Denison, widow of a City of London merchant. She was originally from a North Wales farming family, and with Phillip took to farming for several years at Lyndhurst, in the New Forest in Hampshire.

Arthur Phillip could not resist the sea, and in 1774 he joined the Portuguese Navy on the outbreak of war between Spain and Portugal: the RN did not mind in those freewheeling days. Phillip saw active service, principally off the South American coast – the Portuguese fleet was based at its colony, Brazil. Phillip also saw service in the Mediterranean, and was at the taking of Havana. But his career appears to have been in a trough thereafter, and he probably had to use neighbourly influence to get the command of the First Fleet.

He named the first settlement in honour of the Secretary of State for the Home Department, who in 1783 had been elevated to the peerage under the title of Baron Sydney of Chislehurst. The name Sydney, therefore, was the most elevated thing about the settlement. The Lieuten-

William Pitt, who as Prime Minister of England declared that it was essential to expel the most incorrigible criminals from England as cheaply as possible. He saw New South Wales as the ideal dumping ground.

ant-Governor was a major, the Deputy Judge Advocate had no legal education; the surgeon – there was only one though he had four assistants – was competent for his time. The Surveyor-General, Augustus Theodore Alt, a German, came from a family in the diplomatic corps for Hesse-Kassel. He laid out the settlement and surveyed Parramatta, but was elderly, infirm, and soon sought relief from his labours. The Anglican chaplain, Reverend Richard Johnson, had to act as a magistrate and care for sick and orphaned children. He did his best to cultivate contact with the Aborigines, but was aghast at the baseness of the convicts. Most of the rest of the people in the settlement knew nothing of farming or of supervising convicts, and there were no master craftsmen: a midshipman who had been a carpenter, clerk and architectural student, Henry Brewer, swiftly became provost-marshal, and then building superintendent. All needles and thread, as well as new clothes to be distributed to the women, had been left behind. There were no overseers, no artificers, no gardeners, no lawyers, no flax dressing (not that that mattered, because not even the Norfolk Island flax proved suitable). There was not even a Roman Catholic chaplain for the Irish, and that had been a purposeful decision, so Reverend Johnson was on his own. The Anglicans had their problems with him, however – he had been 'denounced' as a Methodist, possibly because he was fiercely evangelical. As such, it is doubtful if he distinguished much between his Cockney charges, nominal and lapsed Anglicans, and the Catholic Irish, most of whom appeared beyond redemption.

And so a portrait emerges of the first settlers, who were more 'make do' than 'can do' in their attitude to their task. It was not even an *ad hoc* team, that would have been too optimistic a construction to put on it. But they endured, because they had to. Phillip saw to it that there were exploratory forays up the Hawkesbury River, and he dutifully noted the progress of the settlement for his superiors in London. Slowly at first, but then with increasing confidence, they would erect buildings, get the soldiers out of tents, and build sufficient organisation into their little group so that it became a colony. It was June 1790 before another load of convicts arrived: the *Lady Juliana*, appropriately, brought 226 female convicts to help redress the imbalance between the sexes in the First Fleet, in which only 191 of the more than 700 convicts who embarked were women. The First Fleeters had lost so much livestock that before the Second Fleet arrived they had been down to subsistence rations. Phillip had to send to Calcutta for supplies. There were more than 1000 prisoners in the Second Fleet, but one in four died on the voyage, and the remainder fell ill.

Less than two years after the first convicts arrived in Sydney, an emancipist, James Ruse, was given land, and he became self-supporting. (He was one of the few to make it – the large majority of emancipists who were given grants in the eighteenth century failed as farmers or sold up and went home.) The emancipists began to fall into two groups: men and women determined to make the best of their lot, however meagre it appeared to them, and the defeatists, many of whom felt starvation was only a matter of time. The British Government came to agree that New South Wales was a colony and that it would be valuable. That being so, it is remarkable that the Government did not do more to promote the development of the colony, and that it was allowed to suffer for want of people.

Arthur Phillip governed for five years, then returned home, reportedly because of ill health. His wife had died before he left Australia. In May 1794, he married a woman fifteen years his junior (his first wife had been as many years senior to him) and in 1799 he was promoted to

The Reverend Richard Johnson was the sole chaplain for both Irish Catholics and Anglicans of the First Fleet and the first settlement. Probably few hopes were held that life in the colony would promote the urge for redemption.

Rear-Admiral of the Blue. He retired in 1805. Despite the initial disappointments, inevitable with a disparate group in a strange land, he had held the penal settlement together long enough for it to gestate – Hunter, his successor as Governor, was surprised by the development of the place when he took up his post in 1795.

Phillip died at age seventy-five, with a firm record as a dedicated Royal Navy man who might have followed his father's profession as a German-language teacher on the Rhine but for a quirk of fortune. To Phillip goes the credit for recognising the future the British had in Australia. Exactly one hundred and fifty years after Phillip departed these shores another man, also of foreign extraction, would recognise that Australia's future would depend on its ability to attract non-British peoples. Arthur Augustus Calwell was of American descent, and that meant he was of immigrant stock twice over. Ironically, the American line came from Ireland.

CHAPTER 3

Convicts and Squatters

IN THE FIRST TWENTY YEARS of white settlement, fewer than one hundred men chose to live in Australia as free settlers. After half a century of white settlement, Australia had only 12 600 free settlers: four in five of the population were convicts, their rulers, and former convicts. The British Government did not see fit to offer any carrot to prospective free settlers until the 1830s, nor did it do much to build Australia economically. It did not cultivate flax for its sails and was not interested in Australian timber for its hulls. Without considerable inducements there was never much prospect that Australia would get free settlers. America was much more attractive. It was rich, independent, and in the unlikely event that settlers could not make a go of it there, they had

'Les colons de Queensland', from a collection of cuttings from French journals. In the outback, a visitor was an object of curiosity.

the solace of knowing that the sea separating the United States and Europe was just one week wide. And emigrants to America had the comfort of numbers: the more who went, the more who wanted to go. In western and northern New York State alone, the population rocketed from 9000 to more than 700 000 between 1790 and 1820. Many were German or Irish (the Scots-Irish, from Northern Ireland, had already gone, in their hundreds of thousands, in the eighteenth century to settle the Old South as farmers). The population of the United States surged past England's after Independence. Between 1790 and 1820 the number of Americans rose from 4 million to 9.5 million, and thereafter it almost doubled every twenty years. (Australia's population did not reach 4 million until 1905, and in the following thirty years rose to only 6.7 million, despite the advances made over the previous century in shipping.)

Consider immigration in this light: in the century after 1850, 52 million people left Europe for new lands across the seas, and 35 per cent of them, which is to say more than 18 million, were from the British Isles (including Ireland). For every one of them who came to Australia, ten went to America. There was much to offer here, but to the British, with their sprawling empire that touched almost every corner of the globe, Australia was still an afterthought in the early nineteenth century. Quite apart from the fact that Britain had other lands to settle (South Africa and Canada among them, though it can scarcely be said that they did a fulsome job of that either), there was little reason for Britain to entice its citizenry to Australia. America beckoned people: Australia was run in effect by an absentee landlord that did not feel any need to fill the island continent with tenants. Also, Britain's attention was taken up with troubles nearer home. Napoleon blockaded Britain and it took more than a decade to finally bring him down. The British had a second try at subduing the Americans, in 1812-14, failed, and thereby ensured that the United States of America would ever after be regarded as a safe haven for those Europeans who had had their fill of the Old World. In the nineteenth century war was still an acceptable method of solving differences, and Britain had often resorted to it, not always as a last resort. But Australia was not threatened by any power, and showed no rebellious instincts.

The United States had many reasons for developing quickly, and xenophobia was one of them. The British knew they could develop Australia at leisure; but that meant development would be slow. So there was no stimulation to emigration by Britain, and no demand by the peoples of Europe for entry to the wide brown

An English artist, Samuel Sidney's view of emigrants leaving for the Australian colonies.

'The Emigration Agent's Office — The Passage Money Paid'. From the Illustrated London News *of 10 May 1851.*

land. Australia would therefore be developed by a few people from the British Isles – and the free peoples of the British Isles were not about to make a long voyage to any country so far away as Australia that had become part of the British Empire only by virtue of the fact that it was a penal dump for the least civilised inhabitants of the British Isles. Civilised Britons seeking a better life over the oceans were not about to select a penal dump for their new home. If you were a Briton thinking of making a new start, you might as well make a clean break and settle in the Great Republic, where there were riches to be won and few impediments to winning them.

Little wonder then that Australia did not attract middle-class immigrants in the foundation decades of white occupation. For a full half century there were only the rulers, who had been sent here, and the convicts, emancipists and 'currency' or local-born people. Free immigrants constituted only 13 per cent of the white population in 1828, though in the following thirteen years their proportion rose to 37 per cent, and continued to rise. Convicts, who accounted for 43 per cent of all whites in 1828, were only 1.5 per cent of the population by 1851. Most of the free immigrants were ordinary people looking for a new start in life. The unruliness of early nineteenth century Australian society was not confined to those who were being ruled: the antics of the New South Wales Rum Corps, the schemings of John Macarthur, the overthrow of Governor William Bligh in 1807 after a struggle that alienated the merchants of Sydney, all were part of the colourful patchwork of early white settlement. Much of it is glossed over in school history texts with the same sweep that covers up the nature of the bulk of the early settlers. We are forced to conclude that most of the convicts were neither political martyrs nor incorrectly judged victims of Britain's harsh statutes. Vance Palmer it was who said that the best of them were 'people distinguished from their neighbours only by a lighter regard for property or a fainter capacity for self-control in the presence of a landlord'.

Arrival. Some would go straight to Ballarat by Cobb & Co.

And so we see Australia's white population whose totals were:

1788	859
1800	5 217
1805	7 707 (including 757 in Tasmania)
1810	11 566 (including 1470 in Tasmania)
1815	15 063 (including 1947 in Tasmania)
1820	33 543 (including 5519 in Tasmania)
1825	52 505 (including 14 192 in Tasmania)
1830	70 039 (24 279 in Tasmania, 1172 in Western Australia)

But by 1835 Australia had 113 354, by 1840, 190 408, and by 1845, 279 148 – an increase of 146 per cent in ten years. It was done by assisting immigration; it also happened because Australia was becoming known overseas as an increasingly viable proposition for settlers in an era that was dispossessing many in the Old World – the Industrial Revolution was forcing rural people into the cities, and the hardier types preferred to take their chances picking up the tatters of their lives in a new country, in rural or semi-rural occupations.

The flow of free settlers was slow, but by the beginning of the fourth decade enough had changed in the settlement for it to have taken on a different flavour from that of the eighteenth century; the convict odour was not so dominant. It no longer regarded itself so much as an outcast in outlook – the native-born Australian was more confident than his forebears, and physically he would, in succeeding generations, be very different too – he would become the Cornstalk, tall, wiry, sinewy, lantern-jawed. This was a result both of his protein-laden nutrition – in times of plenty, particularly, he thrived on red meat – and a lifestyle that, while not care-free, was less oppressive than he would have been subjected to in Britain. He walked upright. He could aspire to the same things that had brought the free immigrant to Australia, and so knew that his prospects were better here than in Britain. The English and Scots, or second-generation Australians of that ancestry, were naturally torn between Australia and Britain in their loyalties; but patriotism for Australia increased. The Irish were the most pro-Australian of all – they had most to gain, comparatively, from a fresh start in a new land, especially one halfway around the world from the people they saw as their oppressors.

It was during this period that the whites began to open up the bush. Newcastle, first known as Coal River, began as a penal dump when twenty-four of the leading insurgents of the Castle Hill Rising were sent there. The rising, by about three hundred Irish, was swiftly and easily put down. Because such dramas are few in Australian history, a certain romanticism has been attached to it: it was the underdog versus authority, the Irish with their backs to the wall. They went about it in a typically disorganised and hopeless fashion, and the New South Wales Corps, not the finest bunch to police a settlement, welcomed the opportunity to go through their paces. It was a violent field day. The convicts had escaped from the Castle Hill prison farm; there was some talk of setting up a free, independent Ireland, though some thought to return home. The plan was to take Parramatta by surprise, but by sunrise the next day, many had got lost, lost interest, or were drunk. Fifty-six troopers, led by Major George Johnston, head of the Corps, marched overnight from Sydney. The troopers killed fifteen rebels.

As the confidence of the colony grew, so it spread its boundaries: the first few decades of the last century are among the most interesting in Australian history. It was a time full of challenge, and of the birth of the bush legend. There was increasing demand for rural produce – mutton, beef and wool. John Macarthur's name is synonymous with fine merino wool, but the story is not nearly so romantic when examined thoroughly, for chance

Major George Johnston led troopers of the NSW Corps against rebels from Castle Hill prison farm.

Captain John Macarthur, famous for his pioneering work with sheep and for his disputes with authority.

47

'Shepherding in Australia' from the Illustrated London News.

404 858 hectares for fine-woolled sheep. Australia was about to begin its long ride on the sheep's back.

The demand for beef increased too. Itinerant tradesmen began circuit work in the bush. It was an extraordinary period, one of fear and trust. In the bush, nobody white felt really safe, and in that period the Australian tradition of mateship was born. One of the most notable evidences of it was the 'free feed' – travellers, emerging from the scrub after a long journey, would happen on a farm house, and, though there was no farm dweller in sight, enter the farmhouse unbidden and help themselves to whatever food they found.

Lieutenant Philip Gidley King, RN, led the party which settled Norfolk Island, and later became third Governor of New South Wales.

and misfortune had a lot to do with it. Macarthur was what we would today term 'stroppy', and a born intriguer. He was a lieutenant in the Corps who had become a farmer and entrepreneur, and he had no qualms about buying rum, diluting it with water, and selling it at phenomenal mark-ups. He acquired some Spanish sheep, for the mutton, bought 1400 more from a major and tried to sell the lot to the Government for a 66 per cent profit. Macarthur had decided to forsake the colony. The deal fell through because the price was too high. He got into disagreement with Governor Philip Gidley King, fought a duel with his commanding officer, and was sent home in disgrace and under arrest. He was remanded back to the colony, and while waiting for transport was approached by British manufacturers who needed wool to clothe the troops fighting Napoleon. They placed their orders, and after some smooth talking by Macarthur he wound up with a grant of

The doors were unlocked, nobody challenged them. The accumulated cost to the farmer was sometimes high – there were a lot of itinerant workers – but the practice was accepted.

Most of the travellers were men, of course: there was still a massive preponderance of males in the colony. The mateship tradition did not include women. Relations between the sexes, which Europeans to this day find difficult to understand, because of the apparent distance between men and women, probably dates back to this period, when many men went right through their working lives without much contact with women, and certainly little intimate contact. Women were not regarded as equals, but nor were they treated with that deference and Old World courtliness that was so obvious in other 'new' countries, such as the United States. Life was basic, life was hard, and men took great comfort from the close friendships they formed. Captain Cook had named the region New South Wales because he thought the coast lines similar. The continent itself remained New Holland until Matthew Flinders' Australia took hold. Australia was taking shape as a nation, albeit one living in the shadow of, and dependent on, Britain.

'Immigrants landing at the Queen's Wharf'. From a sketch by N. Chevalier, 1863. In that period Melbourne was a prime destination and Port Phillip was synonymous with Victoria.

A moving illustration of emigrants which was published in the Illustrated London News *in 1852.*

A great deal has been written – much of it derogatory – about the squatters. They are in some quarters detested because they took what they wanted – millions of hectares of land – and waxed fat, refusing to contribute much for their privileges, while the less fortunate – the bulk of people of the colony – had to graft for an existence. In Australia, from an early date, envy of the rich and detestation of authority and even those of independent means or disposition was raised (lowered?) to the level of the Tall Poppy Syndrome: a desire to cut everybody down to the same level. But the squatters opened up the country. They took their chances. By 1850, there were forty times as many sheep as there were people, and the annual wool trade was worth nearly two million pounds. The face of Australia was changed. As Winston Churchill recalled in *A History of the English-speaking Peoples*, an

early governor had written that the convict barracks reminded him of Spanish monasteries, 'they contain a population of consumers who produce nothing'. Thanks in part to the squatters, the sheep lands pushed out over the Bathurst Plain, moved south and north. The squatters became the most important part of the community.

Van Diemen's Land became Tasmania, which became a separate colony in 1824, and the prosperity from wool and whaling led to a marked increase in population. From a convict settlement with a reputation even harsher than that of New South Wales it became an island of free people, with a character all its own. The coming of the free settlers to Australia and the end of transportation was a sea change, as important at the time as the decision, a century later, to people the country with Continental Europeans, if need be,

This evocative engraving of a surgeon's bush hut, isolated in the bush, appeared in the Illustrated London News *in 1871: it was also an illustration of mateship.*

rather than depend on Britons.

The squatter was the bold embodiment of the Protestant work ethic and the capitalist dictum, 'to each as much as he can hold' (to which might be added, 'and the Devil take the hindmost', because the Devil already had, the convicts were testimony to that). Eventually the inhabitants of the colonies were all free, better off than they would have been in Britain, and so they came to look on themselves as Australians. Australia was on its way.

The rise of the squatter almost coincided with the end of the convict period. Several reasons have been advanced for the decision in 1840 to stop sending prisoners to the mainland (though they were shipped to Tasmania and Norfolk Island for a further twelve years, and almost 10 000 of them, all males, were landed in Western Australia between 1850 and 1868, thus helping ensure the survival of a colony). Transportation was said to be uneconomic. Free settlers resented the use of cheap labour, which allegedly kept down wages. The convict system was criticised as a method of rehabilitating criminals. Britain was becoming more liberal in its attitude to miscreants. The system was a lottery: some were sent, some allowed to remain at home, and so on. It is entirely probable that the chief reason was the influence of free settlers who did not want Australia to continue as a community of two classes, one composed of contaminants, the other free and free of any impurity. The question remained, however: how to people the continent? (The blacks were dying off, debilitated by the white man's illnesses, the white man's poisoned flour and the white man's gun.)

ARRIVAL AT GEELONG, PORT PHILIP.

Bourrichter &Co. 58, Basinghall St.

CHAPTER 4

Diluting the Convict Flavour

THE BOUNTY SYSTEM, begun in 1835, permitted colonists to organise the immigration of new settlers for their use, and they were rewarded for bringing in manpower. The system fell into disrepute in the early 1840s; there were strong complaints about the quality of people who had been brought out, but as the historian Michael Roe has pointed out: 'Anyway, the migrants came in significant numbers.'

It was logical that Australia should implement a plan that would attract more people from the British Isles, and the one that was chosen was simple and logical, though not without its inconsistencies. The British Government stopped giving land to new settlers in 1831; instead it was sold for not less than 5 shillings an acre (about half a hectare) from 1831. South Australia, founded in 1836 as a free colony, raised the price, at the outset, by 140

Arrival at Geelong, Port Philip (sic).

per cent, to the equivalent of almost 12 shillings an acre, and the British Government followed suit in eastern Australia. The minimum price of Crown land throughout Australia was raised to £1 an acre in 1842, making it about ten times as dear as land in America.

Whereas land prices were comparable in the two countries in 1831, Australia had decided against direct competition for immigrants based on comparably priced land, in favour of a scheme that would raise funds – half the revenue from land sales – for assisted immigration. There were howls from pastoralists and would-be pastoralists, of course – land had been free before, why not continue with that system? Most of the established graziers, however, continued to pay peanuts for the right to huge spreads. There was some risk attached to the scheme, in that Britons with the capital to pay high prices for land might not feel any need to emigrate, since they were obvi-

An emigration depot in old Cork.

ously well-off already. But it worked: Australia got a new class of grazier, and the money to pay the assisted passages of the poorer people who would be needed as workers in this great expansionist experiment. More than that, once the scheme was under way, Australia became more attractive to free settlers who were willing to pay their own fares.

The scheme did not produce anything like a flood of immigrants, and nothing at all to match the American experience, which was a deluge that by the end of the century would become a tidal wave. But it produced a stream and, like any stream, even though it dried up in times of drought, once its course was set it would be there forever, to fill and surge again. So land became the chief attraction for wealthy Britons, and assisted fares and jobs the lure for the less fortunate: Britain's underfed, unskilled and semi-skilled workers, grappling with the social and economic upheaval of the biggest advance since the feudal era – the Industrial Revolution – now knew, from official pronouncements and letters sent home by those who had gone to Australia before them, that you could be reasonably sure of two things in the Antipodes (New Zea-

land adopted the scheme as well): a job and a full belly. One hundred and fifty years ago, that was enough. So land, areas so vast that most Britons, wealthy and poor alike, could scarcely imagine it, and which was Australia's only resource, was to be harnessed as the magnet. It worked, but not nearly so well as another, later magnet that not only stirred the imagination but set men wide-eyed and stuttering with excitement: gold.

The credit for the expensive land-assisted immigration scheme goes to one Edward Gibbon Wakefield, though it was hardly the kind of brainstorm that required the intellect of a Newton, or indeed emanated solely from the fertile mind of Wakefield. As the historian Geoffrey Blainey has pointed out, Wakefield had plenty of time to ponder the economic problems facing Australia, because but for the luck of the convict lottery, he might have arrived here in chains.

Wakefield had a privileged upbringing, was well educated, and had been a British diplomat in Europe. Diplomacy, even at Wakefield's junior level, is a difficult and trying pursuit, and we can only imagine that a rush of blood induced him, at thirty, to abduct an heiress who was still of school age, and carry her off to Gretna Green, where they took their marriage vows, as did so many other couples whose wedding plans matured without the approval of their families.

Australia thus had a system that would ensure development and bring new people. Even after the discovery of gold, however, assisted immigration continued. In the 1850s, 88 475 assisted immigrants arrived in Victoria from Britain, 72 638 went to New South Wales, and 50 354 to South Australia, which had been founded by private interests and preceded Victoria in independent development and importance. The numbers of assisted immigrants to all three colonies dropped drastically in the following decade. Long before then, however, Australia had firmed up, in the minds of colonists and the British Government, as a nation-in-waiting, a country of colonies that was on the move.

Essential traits in the Australian character were set: a belief in equality, a mistrust of rank and authority, and, inevitably, of the rich, which of course was not peculiar to Australia, but was openly

Edward Gibbon Wakefield; an 1823 engraving.

Sketches on board an emigrant ship.

Female Emigration

TO

AUSTRALIA.

COMMITTEE:

EDWARD FORSTER, Esq. *Chairman.*	CHARLES HOLTE BRACEBRIDGE, Esq.	CHARLES LUSHINGTON, Esq.
SAMUEL HOARE, Esq.	JOHN S. REYNOLDS, Esq.	GEORGE LONG, Esq.
JOHN TAYLOR, Esq.	JOHN PIRIE, Esq.	COLONEL PHIPPS.
THOMAS LEWIN, Esq.	CAPEL CURE, Esq.	NADIR BAXTER, Esq.
	WILLIAM CRAWFORD, Esq.	S. H. SHERRY, Esq.

The Committee for promoting the Emigration
OF
Single Women

To AUSTRALIA, under whose Management the Ships "Bussorah Merchant and Layton" were last Year despatched with Female Emigrants, acting under the Sanction of His Majesty's Secretary of State for the Colonies, HEREBY GIVE NOTICE, That

A Fine SHIP of about 500 Tons Burthen,

Carrying an experienced Surgeon, and a respectable Person as Superintendent to secure the Comfort and Protection of the Emigrants during the Voyage, will sail from

GRAVESEND
On Thursday 1st of May next,

(Beyond which day she will on no account be detained) direct for

HOBART TOWN,
VAN DIEMEN'S LAND.

Single Women and Widows of good Character, from 15 to 30 Years of Age, desirous of bettering their Condition by Emigrating to that healthy and highly prosperous Colony, where the number of Females compared with the entire Population is greatly deficient, and who consequently from the great demand for Servants, and other Female Employments, the Wages are comparatively high, may obtain a Passage

On payment of FIVE POUNDS only.

Those who are unable to raise that Sum here, will be allowed to give Notes of Hand, payable in the Colony within a reasonable time after their arrival, when they have acquired the means to do so, as they will have the advantage of the **Government Grant** in aid of their Passage.

The Females who proceed by this Conveyance will be taken care of on their first Landing at Hobart Town, they will find there a List of the various Situations to be obtained, and of the Wages offered, and will be perfectly free to make their own Election; they will not be bound to any person, or subjected to any restraint, but will be, to all intents and purposes, perfectly free to act and decide for themselves.

Females in the Country who may desire to avail themselves of the important advantages thus offered them, should apply by Letter to "The Emigration Committee, London," under Cover addressed to "The UNDER SECRETARY OF STATE, COLONIAL DEPARTMENT, LONDON." It will be necessary that the Application be accompanied by a Certificate of Character from the Resident Minister of the Parish, or from some other respectable persons to whom the Applicant may be known; but the Certificate of the Resident Minister is in all cases most desirable. Such Females as may find it expedient may, when approved by the Committee as fit persons to go by this Conveyance, be boarded temporarily in London, prior to Embarkation, on Payment of 7s. per Week.

All Applications made under cover in the foregoing manner, or personally, will receive early Answers, and all necessary Information, by applying to

JOHN MARSHALL, Agent to the Committee, 26, Birchin Lane, Cornhill.

EDWARD FORSTER, *Chairman.*

NOTE.—The Committee have the satisfaction to state that of 217 Females who went out by the Bussorah Merchant, 180 obtained good Situations within three Days of their Landing, and the remainder were all well placed within a few Days, under the advice of a Ladies' Committee, formed in the Colony expressly to aid the Females on their arrival.

LONDON, 22nd February, 1834.

By Authority:
PRINTED BY JOSEPH HARTNELL, FLEET STREET, FOR HIS MAJESTY'S STATIONERY OFFICE.

---

expressed here. Though many Australians had convict ancestors, there was no inverted snobbery apparent in that: it was something best not spoken of. The assisted passage scheme brought a new class of people; farmers, not a few of them from Ulster, who were loyal to the Crown, had sufficient capital and nouse to succeed on their own, and who had no intention, once arrived, of returning to the Old

Country. The Irish in Australia now fell therefore into two categories, one of which could be termed, unflatteringly, as 'bog', the other with much the same values and aspirations as the English bourgeoisie. The 'bogs', like other workers, were suspicious of, and opposed to, anything that might threaten their own jobs, including competition, or might reduce their wages, which were high because of demand for labour.

So the Australian mateship ideal would, in time, extend to politics and trade unionism; it would be a great leveller. In this, we have a fundamental divergence from the American experience, where the tide of immigrants kept wages lower than they otherwise would have been, and where competition was regarded as a tenet of capitalism, which was admired rather than despised. In America, the growth of trade unions would come late, be violently opposed, and rights that Australian workers took for granted would be resisted well into the twentieth century. But there were plenty of parallels between the immigrant experience in Australia and the United States, and not the least of them was a feeling that the new chum should begin at or near the bottom, and conform with the ideals and notions of established citizens. The biggest difference was the make-up of immigrants to the two countries: Austra-

Between 500 and 600 young Irish women arrived in 1886. The men they met on arrival were a mixed bunch: some respectable, others rough and ready.

Below: *The first Christmas in Australia for a 'new chum': it was very different from 'home'.*

No 3

THE SECOND "HEADER"

No 4

PROTECTING A BROKEN GATE

No 5

LED THROUGH THE MUD

lia continued, before and after the gold rushes, to look first and foremost to Britain for immigrants. The Briton was welcomed in the United States but he was greatly outnumbered in the nineteenth and early twentieth centuries by people from other countries, first from northern Europe, and later from central, eastern and southern Europe.

It was Wakefield's belief that high land prices would lead to the development of smaller blocks of settlements, so that the spread of big blocks into regions far from the principal towns would be halted; the existence of concentrations of small blocks was a prerequisite of civilisation, he said. There were enough Britons willing to go along with the concept. Fortunately, there were other peoples who saw promise in the idea as well.

Wakefield's theory was rooted in a philosophy that has moistened the eyes of capitalists throughout the world, well into the twentieth century. If we were to put it in modern phraseology, we would say that he believed there was no such thing as a free lunch. The price of land would be high enough to ensure that the worker was kept in his place until he had earned enough and saved enough of what he earned to be able to buy his way to the next rung on the economic ladder.

No 6

ANOTHER RIDE ? NO THANK YOU .

Opposite page and above: *The 'new chum' had a difficult time of it — especially if he was an Englishman with airs and graces.*

Institutions would be free, worship would be free, and there would be free immigration. It was as much a social philosophy as an economic one. It was designed to raise the tone of the Australian communities.

In the maelstrom of debate that ensued, Wakefield was supported by reformers and radicals.

Conservative British politicians, most of all Earl Grey, Colonial Secretary, continued to press for transportation to Tasmania and Norfolk Island long after it was evident that the eastern Australian colonies were hostile to it. The Port Phillip settlement and South Australia never took convicts, though there was nothing to stop former convicts from settling in the 'free' colonies. Port Phillip was the closest haven for men and women who wanted to make a fresh start, well away from memories of the harsh life at Port Arthur. But in the 1840s public sentiment ran so high that in the future colony of Victoria free settlers resented emancipists: once a criminal, always a criminal, that was the view. The poor wretches never would be raised from the gutter. In New South Wales prominent businessmen had an economic argument against transportation – it might yield cheap labour for some, but it raised the cost of protecting property.

Associations were formed to agitate for an end to transportation, and in this fierce burst of feeling seeds of both rebellion and federation were clear. Grey compromised with a plan to send more free settlers, but failed to follow through. In early 1852 he was still trying to wear down resistance by insisting that Tasmania take convicts. The contagion would be kept from the mainland by Bass Strait, and he had the support of the squatters, of course, who wanted everything on the cheap. Grey was not the first, or the last, Briton to make a fundamental miscalculation of the events and mood in far-off Australia. No bugles of Australian nationhood rang in his ears; the place was a penal dump with a bonus of undreamed of quantities of fine wool for the motherland. Quite apart from all this, however, the moral argument against transportation had achieved acceptance in Britain, and was irreversible. Before 1852 was out the British Colonial Office, wary that continuing colonial resistance might become unified (and perhaps spill over into unified action on other issues in the future) decided to stop transportation to the eastern colonies. Western Australia, which as a colony almost died at birth, took convicts until 1868 because free labourers did not go there in sufficient numbers at the outset to make it viable.

The ending of transportation was much more than the outcome of moral indignation in Britain and the works of high-minded activists. It was not only partly a result of increased immigration of free settlers, but made Australia safer and more attractive for free settlers. The social face of the convict colonies changed because the convict period ended. The rough bush ethos, in its crudest form, was gone. Australia came to have a more varied lifestyle because it had a wider variety of classes (however hideous the term may be to those who are revolted by class-consciousness). In yielding, however late, to colonial feeling, the British showed that they were not unmindful of their disastrous experience in America, which cost them their richest prize.

When the convict era ended Australia was still very Anglo-Saxon and mostly of English stock, but with marked differences between the colonies. Tasmania had virtually no Irish. New South Wales had proportionately more Irish than any other colony. There was a strong, growing Scots influence in Victoria from 1836. Farmers from the Scottish lowlands came; they had considerable influence in community affairs. The two non-convict colonies, Victoria and South Australia, had at their helms free settlers who from the outset put their stamp on their respec-

The Cricket Ground, Richmond, Melbourne, was a social and sporting venue.

tive settlements for all time. They were industrious, high-minded, public-spirited and often strongly religious. They believed in education and self-improvement. God helped those who helped themselves. They were, in their time, the embodiment of a term that did not come into popular usage until the 1960s: they were WASPs, white Anglo-Saxon Protestants, and to them the work ethic was a plank of life, so much a part of their marrow that they would never have thought to question it.

The stream of free settlers was encouraged not only directly by government, through land sales, but also by schemes such as Caroline Chisholm's Family Colonisation Loan Society, which began sending out 'superior' immigrants in 1850. All of this marked a transition. Squatterdom did not die quickly, and scruples about using Chinese and Indian coolies and kanakas did not evaporate

overnight. These pools of sweated labour had given Australia a cheap solution in times of manpower shortages, but were on nothing like the scale of slave labour in the United States. The working man's antipathy to cheap labour was a seed of trade unionism, which sprouted early in Australia. To free settlers, convicts were always suspect and the descendants of convicts melted silently into the Australian mainstream. There were never sufficient numbers of coolies and kanakas to form a broad, brooding workforce that could constitute a social threat in later years, nor was the economy dependent on them. The emigration to Australia of free settlers was much slower than it was to America in the 1830s and 1840s, but the first big tide of immigration was just around the corner. Out of it came the only armed conflict that threatened, however fleetingly, to boil over and perhaps uproot society: Eureka Stockade.

CHAPTER 5

Continental Europeans

SOUTH AUSTRALIA'S beginnings set it apart from all of the other Australian colonies. It was the fourth colony founded and was established before both Victoria and Queensland, but it grew out of inspiration, ideology and a desire to experiment, all present in the hearts and wallets of the businessmen who conceived it. These men were virtually promised self-government if they could attract a population of 50 000. The British Colonial Office was joint administrator of the colony, but the finance for it was raised through the South Australian Company, over which loomed George Fife Angas, one of the most extraordinary figures in Australian history.

He was a Baptist and a businessman. In most Australian histories he is accorded a

George French Angas' 1846 lithographs of Klemzig, a village of German settlers near Adelaide. The orderly nature of the inhabitants is apparent.

few paragraphs only, and in some just a few lines. He was not colourful, and nothing much of his personality emerges from general history texts. But in rarer works, a keen picture forms of an energetic visionary, persistent, patient and painstaking. Looking at some of his business correspondence, there is a tendency to deduce that he was open and vulnerable to crooks and charlatans, or was too trusting of slow-moving underlings in South Australia in whom he had placed his trust. In modern parlance, he seemed the sort of man who might be taken to the cleaners by a second-in-command, and then charged for the cleaning fluid. But we must remember that he lived in an earlier era, when the pace of events was slow and communications between England and Australia took many months.

Angas was a rare combination of Christian and businessman. He placed his trust in the Lord, and chose carefully those whom he entrusted to look after his interests in South Australia. He was meticulous in his correspondence with them, going over each detail that interested him, to reassure himself that his experiment was succeeding. His religion was the core of his being. He never pre-judged, he gave the benefit of the doubt, and he never lost heart. His religion was so important to him that when all else failed he risked substantial capital of his own to provide a new start in South Australia for a group of foreigners who, though religious, were not of his own denomination. Why did he do it? 'I felt at one time great difficulty in taking up their cause,' he wrote of the Germans, 'but ... my duty is to love all men who love the Lord Jesus Christ, of every age, kingdom, colour, language and sect. Men who for his sake have suffered the loss of all things, may be supposed to be sincere ...'

The people he supposed to be sincere were, indeed, so sincere that they repaid his trust many times over. They were the first organised group of Continental European settlers in Australia. Their leader and mentor was Augustus Kavel, a Lutheran pastor from Zullichau, deep in eastern Germany and under the control of Prussia. By order of Frederick William III, all Protestant churches in the kingdom were to conform with rules laid down for the reformed church, and adopt its liturgy. Thus was enforced, in 1830, the union of the Lutheran and Calvinist churches. This coercion lapsed after ten years. By then, however, there had been a steady flow of Germans to South Australia, a very different colony from New South Wales in which organised religion had been neglected from the outset. But it played a central part in the daily life of many of the first South Australians, and that is why Adelaide, when it began searching for a phrase with which to market its tourist appeal a century later, decided that its single most visible distinction lay in the indisputable fact that it was Australia's 'city of steeples'.

The first German immigrant in South Australia is supposed to have been Daniel Henry Schreyvogel, a clerk in the South Australian Company who landed on Kangaroo Island in July 1836. That year there were 884 immigrants from Britain, 71 of whom had sufficient faith in their future in the colony to pay their own fares and settle in it in its first year. It was Schreyvogel's father who took Pastor Kavel to talk with Angas in London early in 1836. The company recruited a geologist or mineralogist, Johann Menge, and German miners, labourers, vine-dressers and flax growers. The following year about fifty Germans arrived, some with families, and they included a blacksmith, four bakers, two carpenters, a bricklayer, some coopers, wheelwrights and shepherds.

A supplement to the first annual report of the directors of the South Australian Company, in 1837, says: 'From the steady and industrious habits of the German labourers and farmers, they will prove a valuable acquisition to the villages of the company's locations.' How different this was from the first settlement in Sydney.

The men and women who were helping South Australia on its way had names like Drescher, Stein, Schlotz, Rehm, Kleinschmidt, Hoffmann and Ahrens. Kleinschmidt was a labourer when he arrived. He put up the first government offices in the colony, farmed, started a brewery there, and a tweed factory. He and Dr Julius Drescher, the so-called 'superintendent of Germans', were among the most successful settlers.

Pastor Kavel gets the credit for the German influx because he led his faithful flock there in 1838. His first notion, however, had been to take them to the United States – a brighter, closer beacon. But they came, the first of them in the ship *Prince George*, to Port Misery, aptly named because it was a mangrove swamp. After travelling to Hamburg to embark and spending six months at sea, they must have been even less favourably impressed

George Fife Angas, one of the most distinguished exponents and planners of immigration in Australian history.

than the first whites who stepped ashore at Port Jackson. But there could be no turning back: the Germans had had trouble getting documents to leave Germany because the Prussian Government despised dissenters. It was November 1838, hot and steamy on the Port River. They sent scouts to find suitable farmland and chose some of Angas' land, only 8 hectares, by the River Torrens, a few kilometres from Adelaide. The soil did not seem particularly good and the cli-

mate was viciously different from Klemzig, the village many of them had left behind, but they named the settlement for Klemzig anyway, and began to dig and chop.

Another ship arrived a month later. The Germans decided that the Adelaide Hills offered better prospects. They did not have the money to buy oxen or horses, or even to rent some, so they piled their possessions into carts and pulled them, by hand, up into the hills, retracing their

steps at intervals because there were not enough hands for all the handcarts. It took two hundred of them about three months. They named their new settlement Hahndorf (Hahn's Village) in honour of the captain of the ship *Zebra* which had brought the second group to South Australia. Food was scarce: they lived off the land, on kangaroos, possums, even roots. But they planted, they constructed, and in a few short months the strongest of them were turning up in Adelaide with vegetables and dairy produce to sell. When they had to, they made the 30-kilometre journey with the produce on their backs. The English-speaking townsfolk gaped. They could not understand German, much less the strange dialect they heard. Winter swept in, the rain and the cold, and still these people came, down from the hills, always with produce to sell; then back to their fastness in the hills to farm and build. Who were these people? Nothing stopped them, nothing even daunted them: nothing was too hard, absolutely nothing.

In time, not a long time, the Anglo-Saxons came to understand that this minority group not only did not feel inferior, but did not need the recognition of Anglo-Saxons.

Most of the Klemzig people had moved inland as soon as they found they had made a wrong choice of land. The ships kept coming, new settlements sprang up. Pastor G. D. Fritzsche, of Posen, arrived with more Old Lutherans, as they were known, in 1841. Some of Fritzsche's pastor colleagues had been imprisoned, and by now the German settlements in South Australia had proved viable enough for other persecuted folk in the homeland to feel the long voyage was worthwhile. A Lutheran community adjoining Hahndorf was named Lobethal (Valley of Praise) in 1842; in the next two years other communities were born, with names such as Bethanien, Langmeil, Schoental. There were about six hundred settlers a year, on average, in 1845, 1846 and 1847, and twice that number in 1848, the year of revolutions for liberalism in Europe, and so the figure quadrupled in 1849. Not a few of them were middle

Opposite page and above: *These three lithographs of the Barossa Valley, South Australia by George French Angas show shearing time, the Angaston township and the opening of the chapel at Angaston.*

class: 5.3 per cent were professionals, 23 per cent worked in commerce, 28 per cent were farmers and 36 per cent were artisans.

Thus, by the end of 1851 there were about 9000 Germans and their Australian-born offspring in South Australia, and they represented about one-seventh of the total population. The board of the South Australian Company desired them for their sobriety, steadiness and perseverance. The names of many of them were distinctly eastern German: Leditschke, Nitschke, Koslowski, Zwar. Many of them were Wends, of Slavic ancestry. They preserved the Wendic language, even after generations in Australia. But in time, as the word spread in the Old World that you could make a go of it in South Australia, immigrants began arriving from Saxony and Mecklenburg as well as Silesia and Posen.

They were not pastoralists, not big-land farmers as the British were. In 1861, only sixty-eight Germans of the thousands in the colony were what we would call graziers today. The Germans took small blocks. Caution, frugality, conservation were everything to them, and their concept of farming complemented that of the pastoralists who farmed with exports in the foreground of their vision. It did not matter to the Germans if their land was heavily wooded or thick with

Christmas Eve in Australia, 1868; from the Illustrated Sydney News.

Robert Hillingford (1825–1904) painted this watercolour of emigrants to South Australia.

brush, so long as it was fertile. The dense foliage would lower the buying price. They would work like people possessed to clear it.

After the first of them, very few were religious refugees, but most were Lutheran, and few people had ever been known to work as hard. They were clannish. They maintained their German customs; singing and music were very important to them in what time they took for leisure — even that was carefully organised, like just about everything they did. They were never idle, so it seemed. In time it was the settlers of British ancestry who sought out the Germans, and an invitation to the liedertafel, the festival of song, was a mark of acceptance by the Germans.

Angas had sold his coach and resolved to live plainly and economically so that 'I may make the property which God had graciously given me the means of refreshing many a barren soil and cheering many a thirsty soul.' He was at his most effusive when doing good works in the name of his Maker. He need not have worried about the Deutsch. They worked from sun-up to dusk to repay his faith in them.

The Germans set in motion a wine industry that greened the Barossa Valley and became the most important of its kind in Australia. Kleinschmidt's tweed factory, at Lobethal, became the Onkaparinga Mills; it was the first spinning works in South Australia.

Because the Germans were so careful and conserving, you cannot walk the streets of their villages in South Australia without being struck by evidence of who they were and what they did. Examples of the implements they used, relics, ornaments, documents, abound in small museums. They left lots of records, carefully prepared. Some of the houses they built survived more than a century; well-built cottages with tiny rooms, and often with the sleeping quarters and eating space combined. Their town council meetings often lapsed into German, and records of these had to be translated into English for the town clerk. They were proud of their schools, of their skills, and with their discipline they had a natural leaning towards volunteer military groups. Because they tended to settle as families (60 per cent of them came in family groups) they helped populate a colony that desperately needed more people if it was to grow.

Even though many of the Germans drifted to Victoria during the gold rushes in the 1850s, and some moved to new farmlands in other colonies, the German-Australian flavour in South Australia did not wane. German immigration to South Australia did drop to a few thousand a decade in the late nineteenth century, but even so, upwards of 20 per cent of the population was German-Australian at the beginning of World War I, and the presence was so strong, so influential, that it had made an indelible mark. It is a sad irony that Australians of German descent then came to feel some of the bitter discrimination that had forced their ancestors to leave Germany. Scores of names of towns were Anglicised. Hahndorf, for example, became Ambleside, and Germantown, on the Hume Highway in southern New South Wales, was changed to Holbrook. Many South Australian names were changed back again in the 1930s.

The essential fact about non-English-speaking whites, which Australians did not begin to accept until well after World War II, was that their nationality really matters little. The national borders in Europe have always been changeable, with Poles becoming Germans or Russians, French becoming Germans and then French again, and so on. What really mattered was what the immigrant could offer Australia in return for the new start that Australia was offering him. Did he have skills in the workplace? Could he adapt sufficiently to a new and in many ways very different country? We can be more objective if we perhaps forget the name of the first homeland and ask the simple question: what sort of people are these? The English-speaking townsmen in Adelaide found that out very quickly when white settlement in Australia was

Port Adelaide, c. 1845, as S. T. Gill (1818–1880) saw it in this watercolour.

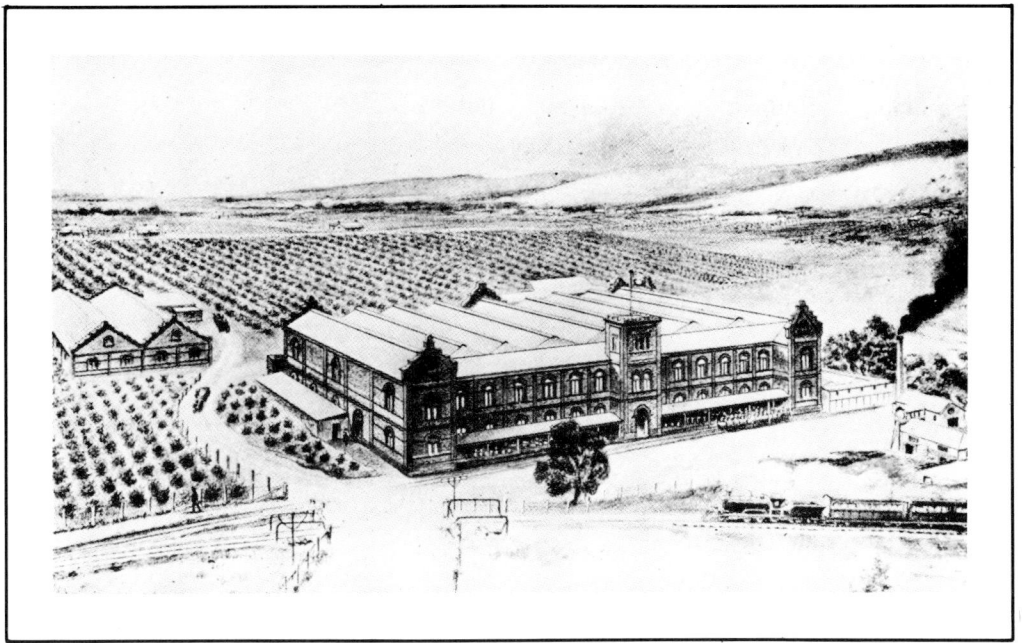

Chateau Tanunda, South Australia.

just fifty years old. The Germans were eminently suited to the pioneer work required in a new settlement, and that was what mattered. In most ways they were the best immigrants of all. The pity is that Australia did not take in many more of them. Then the fear of foreign bogeys would have died a natural death, through familiarity with different ethnic groups and because there is security in numbers: security dilutes xenophobia.

There are problems, of course, when the new country and the old one come into conflict, as has happened twice between Germany and the English-speaking countries. By the time World War II broke out, a full 38 per cent of Americans could claim some German ancestry, so great had been the exodus from Germany over three centuries. The German bunds were strongly pro-isolationist. But this was something with which the United States had always been able to cope (even if not with complete success) because Americans grow up accepting that they are derived from many different peoples but are, above all, Americans.

Dr John Cole, of Brisbane, who has made a detailed study of aspects of German immigration to Australia and the United States, says German-Australians were less cohesive than German-Americans because there were fewer of them – Germans assimilated faster in Australia than in America. (This means that on two counts – numbers of Germans and the degree of their assimilation – Australia had less to fear from its German-descended folk during both world wars than did America.) Dr Cole says 49 per cent of people in Boonah Shire, in southeast Queensland, are, like him, of German ancestry. Queensland, a pioneer State in its nineteenth-century attempts to attract immigrants from Continental Europe, has many towns with a distinct German background, among them Boonah itself, Kalbar, Rosewood and Marburg in the Fassifern district to name just a few. The Germans who went to Boonah in the late nineteenth century were education-conscious, got a 'provisional' school by 1878 by dint of lobbying and strength of numbers, and were farmers, not pastoralists. If you walk down the main street of Boonah, a few kilometres off the Cunningham Highway, you'll find evidence of them everywhere, not least in shop signs: Pfeffer Pty Ltd stands next to Humphries and Tow – the Tows are descended from a fourteen-year-old German who emigrated, without his parents, more than seventy years ago. The licensee of the Commercial Hotel is Anita Stenzel.

There are the Vogels, the Richters, the Kuhnemanns; the phone book must be a typesetter's nightmare unless he's of German extraction – Scholz, Schelbach, Scholl, Schiefelbein, Schisser, Schimke, Schubel, Schubring, Schulz, Schumacher, Steinhardt. Boonah was founded by the Blumberg brothers, who set up a store there and named it Blumbergville. (Kalbar began its existence as Engelsburg.) Dr Cole believes that the Germans' conservatism has had a marked effect on Queensland politics, and with most conservative State MPs, including Sir Johannes Bjelke-Petersen, coming from electorates or areas with a distinct German flavour.

The Germans in Queensland kept their cultural traditions, just as they did in South Australia, but they assimilated – as early as the 1890s Lutherans were turning to Methodism, by 1914 one-third of German-Australians in the Fassifern had become Methodists, and by 1945 two-thirds were Methodists. The Germans in Queensland were, like their kinfolk who settled South Australia half a century earlier, hard-working and frugal. They were not pan-Germanists; Germany had a low-key desire and record as a coloniser. The first English word the Germans in Queensland learned and penned home to their relatives was 'farmer', because it denoted their status, and gaining respect was all-important to Germans. They were people of what we should term lower middle-class values and outlook, conscious of position in society, conservative, not

people of the grand outlook, not aspiring to great wealth. First become self-sufficient, then produce commercially, that was the limit of their business instinct for the most part. They were proud of their accomplishments, and erected monuments to their leaders. They were deeply hurt when, generations after they had established themselves in Australia, Australians of different stock looked on them as traitors, simply because they had German names. They were as Australian as people with English names.

One solution to this or any other problem was to Anglicise the name. Gnech became Nash, Heinrich became Henry, Wilhelm almost went out of existence, which was indeed the fate of August, and Karl reappeared as Charlie. There was always bound to be, in any event, a subtle merging of Anglo-Saxon and German values, and that is true of other 'foreign' nationalities too. You will not hear Australians of the fifth-generation in Queensland who are descended from Italians speak of themselves as Italian-Australians, nor would a South Australian or south-east Queenslander with the name Schmidt refer to himself as a German-Australian if he came from a family that has spent a century here. Australia, though it has exhibited bigotry and racism during its history, is relatively divisionless.

It is more than eighty years since President Theodore Roosevelt told his countrymen that the United States had no place for 'hyphenated Americans', but only for Americans, and he intended to see that the crucible turned out Americans. He need have had no fears. In America, 'old' families revere their pioneer origins, and it does not matter one whit whether their origins were English, German, Dutch, or some other nationality. In Australia we may be reaching a position which approximates that of America, and, in the near future, may

The Seppelt winery, Barossa Valley.

even begin to revere the fact that there was, among our pioneers, a diversity of nationalities. Had there been a greater diversity, had we depended less on Britain and Ireland for immigants, that would surely have provided a bigger and perhaps stronger base on which to populate the country, and our population might have been much greater today than it is. All the more reason, therefore, to remember those non-Anglo-Saxon people who, last century, were brave enough to make a new start on virgin land in a raw continent, alongside British people of similar pioneer instincts, and who made a go of it, left their mark, and helped build Australia.

Mr E. H. HARGRAVES,

THE GOLD DISCOVERER OF AUSTRALIA

FEB 12th 1851

Returning the salute of the Gold Miners on the 5th of the ensuing May.

DRAWN & LITHOGRAPHED BY T. T. BALCOMBE

CHAPTER 6

Gold!

As AUSTRALIA entered the second half of the nineteenth century, and took stock of itself, it was obvious that a transformation had occurred since the first five decades of white settlement. The rough bush ethos had softened; the wilder excesses and fears that had persisted long after the establishment of the penal colony were moderating. The years when any traveller could expect to find a homestead door unlocked, enter without fear of challenge and fill himself with beef or mutton were fading into memory. So too, to a degree, was the unspoken feeling that Australians were a tiny band of outcasts at the furthest extremity of the empire.

The country had begun to attract a different kind of immigrant – one almost as different in outlook, aim, disposition and background as the early rulers had been from the motley band of felons they had

E. H. Hargraves, the man whose discovery of gold in New South Wales initiated the gold fever.

governed. The new class of free immigrants did not depend for their existence on the colonial, civil or military infrastructures. They could exist beside the boisterous generation of native-born whites. Less than a quarter-century earlier, convicts had accounted for about 40 per cent of all who toiled in the colony of New South Wales; now they were a small minority of 1.5 per cent (transportation to the mainland had ceased in 1840). For the first time, almost half the population was Australian-born.

Western Australia had been annexed only twenty-one years earlier, in 1829, giving white settlers some additional sense of identity with the continent. New South Wales still stretched all the way from Cape York to Port Phillip, and encircled all land borders of South Australia, which had been proclaimed in 1836. Port Phillip and nearer settlements were known by the romantic nomenclature of Australia Felix, and were awaiting self-government as Victoria. Tasmania was still Van Diemen's Land, Queensland had yet to exist.

Sydney, fount of the white outpost of Australia, the nation-in-waiting, had about 54 000 residents in 1850, Hobart and Melbourne each had 23 000, Adelaide 14 500. The total population of Australia was 405 000, a scarcely impressive figure by which to mark sixty-two years of progress. At least the inhabitants were able to draw a sense of security from the knowledge that the numbers were increasing faster than they ever had – as recently as 1830 the white population had been a pitiful 70 000 – but in most respects the changes that had occurred in Australia, in its people and its pattern of

settlement, had been slow. Wool had established itself as the Australian staple, but the Industrial Revolution, as measured by output, had thus far failed to materialise. When the colonies came to select an example of their manufactures to represent Australia at the Great Exhibition held in London in 1851, they could proffer nothing more substantial than a case of cabbage tree hats.

Nothing could have prepared the colonists for the enormous changes that lay immediately ahead of them, and which happened when they did because a humourless but optimistic English immigrant followed his rainbow all the way from New South Wales to California and back, to Lewis Ponds Creek, near

A gold licence issued in Victoria, 1853. At a pound a month the licences were hardly cheap, considering that a shepherd's income was £26–4–0 plus rations.

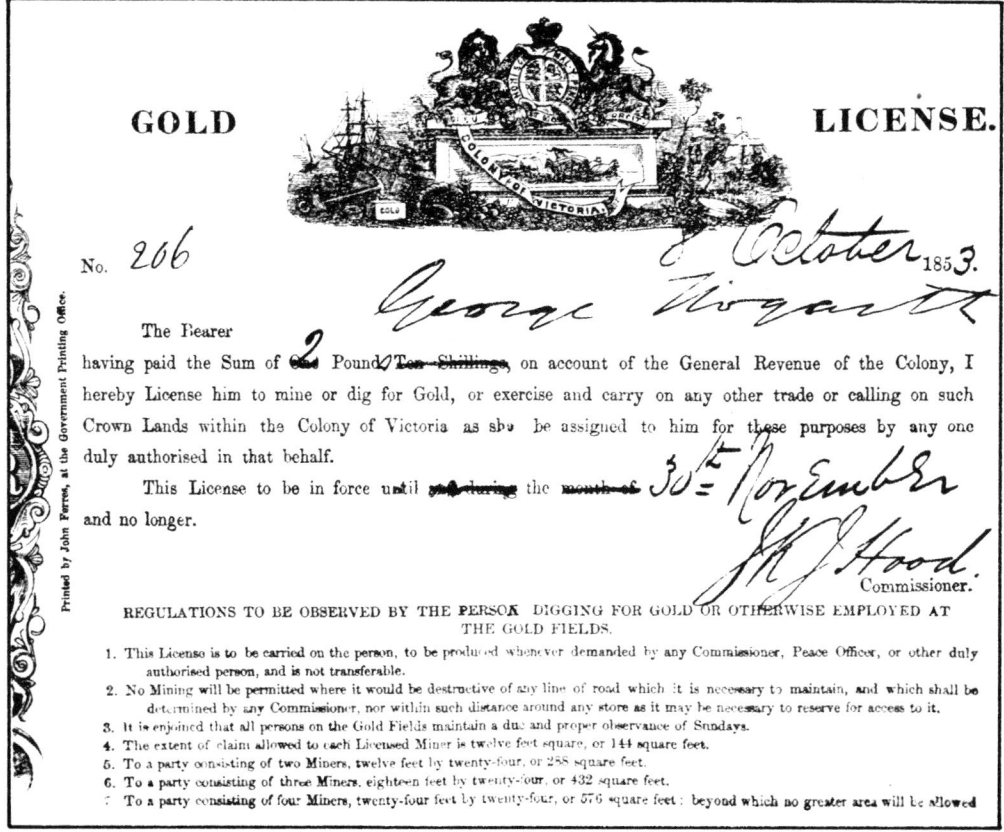

Bathurst, mid-western New South Wales. There, in the bottom of his gold prospector's pan, Edward Hammond Hargraves found what he had been sure to find. There were only a few specks of gold, but all around there was enough to infect the colonists with the most pleasurable epidemic of yellow fever, for Hargraves had accurately predicted that as the general features of the California fields resembled those in several districts of New South Wales, then what lay in the Australian soil might well be the same too. It was 12 February 1851, the start of an era.

Hargraves, who had a huge conceit to match his physical appearance, was greedy and indolent, but he was also a man with a keen sense and a quick eye for the main chance. He had been part of the emigration to the Californian lands being fossicked by forty-niners. Australia had lost an estimated 6200 souls because of the lure of easy pickings in the Golden State, which had, in 1850, yielded about £20 million worth of treasure. John Fairfax, the sermonising owner of the *Sydney Morning Herald*, had grown weary of publishing editorials beseeching the local populace to remain at their workplaces instead of expending their meagre savings on the fare to San Francisco. The phrase 'El Dorado' had a ring to it. It struck a stronger chord in antipodean breasts than any that had been wrung through newspaper presses ...

Hargraves belongs to history because his find and those that followed it reversed the human flow across the Pacific and did a lot to add to Australia's human resources. But at first officialdom baulked, for fear of what gold fever might lead to. It was May 1851 before news of gold in abundance was allowed to reach the public. The Government's chief fear was social disorder, with the workers deserting their jobs and families, leaving crops to rot in the soil, and with the secondary, and gloomy, prospect of the hinter-

Above: *Life on the diggings.*

Arrival of the N. Boynton *in Port Jackson with the first emigrants from America. Though Americans flocked to the gold rush, few remained afterwards.*

land being opened up to hordes of anarchic go-getters. The notion that a rush might be a golden opportunity to swell the population without the need for assisted passages and all the other expenses associated with immigration programmes did not, apparently, weigh heavily, if at all, with the authorities. They resigned themselves to the growing suspicion that the human influx would generate a lot more work for public officials, and accepted their fate.

As for Hargraves, he would wind up with a £10 000 grant and a pension for life, and he would, oft-times, betake himself to yet another banquet table in a remote town to belabour his all-too-eager audiences with the full import of what he had achieved. He was a man of modest talents and immodest disposition who happened to have been in the right places at the right times and who, in his moment of glory, was a veritable parody of greatness.

The impact of what he started would be felt for some time. It could be measured by much more than the quantity and value of gold that the diggers loaded on to the scales, gold that they sometimes found sitting on the soil, waiting for them to stumble on it. The effects of the bonanza would be social, political and racial. Australia existed before 1851, but few people apart from the British had ever thought to look far enough south on the map to see it. Now they had to. In the ten years between 1851 and 1861 the number of people in Australia almost trebled, from 405 356 to 1 145 385. The rise in Victoria was more than six-fold, from 80 000 to more than half a million. The goldfields of eastern Australia would extend from northern Queensland to

Sly grog selling on the goldfields.

southern Victoria, and as far west as Glenormiston in Queensland and Paterson Point at the top of South Australia's Spencer Gulf.

Gold! It electrified imaginations overseas, particularly in countries that were overcrowded or torn with strife. It took a little time for the news to reach London, San Francisco, New York and Shanghai. Most of the thrill-seekers waited a while, to assure themselves that the Australian finds were not a flash in the pan. Besides, Australia was still a hazardous sixteen-week voyage from Europe, and belonged in a part of the globe that most peoples still regarded as the vast unknown. But as the reports grew stronger and more frenetic, men threw up their jobs and headed for the wharves. When the flood began, in 1852, it would have a wider social and financial base than anything Australia had been host to before. Members of the professions were not immune to the glow that the news produced. Respectable, well-heeled men rubbed shoulders with skilled craftsmen and soldiers of fortune who stormed ashore at Port Jackson or Port Phillip and made all haste to the rich lodes in the Australian plains.

The people who came were from communities as widely scattered and racially or ethnically diverse as New England, USA and Olde England; Bavaria and Bologna, Shanghai and San Francisco. It may seem strange, in hindsight, that some effort was not made to keep the gold seekers at bay, given Australia's oft-demonstrated penchant for minimal immigration so that domestic living standards could be preserved. Perhaps the authorities realised that any attempt to keep all the gold for Australians would

only denude every other workplace of its labour. The authorities knew that most of the gold, being in Crown land, belonged to Queen Victoria, but nobody was going to hang back because of that. The next best thing would be to impose a licence tax to siphon off some of the bonanza at minimum cost to Her Majesty. It was this tax, as well as other grievances, that triggered the armed conflict at Eureka Stockade, Ballarat, in the summer of 1854.

It is worth noting that shepherds received only £18-24 a *year* in 1850, plus rations, and this rose to only £26-40 plus rations in 1853. The licence tax was £3 a month in Victoria, or almost the equivalent of a shepherd's wages, and a sum to baulk a working man who had likely dug deep into his savings to purchase tools and provisions at exorbitant prices so he could join the diggers. If he was unlucky in the gold lottery he was likely to resent the licence tax and the men who collected it. The other group on whom the white diggers vented their frustration, particularly when pickings were lean, was the Chinese, who also copped it when unemployment rose. There were dozens of riots, the worst of them at Lambing Flat (Young) in New South Wales, in 1860 and 1861.

New South Wales imposed a double tax on aliens, and Victoria unsuccessfully attempted the same from New Year's Day, 1852. The militaristic methods of administrators, the lack of an effective miners' voice in the formulation and administration of mining regulations, the fact that police received half of the amounts of fines imposed on those who defaulted on the tax – all these irritants bred a deep resentment. Little wonder the miners began to organise. Victoria led the other colonies with a £10 poll tax on Chinese and a quota on Chinese immigrants which limited the intake to one for each 10 tonnes of ship's burden. New South Wales and South Australia passed

S. T. Gill's 'Fair Prospectors', 1852, the year the rush began. Fortunes were also made equipping the prospectors and keeping them in food and liquor.

'Wool Drays' by S. T. Gill. Bullock drays were the mainstay of overland transport for heavy loads.

similar Acts after Chinese began landing in their ports and trekking overland to Victoria.

The thousands of men who poured in from across the Indian and Pacific oceans (few women accompanied them) found that, as with all lotteries, only a very few struck the jackpot. They learned that back-breaking toil under a boiling antipodean sun could indeed bring forth riches from that grey landscape, but in the excitement of those novel times the tendency was to 'work and bust' just as shearers and stockmen had before them. The men who were trying, at first frantically, later with patient resignation, to find the nuggets that would ease their labours for the rest of their days were loath to yield large sums to a greedy, uncaring administration that scarcely acknowledged their difficulties and basic rights as decent, hard-working and wholly legitimate soldiers of fortune.

Well, who were the gold diggers? They came in such numbers that the census takers had trouble with their figures. Immigration to Australia in 1852 was seven times as high as it had been in 1851, the year of discovery, and before the fever began to subside there would be upwards of 5000 Americans in Victoria alone, more than 6000 Germans there, vast numbers of British and Irish, and somewhere between 25 000 and 40 000 Orientals, mainly Chinese (the former figure was from the 1857 census, but some historians accept the higher figure). The gold-hunting Germans numbered about 27 000 throughout Australia by 1861, and that was about one-third of all foreign-born settlers, a proportion that would be maintained for most of the rest of the nineteenth century. (Germans tended to immigrate in families, unlike Italians, and so had less reason to return to their native States.) To these relatively large numbers of Germans must be added the second-generation German-Australians who had been born in South Australia after their

Above: *Every class of man came to seek gold in Australia, despite the uncertainties of the long voyages and the lottery of finding gold. Tom Jones yarns companionably to the sailors on board the* Fortune Seeker *but the Hon. Adolphus Augustus Fitzfiggins maintains a proper distance on the poop.* (Mitchell Library)

Opposite page: *The joys of working underground demonstrated.*

A concert being held to celebrate a new rush. The miners worked hard and played hard.

parents emigrated in the late 1830s, mainly from Prussia, Silesia and Saxony. Many had been religious dissidents. The gold rush Germans, like those who had come earlier to farm in settlements around Adelaide, were typical of other members of their race who were now spreading to new lands throughout the western hemisphere – industrious, hard-working, abstemious, meticulous to the point of fetishness. (Abraham Lincoln would come to regard the enormous numbers settling the American hinterland as his favourite type of immigrant.) Not a few of the gold rush Germans had stories of their own to tell about meddlesome officialdom in the land they had left behind. The goldfields were great levellers, and people spoke their minds freely; these were self-contained communities, and a new kind of society.

The Irish diggers, some of whom had

emigrated to the United States years before they sailed south for Australian gold, had strong reason to distrust officialdom too, especially when it was administered by Anglo-Saxons. The British military, British landlords, imposition of British value judgments – they knew it all, had come from a country with what amounted to a tradition of suffering because of the British. It did not take much of a spark to ignite the Celtic spirit.

The Orientals (or 'Celestials' as they were known) were the largest group from overseas after the English, Scots and Irish. They suffered discrimination from whites who complained about discrimination from officials: white diggers felt there was nothing hypocritical about this, since it was undeniable that yellows were inferior. The Chinese took no part in the Eureka conflict.

The European diggers had come from countries as geographically and culturally diverse as Italy and Sweden-and-Norway (as they then were). Not a few Scandinavians found a more secure existence after they trudged from the sun-baked fields and set up small businesses, catering for other diggers – they usually did well. Their names survive in Ballarat, Bendigo, Castlemaine and other old mining towns, and their descendants prospered as storekeepers, produce merchants, publicans, insurance agents and tradesmen.

No group of foreigners, however, stirred as much interest in Australia in the mid-1800s as the Americans who came in search of gold, and American newspapers of the period reflect a fascination with Australia and what the future might hold for it.

Australians and Americans were not strangers to each other before the discovery of gold in Australia. American whalers had roamed Australia's southern coastline, American trade was healthy, and thousands of Australians had gone to California for the gold there. (It ought to be added that the British colony of New South Wales was better known in California in 1850, the year that California attained Statehood, than it is now, for the unfortunate reason that some Australians who went there relapsed into their former habits, with a criminal disregard for the impression they were creating. They broke the laws so often that postal authorities went so far as to refuse to take up mail for New South Wales.) When the human tide began to run in the opposite direction, some American editorialists at first declined to believe that the Australian gold rush could be surpassing California's fine flush (Americans already accepted that everything was better in America). But by 1853, when it had become obvious that the gold was not running out, leading American newspapers turned their attention south. The *Boston Post*, for example, opined: 'Soon republican institutions will be there ... monopoly, under the impious plea of divine right, will not be allowed to filch bread from the mouths of those who earn it – as is done in England now; as the development of principles is sure, [there] will arise a new government, another America, that will rejoice and profit together with its elder brother Jonathan, in free trade and free institutions.'

By 1855 American clipper ships would be sailing from New York to Melbourne in as little as seventy days, and American-built clippers (from the phrase 'to move at a fast clip') in Port Phillip would be a familiar sight. James Gordon Bennett, the New York *Herald's* owner-editor, would write of Australia's future as a 'great country ... a new home for the Anglo-Saxon race'. Australia, the *Herald* said, was 'a real Ophir, from the hills and valleys of which gold is rolled out, not by penny weights, as in North Carolina, not by ounces and pounds, as in California, but by the ton ... This is the golden age, and Australia is the real El Dorado'.

The American stood out wherever he

went in Australia. In the streets of Melbourne, which were swarming with new arrivals, he could be detected by his bandana, colourful clothing, and also by his careworn countenance, which underlay an air of alertness and confidence that were prerequisites for and the mark of success in America. 'Hawkeyed and bilious looking' was how one Melburnian described Americans in mid-1853, and went on to say that they were 'rapidly becoming a recognised section of the community' and that the streets contained a 'large sprinkling' of the energetic fellows. Their pallid, careworn features he attributed to the seal of 'the worshipped dollar'. The self-assurance exuded by Americans upset a class of Australians used to more modesty, and the speed of their work on the diggings aroused comment. In Sydney they were noticeable for the flashy Mexican-style trimmings of their clothes, which caught glances half a block away. The *Bathurst Free Press* noted that the Americans were 'a sober and industrious class' who had contributed in no small degree to the promotion of mining interests in the Turon. William Charles Wentworth was not so kind: the Americans, he sniffed, 'neither improve the blood nor the morals of the country'. Obviously, they were not being ignored.

The Yankees and Californians, by most accounts, *were* a sober and industrious lot on the diggings, and their style then, as during later 'invasions' during World War II and the Vietnam War, would captivate some Australians even as it stoked envy and apprehension in others. Some of the locals mocked Americans, in accents

Below and opposite page: *The Cooliban diggings on the Cooliban River, Victoria, and packhorses climbing a mountain road to the diggings, North Gippsland, Victoria. Everything but the men and their equipment is makeshift.*

that harked all the way back to an England of a bygone age, but others could not resist imitating them with sincere flattery. They were from the New World, but had retained the Old World manners and courtesies, not least towards women, which must have made native Australians of rougher and ruder stock look to their own behaviour.

All in all, the written reports of their conduct that have survived seem to substantiate a feeling that the mood and style of an emerging race, American or Australian, may be set very soon after the birth of a nation. As E. Daniel Potts and Annette Potts said in *Young America and Australian Gold*, their book about Americans in the gold rush of the 1850s, Australians were slow to realise the benefits of complex machinery and advanced mining methods that required capital and work done in large companies. One digger who had worked in California and went back there in 1855 after trying the Australian fields felt that Australian diggers, his own com-

patriots, were a 'spiritless, haggling set, and seemed unaware of the advantages of co-operation'. He said, 'I now and then see that such and such a party of American diggers, have cut this race, have tunnelled that hill, and brought down a stream of water so far, and hopes expressed that our own people will imitate the example ... But they go on in the old style, scratch the ground, and peddle, and prospect, and finding nothing, march off.' In Melbourne tipplers were surprised to be served by American waiters who oiled and curled their hair and served concoctions with a flourish, evincing evident pride in their station. Some Australians were content to imitate the superficialities of a people whose predominant ethic and spirit they but scarcely perceived or understood – just as a later generation would take to hamburgers and Coke, and allow that patina to stand as their image of America.

The Americans, however, underneath their obvious attempt to express their

individuality, were made of stern stuff. They were organised, industrious, energetic, proud of their republic, which was scarcely more than half a century old and well established by then. A century later Americans would boast of the visible benefits of free enterprise values, freedom of choice, while warning of the perils of socialism, collectivism, and other 'isms' that were not prefixed by the word 'capital'. But in the early 1850s American diggers in Australia spoke up for republicanism, which they equated with freedom and prosperity. Their words found ready ears among the Irish diggers and some of the idealists from Continental Europe whose native countries were still shackled with inequality and oppression.

It is difficult now to evaluate the role Americans played in the Eureka conflict. It was even more difficult back in early 1855, when Victorian authorities were attempting to determine just who was responsible for whipping up the miners' fury, and the extent of their aims. It ought to be said at the outset that whatever the fervour of republican sentiment that beat in the breasts of some of the miners' leaders, Eureka can in no sense be portrayed as an independence movement that boiled over into bloody revolution and then failed because of a lack of military expertise. An insurrection it certainly was – the diggers, or some of them, rose in open resistance to established authority, and it was an incipient rebellion, no doubt of that. But the verdict of history surely must be that the miners arose because they had legitimate grievances, primarily against the licence tax and the people who administered it. It was a revolt, or an uprising, but a revolution in the making it was not. It is difficult to believe that Eureka would have the place in Australian history that it continues to maintain had it not been for the fact that egalitarian diggers raised the Southern Cross flag, swore allegiance to it on bended knee, and can be said to have shed their blood on Australian soil for the sake of Australia. Eureka has its place in Australian history because it was the bloodiest of the few organised struggles on Australian soil (between whites, that is: many more Aborigines died in the worst armed struggles between them and settlers). At Eureka twenty-two to twenty-four diggers died and twenty were wounded, while five soldiers died and eleven soldiers and one policeman were injured. Eureka is up there in the history books somewhere near the 'legend' of Ned Kelly, who would scarcely occupy his place had he not been expressing, in some way, the opposition of the deprived masses to the harsh authoritarianism of their rulers. However valid the sentiment, it was not one to start a revolution, nor on which to build a philosophy for a new nation.

At the last monster meeting of diggers of all nationalities on Bakery Hill, Ballarat, before the battle of Eureka, the man who asked the diggers to burn their licences was Friedrich Vern, a Prussian immigrant given to haranguing large crowds with his talk of what amounted to 'red republicanism'. Of all the foreigners involved at Eureka, the Germans were the most conspicuous, and there was strong feeling among them that there must be redress for legitimate grievances.

Raffaello Carboni, an Italian intellectual and former member of the Young Italy movement, had gone into voluntary exile in London before coming to the goldfields; he was (according to the historian Manning Clark) a foe of aristocratic tyranny rather than a friend, let alone a lover, of the people.

Peter Lalor (pronounced 'Lawler'), the elected leader of the nascent rebellion, made it clear that for him democracy did not mean 'Chartism or Communism, or Republicanism' – he was opposed to tyranny of the kind he had known as a boy in Ireland, and as far as he was concerned the same kind of Anglo-Saxons were trying the same thing in Victoria.

Peter Lalor, the elected leader of the diggers at Eureka.

Vern and Tom Kennedy, a Scot, were radical leaders. Lalor was, politically, no radical, and he disdained the more high-blown rhetoric about the rights of man. Carboni thought the 'blather' and 'yabber yabber' of the big diggers' meetings was part of the 'storm of life'.

Even those diggers who had little mind for the ideological aspects of these meetings could identify readily with the sentiment that something must be done about the licence tax and those who ensured that it was paid. A grimy, bone-weary digger who was summoned to show his licence paper to the symbol of authority felt his blood rise when he was confronted by some pot-bellied poltroon who had a secure job, a regular wage, and lacked the stomach for the hardship of the digger's life.

Estimates of the number of Americans at Ballarat vary, but there were probably at least six hundred. If this figure is anywhere near correct, Americans were certainly well represented in the agitation that preceded the conflict, because the Independent Californian Rangers numbered between two hundred and three hundred, though how many were native-born Americans, as distinct from Irish or Scots immigrants, is not known. The ran-

gers were led by one James D. McGill, who was said to have been a lieutenant in the American infantry. He was a tall, heavy man whose size commanded respect and who displayed a smart mind in the eloquent toasts he proposed at the banquet table (banquets were a favoured entertainment with gold seekers). His knowledge of drill led to doubts about whether he had really trained at West Point, the American military academy, but it is known that he drew the plan for the defence of the Eureka Stockade.

An American named Nelson was made captain of the First Rifles a few days before the shoot-out. He had been a carpenter, was vigorous, and his corps was considered one of the best. Some of the Americans who 'enlisted' had colourful backgrounds, including action in the war with Mexico. Others apparently had to be dragooned into units, joining rather than surrender their guns, or because they did not want to endure snide remarks about cowardice. 'Be in it' was a catch phrase at Ballarat.

There is no doubt that many Americans saw parallels between early America and the Colony of Victoria, and they had much in common with the Australians they met. There was the same egalitarian instinct, the same pioneering spirit and, beneath the casual attitude to life's trials and dangers that each liked to affect, a feeling that up-and-at-'em was the way to go. In spite of a swaggering tendency the Americans had a resolve: they were a good deal more organised, more sober, more serious, more confident. The Americans' forebears had seized their moment in history in 1776; those antecedents had been a polyglot lot, and only one-third of them had been fired up enough to take a firm stand for independence in any event, so perhaps the same seed that was sprouting in hearts on the Ballarat fields would grow into something more substantial. The republican spirit tended to overflow at American July 4 celebrations in Vic-

V. R.

Colonial Secretary's Office,
Melbourne, 11th December, 1854.

£500

REWARD

FOR THE APPREHENSION

OF

Frederick Vern

WHEREAS

A Man known by the name of VERN, has unlawfully, rebelliously, and traitorously levied and arrayed Armed Men at Ballaarat, in the Colony of Victoria, with the view of making war against Our Sovereign Lady the QUEEN :

NOTICE IS HEREBY GIVEN

That whoever will give such information as may lead to the Apprehension of the said VERN, shall receive

A REWARD OF £500

being the Reward offered by SIR ROBERT NICKLE.

By His Excellency's Command,

JOHN FOSTER.

DESCRIPTION OF VERN.

Tall, about 5 feet 10½ inches, long light hair falling heavily on the Side of his head, little whisker, a large flat face, eyes light grey or green and very wide asunder. Speaks with a strong foreign accent. A Hanoverian by birth, about 26 years of age.

The 'wanted' poster for Frederick (Friedrich) Vern. Vern was a radical orator who urged the diggers to seek redress for their grievances, inflating the emotional atmosphere of the day. The authorities wanted him for inciting the riot at Eureka.

toria, euphoric and long-winded affairs which invariably drew high-ranking Australians as guests-of-honour. The Americans were, however, restrained on the diggings, and careful not to give offence. 'An exceedingly quiet and respectable class' was how Edward N. Emmett, who later became Mayor of Bendigo, described them. The Americans, it seems, approved of British rule of law, contrasting it favourably with the rough justice dispensed by vigilante groups in California, where lynching was not uncommon. Only one in nine of the Americans in Victoria was at Ballarat, but they were able to form units.

Sufficient has been written about why the diggers' armed struggle failed so lamentably. On the morning of Sunday, 3 December 1854, McGill led most of the Independent Californian Rangers on an expedition designed to intercept a group of government reinforcements said to be arriving from Melbourne. The other American leader, Nelson, was also away and missed the action. Some Americans took a dim view of Lalor for blaming McGill, his second-in-command, for the debacle, and Lalor himself was criticised as having been unsuited for the command for lack of firmness and boldness.

The essential difference between the opposing camps was that the soldiers and police had a definite plan of action and attacked, while the rebellious diggers' numbers had dwindled from two thousand to a remnant of one hundred and fifty. The shoot-out, when it came, lasted fifteen minutes. Some of the diggers were so stupefied from a binge the previous day – no isolated instance – that they were useless. Among the twenty-two or twenty-four dead diggers, ten were identified as natives of Ireland, two of Germany, two of Canada, one of England, one of Scotland, one of Australia. Raffaello Carboni of Italy and London had his cabbage tree hat blown off his head by a trooper who fired at him as he raced for his tent. Lalor was shot in the arm and was hidden from the troopers who hunted for him. Vern of Prussia and Kennedy of Scotland, the radicals, eluded the men who wanted them captured.

Lalor would later make little of the role of foreigners at Eureka, saying that 'there were only about thirty in the movement'. More than one hundred men were captured. One American, Charles Ferguson, bluffed his way out of a prison sentence by claiming that the rioters had abducted him. The thirteen men sent for trial charged with high treason included Carboni, James Campbell, a black who said he was from Kingston, Jamaica, and an American, John Joseph, also black. If there was some feeling in Ballarat that the Americans had been among the chief agitators because they wanted independence for Australia, officialdom was not concurring, or preferred not to probe too deeply, perhaps to avoid upsetting the official representatives of that friendly foreign power. In any event, now that the diggers' revolt had been soundly crushed, and there was unlikely to be any recurrence, the authorities had less to fear. The Governor of Victoria, Sir Charles Hotham, seemed to favour Americans. McGill was not even on the wanted list, and on 16 January 1855, some six weeks after Eureka, was reported to be 'boasting all over Ballarat [sic] that the Governor had granted him an amnesty'. Vern remained at large. All Carboni lost was his sang-froid and his cabbage tree hat.

Joseph was accused of wounding Captain H. C. Wise, a popular and kindly disposed officer who took part in the attack on the stockade. There was evidence that Joseph had been positively sighted drilling with a double-barrelled gun. Two prosecution witnesses swore to having seen Joseph fire at Captain Wise. The prosecution, however, aimed too high in attempting to prove high treason. For that, the insurrection would have had to be accompanied and preceded by overt acts which had a public object, and the use of force planned and organised by previous concert and conspiracies, and having a general object. Had there been charges less difficult to prove, the prisoners might have been executed or incarcerated, and would have become martyrs rather than the folk heroes.

Joseph, who was variously described as being from Baltimore, New York and Boston, was the first to be tried. He had come to Ballarat to run a refreshment tent and was now charged with having made war against Queen Victoria of Britain et al, with having tried to injure her and force her to change her counsellors (a

J. Henderson's 'Eureka Stockade Riot', 1854. The shooting lasted only a quarter of an hour. The rebels numbered 150 and lost at most 24. Civil war it was not, nor even civil uprising. (Mitchell Library)

euphemism for trying to overthrow the government). He impressed those in the court with his dignity, and was acquitted after the jury had been out only half an hour. The twelve accused who followed him were released too. In his report to Sir George Grey, the Colonial Secretary in London, Sir Charles Hotham, confined himself to a single paragraph about the episode. The American press, after some early high hopes for revolution, discounted Eureka as the work of political rowdies. The New York *Daily Tribune* said the 'rising' had an 'air of turbulence' which was more like a riot than a revolu-

tion. The character of the rioters might incline more to anarchy than to a regular republican form of government, the newspaper said, but the wild excess of passion displayed at Eureka would be redeemed for posterity if it brought about Australia's independence, thus securing democracy for future generations and the attendant blessings of peace, prosperity and progress.

Bennett of the New York *Herald* wrote that Eureka was an 'outbreak' caused by the imposition of an unfair tax on the miners as well as by the despotic way in which it was enforced. He concluded by forecasting that 'the struggle ... with the mother country' would come sooner or later, and hoped that when it came Australia would be as fortunate in the choice of its new institutions as America had been in hers. Bennett, writing half a world distant from the bloody ground of Ballarat, got the proportions of the brief struggle at Eureka Stockade into the proper perspective; the forecast he got wrong.

American newspapers apparently did not have a lot to say about the role of Americans at Eureka. Americans not only detested failure, but knew, all too well, what armed rebellion against Britain entailed: intense, protracted and well-organised warfare. Valley Forge is a national monument. Ballarat has Sovereign Hill, a monument to the gold rush.

Americans in America quickly forgot Eureka, and a haze descended on the events on Bakery Hill. A Dr Kenworthy, we do know, went to Melbourne to negotiate with Governor Hotham for those of his countrymen who had joined rebellious Australians, Britons, Germans and others. Germans continued to arrive in Australia long after Eureka; most of the Americans returned home, not a few to fight in the Civil War of 1861-65. But among those who remained was Davis Calwell, from Pennsylvania, who shared a hut with his brother Dan near Eureka before Dan went on to New Zealand to try his luck at sawmilling.

Davis Calwell got 28 hectares in 1866, on the Western Moorabool River, and in 1874 he applied for citizenship. He became a shire councillor, and would live to see his grandson, Arthur Augustus, who would later become chief architect and builder of the biggest immigration programme in the history of the British Empire and Commonwealth.

Looking back, it must be said that Australia missed an opportunity to capitalise fully on the attention that was focussed on the country by the gold rush.

The world had come to know that a large, richly endowed and largely unpopulated continent was being peopled far from the woes and miseries of Europe. Australians had seen for themselves that people who were not British were not inadequate for the task of nation-building. Assisted passage schemes had continued during the gold rush – some who took advantage of them were Americans, and it was obvious that a huge emigration from Europe was under way. But instead of grasping its chance, Australia let the prize go. The human exodus from the eastern and northern shores of the Atlantic would be directed elsewhere. The United States of America was bold and unafraid, knew its foundations, knew what it wanted and where it was going. Australia, building on the remnants of a penal dump, did not know what to do about a national philosophy apart from what had been forced on it by a harsh land or was handed down from England. The gold rush was a spurt. Immigrants would keep coming, in trickles and spurts, but not enough of them, not for another century.

CHAPTER 7

The Chinese and Gold

THE GOLDFIELDS gave Australians their first taste of multiculturalism. It was strange and too much to digest. They spat it out.

No Australian digger expected goldminers from foreign countries to dress, speak, work and enjoy precisely the same recreations as he did. The Australians resented the intrusion of so many foreigners on fields that were loath to yield up their treasure, or were almost worked out. There was a lot of suspicion between men who regarded the gold rushes as their only chance of a lifetime to dig themselves out of the humble sinkhole in which fate had placed them at birth. Australia by the mid-1800s was prosperous by the standards of most Europeans, but the hardships and dangers of life are scarcely imaginable compared with the living standards that are taken for granted

Chinese immigrants landing at Cooktown, Queensland, 1875.

today. Which is to say, there was food and shelter for those who had work. Outside the cities, however, serious illness, even if treatable, often meant death because of distance from a doctor. Schooling was a real problem.

As late as 1860, when the gold rushes were losing their shine, when the population and wealth of Australia had increased quickly, there was still no compulsory education. Such schools as existed operated under three umbrellas – Protestant, Roman Catholic and National – because of the sectarian disputes about how schools would operate, and what they would teach, if all schooling was to be financed and administered by the State. This sectarian suspicion and bitterness ran deep. There was a great deal of debate, some of it in print, about the machinations of Irish Catholics, who, because they tended to have large families, looked on a job in the Public Service as a lifelong guarantee that they and their children would never sink, poverty-stricken and jobless, into the gutter. Their concern was quite natural; the protection a public service job afforded them was no different from that which it afforded non-Catholics.

All parents except paupers had to pay fees to keep their children at school, and the average, five cents a week, was not high compared with the wages of the day, which were high compared with wages in Europe. Nevertheless, at least half the children of lower-income families in Sydney in 1860 did not attend school. Their chances of advancement in the workforce would depend on natural ability and luck, but were in any event severely limited. They would enter the workforce early, and be forced to stay in it until they were too old to be of any use. Those who were not exploited by their parents as child labour were free, in the cities, to drift to wherever instinct and the companionship of other unfortunates led them, which not unusually was into crime.

For children fortunate enough to go to school, the fruits were dismal. Conditions at schools varied, of course, but some classrooms were so cold and dingy as to be unhealthy, while others lacked materials. Teaching standards were often very low. Some children did not even learn how to read, write and add and subtract. Their parents were even worse off.

It was a national scandal in a country that was not yet a nation, and thus revealed itself, three-quarters of a century after white settlement, as still semi-barbaric in important respects. It was not schooled, let alone educated. There was plenty of talk on the goldfields – which promised to make up materially for what had been missed early in life for want of schooling – about democracy, manhood suffrage. The aristocracy of labour, as evidenced in the mechanics institutes and libraries which flourished in the big goldmining towns, helped raise the consciousness of the working class. Alas, it

did not always raise the level of their conscience. They had battled it out at Eureka, and in less violent conflicts wherever there were goldfields, for what they saw as their rights. The universal cry was that they, the workers, should be as free as possible, and without undue impediment or burden from their rulers (chiefly in the form of the gold licence) to take what they could from the soil. Life on the diggings was harsh enough without well-fed inspectors employed by soft-living toffs making it more difficult. The soldiers of fortune who flocked to the diggings from Europe and North America took up the cry, and stood shoulder to shoulder with the Aussie digger. The Chinese did not. They weren't asked to, and they tried to keep out of harm's way, which meant out of trouble with all occidentals, diggers and troopers alike.

So we have the picture on the goldfields of a pretty primitive mob, even by the standards of civilisation in Australia all those years ago. They were a wild bunch. They were tent-dwellers, at the mercy of the elements on many fields. What with the foul physical conditions, the hard work, the desperation and the ever-present strong drink, there were plenty of

A CHINESE SWELL

ON THE WALLABY AGAIN.

94

irritable men, unstable of temperament, and a lot of them were ready to take out their anguish on their colleagues. The bar-room brawl or the more orderly stand-up slugging match around the back were the favourite methods of ending quarrels or letting off steam. The Marquis of Queensberry's boxing rules were not formulated until 1867, and even if they had existed during the gold rushes, it is doubtful if anybody would have known of them, much less paid any attention to them. A kick in the guts was a cause for guffaws from all those assembled, except one.

Into this rude environment came the Chinese. There were estimated to be only 2000 of them in all eastern Australia in 1851, when gold fever struck. Three years later the number had doubled. When the lure of gold was at its peak, they outnumbered several times over such well-represented nations as the United States. They were impossible to overlook because there were so many of them, and they stood out because they were so different, in looks, dress, customs, size, even their *modus operandi* on the fields. They became a target, first as an Aunt Sally, and finally as a yellow demon. What happened to them was as shameful as what had happened to the blacks in Tasmania: the whites tried to evict them, and finally decided to kill them. The Chinese got it from both other races on the continent. Sometimes they were killed by blacks before they reached the goldfields, and cases of cannibalism were reported. Anybody from China hoping to make his pot had to have steel nerves or security of numbers to want to stay long in 'Terror Australis'. Unfortunately, their numbers, through no fault of their own, proved their undoing. They were damned, either way.

Why did the public officials responsible for good order on the goldfields not do more to prevent violence against the Chinese? Why were the Chinese permitted to come in the first place if they were

A CHINESE NURSE

Above and opposite page: *Sketches from the Queensland diggings.*

to be subjected to so much derision and violence? Perhaps the answer lies in the fact that order on the fields was always suspect, and the oriental presence was regarded by whites in much the same way that it is to this day, which is to say, 'We don't mind a few of them, but more than a few ...' But, for all the distrust between the races, international travel was relatively uncomplicated in the nineteenth century, once you had the passage money.

By 1854 the debate about the flow of

This Chinese doctor's retinue must have seemed very strange to people more familiar with barber-surgeons.

Chinese to the goldfields had reached the point where colonial governments were ready to restrict it. In New South Wales, where white convicts had by their numbers set the tone of much of colonial life for decades, Henry Parkes told Parliament that the Chinese would degrade labour and seriously endanger the moral well-being of society. No doubt he was applauded. The Victorian Legislative Council went further, imposing a £10 poll on the masters of ships for each Chinese immigrant they landed, and only one Chinese immigrant for each 10 tonnes of ship's burthen was permitted. For the Chinese, there was a simple, but arduous, loophole: they landed in South Australia, at Port Adelaide and Robe, and walked about 800 kilometres to the Victorian fields. They carried their possessions in their age-old way, hung from the ends of a pole that was balanced on their backs. They moved on the trot, Indian file, hundreds of them, chatting continuously to blot out the boredom and the weariness.

Manning Clark tells us that they had their own rules at Ballarat and Bendigo to try to keep themselves in order on the fields and out of trouble with the whites. Thieves were fined and beaten thirty

times with the rattan, which could raise welts. They were not to leave rubbish, including food scraps, outside their tents, and were not to urinate or defecate nearby: punishment for transgressions was twenty strokes of the rattan. They were not to wear Chinese trousers within sight of whites, who disliked Chinese garb (a sure sign of prejudice).

The Chinese had no reason to risk trouble, because they had nothing to gain from it. The Chinaman was an alien: with his singsong voice, pigtail, coolie hat, strange garb, a preference for walking around in bare feet, and a habit of hawking and spitting noisily, he was a target of derision. To the white diggers, the Chinese might well have been from another planet. The Middle Kingdom was the world's oldest civilisation, but on the rough and ready Australian goldfields, nobody knew, or cared, about that.

There were times when white diggers were invited to sit with the visitors and eat their food, prepared in the Chinese style, and in Australian towns a Chinese procession was a treat, the most exotic entertainment of them all. But suspicion was always there, just beneath the surface. It was never going to take much to inflame

G. Lacey: 'Hullo! Jem, here's a speck–Crikey!' Panning for gold.

Gold washing at Summerhill Creek. Much of the gold found in the rushes was alluvial.

it, and it boiled over, eventually, at Buckland River, north-eastern Victoria, though you won't find the place on tourist maps issued by the State today. It was 4 July 1857. Eureka, which had erupted not least because of a hatred of the licence tax, was still fresh in memory. Exactly a month earlier, John Pascoe Fawkner had urged the Victorian Legislative Council to control Chinese immigration and there was serious talk of putting a £1 a month tax on each Chinese digger (it was reduced to £4 a year) to pay for their protection. The Chinese responded, humbly, in a petition to Parliament in which they said they had heard that their hosts were good and kind to everybody, and that they, the Chinese, could not afford to eat if the tax was imposed.

Before there was time for any semblance of objective debate about the discrimination intrinsic in any such proposal, the bush telegraph buzzed with a report that a Chinaman at Buckland had committed an unnatural and criminal act, verified by a woman. The diggers lost their balance at an angry meeting and, incensed beyond reason, descended on the Chinese huts.

There were, by some accounts, about a hundred whites and fully two thousand Chinese, but the whites were armed with rifles and pieces of timber. They drove the Chinese along the river, burnt the huts and looted the camp. Even the local press was aghast. It was two days before police arrived. Protecting yellow barbarians from white ones was not a task that excited the moral indignation of society's employed protectors.

A Chinese procession in Ballarat for a charities fete in 1875. The exotic glamour of ethnic costume and regalia has since become an integral part of many public festivities all over Australia.

Two more sketches from the Queensland diggings.

The white man's dislike of the oriental stemmed in part from allegations that he had unhygienic habits. It is safe to say that because the Chinese was so different, the white man would always have been sure to find something to justify discrimination. The same charges were made by white Americans against the Negro, and in the southern States of America they boiled over into repeated atrocities against Negroes, to which police there turned a blind eye. Therein lies the explanation: in those southern States there were millions of Negroes, on the Australian goldfields there were thousands of Chinese. The presence of large numbers of Americans, Germans, Irish, was fascinating, a social *mélange*. Large numbers of Chinese constituted a Yellow Peril, and the Tartar hordes must be turned back. The white man, forging a lonely outpost of British civilisation on a vast continent, felt like Canute. Roll back the wave before it's too late, that was the feverish instinct. They're different from us, strange, and they'll overrun us. The Chinese would scarcely have evoked more suspicion, distrust and finally hatred had they stepped off a spaceship from some other galaxy. White miners at Bendigo threatened to throw them out. Parliaments were bombarded with petitions urging the elected representatives of the people to stop the flow. The Chinese were heathens, and they smoked themselves into glassy-eyed insensibility with opium pipes. The fact that Australia in general, and the goldfields in particular, was not a model of Christian belief or practice, and that many diggers drank themselves into sprawling incoherence every week, took the pleasure of harlots and lived like animals, was a hypocrisy nobody would have dared mention in a diggers' saloon, unless he wanted to be punched to the floor and kicked silly.

So the Chinese were subjected to a sort of 'import duty' that assisted the public revenue; many of them drifted from the goldfields, and cheap labour was a cornerstone of the squattocratic ascendency. Others kept digging, moving, single file, from spent fields to new ones, like the hardiest of diggers.

The trail led, eventually, to Kiandra, deep in the Snowy Mountains of New South Wales, which was packed with upwards of 10 000 diggers when the rush there was at its peak. By late 1860 it was being deserted by even the most resolute

This wood engraving from the Australasian Sketcher *of 1876 is entitled 'A Game of Euchre'. Perhaps this kind of multicultural comradeship did exist to some small extent on the goldfields.*

adventurers. There had always been another field, but by now, a full decade since the first Australian gold rush began, many sensed that the rainbow was evaporating, and that anybody who did not find his spot soon would have spent years of back-breaking toil for nothing save his sustenance.

They trudged over the mountain, hundreds of kilometres, heading north-west, to a place where men had struck it rich, so the newspapers said. The place had a soft-sounding name, gentle, pastoral: Lambing Flat. But it was an unruly field, even by the standards of the day. The miners who had come from Kiandra had endured bitter winters, slushing through snow for their provisions, huddled around fires at night when the temperature dropped to

Another sketch of the rushes showing the alien Chinaman 'welly hard' at it.

The Australian News, *9 July 1877, used this illustration to demonstrate Chinese immigrants 'invading' Queensland.*

freezing. Now, after the long journey cross-country, there would be the dust and flies of a hot summer to contend with in territory vastly different from the one they had forsaken. And the proportion of Chinese on this field was unusually high. How many goldseekers went to Lambing Flat we will never know, but by mid-1860 there were about five hundred Chinese there, one for every two or three whites.

It was at this time that New South Wales building workers were leading the drive for the eight-hour day, and these workers were successful the following year, 1861, despite the growing tendency of employers to combine. There was a silent war between unions and employers: to the working man, cheap labour was treachery. There had also been a recession at the end of the Fifties, and hard times breed mean men. The diggers worked shoulder to shoulder along the banks of the creeks at Lambing Flat. In

November the weather turned hot, and tempers frayed. The white diggers posted their anger, in notices that the Chinese must get out. (We assume that the Chinese had them translated.) The Chinese clung together, as always. There was a lot of loose bragging and easy liquor in the white sections of the field. Chinese tents went up in flames.

The white diggers began to organise, and as their numbers swelled at rowdy meetings, so their sense of proportion declined. Safety in numbers. Diggers everywhere were agitating for reforms because they lived in primitive conditions, and were so isolated that there was little communication with the outside world. Their gold was taxed, and on top of everything else they had to compete with the yellow-skins. They formed the Miners' Protective League and totted up their grievances, on paper, in a mish-mash of rhetoric that included a call for equality,

Above: *Conviviality thriving on a cheque from the sale of gold.*

Below: *An illustration of the Lambing Flat riot.*

Line drawing of Lambing Flat riot.

fraternity and liberty, but from the terms of which they specifically excluded anybody from China. The atmosphere was so tense that the Premier, Charles Cowper, travelled to Lambing Flat to test the wind for himself. When he returned to Sydney and addressed the Legislative Assembly, it was obvious that Chinese immigration was not about to be restricted. Sydney was a long way from the goldfields. When word got back to the white diggers, they decided to take the law into their own hands.

They gathered, thousands of them, on the last day of June 1861, a Sunday. They flew the flags of several white nations, Britain, Ireland and the United States, and another flag not unlike the Eureka one. They stoked their passions with speeches and band music, then, armed with crude weapons and whips, descended on the Chinese quarter.

The atrocities they committed defied description, and made a mockery of any notion that they were done in the name of a civilised race acting against an uncivilised one. The whites, using spades and whips, slashed at their quarry, and struck down at least one child. One Chinese was reported killed. The stated

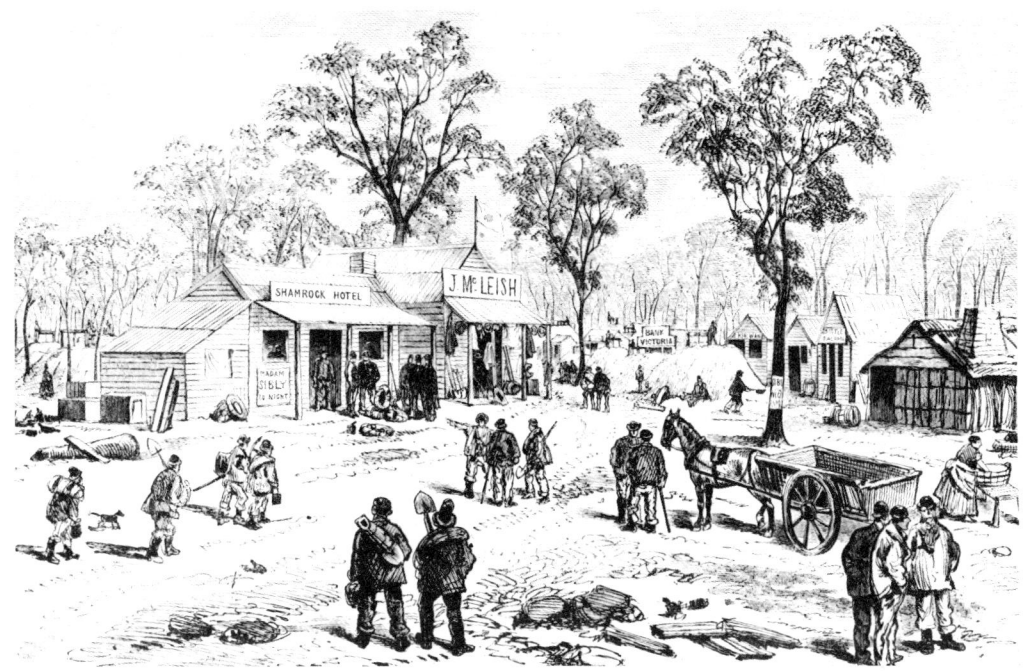

A sketch of the main street of a Victorian gold rush town.

aim was to force the Chinese to leave: every possession in the camp that the invaders could get their hands on, including clothing, food and books, was piled on to a bonfire. The diggers hoped their stupid, violent action would trigger an uprising against orientals throughout Australia. Instead, it cost them any support they may have had among legislators in Sydney, who were naturally concerned about what London would think of a colony, new to self-government, that permitted mob rule.

There was no intention by legislators to encourage a multi-racial society, in contrast to the situation in the late twentieth century, but there is a clear parallel in the public attitude towards Asians in that a small number of Asians in Australia are considered tolerable, but that is all.

In 1861, however, the use of violence against Asians was not so widely considered reprehensible as it would be now. The police arrested only three people in connection with the attack. The diggers held another mass meeting and decided to demand the release of the prisoners, and when the police quite correctly refused, diggers attacked the camp where the prisoners were held. In this protracted riot a digger was killed, and the situation got entirely out of hand. It had been more than a fortnight since the attack on the Chinese, but the number of police who had responded to it, like the number of arrests, had been small. The diggers had the numbers, and they showed no signs of guilt about what they had done. The opposite: upwards of 3000 of them moved on the camp the following day. The police retreated with the prisoners, and set out for Yass, about 100 kilometres to the south-east.

On the diggings there was near anarchy as the men set up vigilante groups. At Yass, somebody obviously feared that thousands of felons from Lambing Flat would materialise at any moment, to raze the gaol and take the town with them. The prisoners escaped from gaol, leaving the same way they had come in. Somebody left the doors unlocked.

Chinese victims of the attack at Lambing Flat turned to the Legislative Assembly by way of petition. The victims got no redress. One of the Chinese, a Roman Catholic married to a European woman of the same religion, was among more than fifty victims who described the attack, listed the possessions that had been destroyed, and requested compensation, to no avail.

Five men were prosecuted at Goulburn in September 1861, on charges of riotous assembly. Their trial went for two days, at the end of which the jury found them not guilty.

One of the white diggers' representatives was Mr E. A. Baker. He and another white digger were sent to Sydney to ask the Governor, Sir John Young, to refrain from declaring martial law on the goldfields, and to request a royal commission into their grievances.

A half century after the riots, Baker wrote, in the *Australian Star*, that the enraged whites had been armed with pistols, axes and tomahawks and, at one point, had threatened to 'settle not only the police but the gold commissioners as well'. The white diggers' attack on the Chinese, he wrote, 'drove the celestials before them like a flock of sheep'. The miners had quickly raised £600 for the legal defence of thirteen miners accused of taking part in the riot, and only one had been convicted. According to Baker, the man convicted was a watchmaker from the town, 'a half-witted fellow ... who gave himself away by his foolishness'. After the twelve acquittals there had been a great celebration. A bullock had been roasted whole and eaten at the fireside, grog 'flowed like water' and there had been 'inflammatory but harmless speeches ... and thus ended the Lambing Flat riots.'

E. A. Baker went on to become a Member of the Legislative Assembly of New South Wales before he wrote his account in 1909.

In a nutshell, a small army of whites had attacked a smaller number of Chinese, the police arrested a few whites as ringleaders, some escaped, and there was a joke-trial of the rest. It was a disgraceful blot on a colony that had been granted self-government on the assurance that it would uphold the British rule of law. Where was the 'British sense of fair play'? That this was a travesty was not lost on the cooler heads in Sydney, but in most of New South Wales the riots failed to rouse the public conscience in support of human rights for non-whites. Chinese might be people, but they weren't the same sort of people as those who deserved 'fair play'.

About 2600 coolies had been brought to Australia as indentured workers before the gold rushes. Chinese came and went, and it was difficult to keep tabs on their numbers, but in the 1871 census, there were only 44 women, compared with 28 307 men. Why whites entertained any notion that the country would be overrun by a group that was threatened with extinction for lack of a reproductive capacity is a mystery.

The Queensland Government legislated to ban Chinese from any new goldfield for the first three years of diggings, but this was rejected by the British in 1876. Eventually, China complained to Britain about discrimination in Australia.

The numbers of Chinese in Australia appear to have increased in the late 1870s and the 1880s to about 38 500, but declined after further restrictions which constituted one of the few agreements of any importance between the colonies before Federation. The Chinese were concentrated almost entirely in the three eastern States; when the gold was gone, some headed for the capital cities, others took up market gardening and shop keeping in country towns, and prospered. As a minority, they knew enough to keep their heads down. In time, Chinese carved out small empires as businessmen and became community leaders, thus gaining

An early twentieth century Chinese market gardener in the Northern Territory.

a measure of respect from their fellow Australians. But it was uphill most of the way.

Few Australians ever bothered to inquire about the customs and traditions of orientals. Indeed, it is unlikely that more than a few Australians could name all the countries of South-East Asia until Australian troops got bogged down in one of them in a major war in the 1960s. If pre-judice is breaking down only now, I am afraid it is to the jetliner and cheap package holiday that we must attribute much of the credit. The yellow peril theory is dormant partly because Australians fought in the Vietnam War to prevent the peril eventuating: the war was lost, but the hordes have yet to materialise. Thinking Australians are still awaiting an explanation from their elder statesmen.

CHAPTER 8

A Little Bit of Italy

QUEENSLAND has always regarded itself as a pioneer State, a place for rugged, no-nonsense settlers whose wealth has come almost exclusively from farming and mining. It certainly has been a pioneer State for non-British immigration, and some of the most interesting and successful schemes to lure settlers from Continental Europe were hatched not in the more populous States of New South Wales and Victoria, but thousands of kilometres north of Brisbane.

The gold rushes did not have nearly as much impact on Queensland as they did on the other eastern States, and it became obvious to business leaders north of the 29th parallel, after Queensland was formed in 1859, and expanded in 1861, that although the colony had rich natural resources, it would want for manpower unless special steps were taken to attract

An Italian family picnicking beside the Murrumbidgee River in the late nineteenth century.

more settlers. Queensland is more than twice the size of New South Wales, and more than seven times the size of Victoria, but at its birth had only about one-twentieth of Victoria's population and only one-twelfth as many people as New South Wales. Only Western Australia was less populous.

At the apex of the Queensland economy were big landowners and squatters, and it was they who demanded that the Government take responsibility for ensuring that they had an adequate supply of cheap labour by introducing coolies from India. Captain Robert Towns looked for a closer source, and found it in South Sea islanders; 2000 of these kanakas were brought in during a five-year period in the 1860s, and they were treated harshly. They were indentured, but it was not until 1868 that they were assured, by an Act of Parliament, of wages of £6 a year, repatriation at the end of their contracts, and improved conditions on the ships that

An illustration from The Bulletin, *30 April 1881.*

brought them and took them home. Their lot improved because of protests by white workers and clergymen.

There had been a trickle of Italian immigrants from the early years of the nineteenth century, and they were to be found in small but growing numbers throughout the mainland. In Queensland, they became a mainstay of the cane-cutting industry after the kanakas went home to their islands. There was, as there always has been during economic

A kanaka house in Queensland.

downturns, a great deal of antipathy towards the Italians during the Depression of the 1890s, and there had been a sufficient flow of them from the 1870s to make them a readily identifiable group in north Queensland. Their letters home, to Veneto and Sicily, told of their hardships, but they kept coming because a labourer could earn 8 shillings a day, more than six times as much as he could earn in the old country, and enough, if he saved carefully, to get him a roof over his head, a bit of land or even a small business. And they saved – their care with money was legendary, and to some Anglo-Saxons was irritating and threatening.

In the 1960s, when Italians were arriving in Sydney and Melbourne by the boatload, and every Italian in Leichhardt and Fitzroy had an accent thick enough to cut your pizza, it was always a surprise for tourists from the south to stop on the way through towns like Innisfail, one of the last stops before Cairns. There they would find men and women in service stations and restaurants who were, in features and physique, very much like the

immigrants arriving in the southern cities, but when they spoke their accents were broad and rural, as drawling as a drover's. And that, more than the standard worker's gear of singlet, khaki shorts and heavy boots, stamped them as true-blue Aussies. But their forebears, the ones who paved the way for them, had a tough time of it for a couple of generations.

For a start, the early Italians found difficulty gaining acceptance among Anglo-Saxon pioneers, and this included social clubs and civic groups. Nor did they appear to want to join, since the Italian family unit is firmly welded and strives for self-sufficiency. The Italians came with a reputation as willing workers, men with strong backs and big calluses. They would toil from sun-up to dusk, six days a week, and even on the seventh they would find odd jobs to do. They stayed away from the pubs – and they also stayed away from church in such alarming numbers that a visiting priest, the Very Rev. Father Mambrini, calculated in 1923 that in Ingham only four per cent of his flock had received the sacraments since they left Italy up to half a century before! 'Bearing this in mind, it is a wonder that they are as good as they are,' he wrote, noting that they were by temperament good citizens, and were hard-working, but had easily come to the conclusion that one religion was as good as another because they had observed that 'probity and good intention mark the lives of their Protestant neighbours'. As he saw it, the national spirit of Australians was against Italians, whose souls were 'naturally religious', while Australia was becoming more pagan every day 'on account of the flourishing condition of material things'.

When Italians did join the mainstream of community endeavours in north Queensland, the effects were startling. Two businessmen, Armati and Fraire or Frere, suggested to the Chamber of Commerce in Townsville in 1890 that Italians could be brought out to make up for the loss of the kanakas. Fraire sailed to his native Piedmont, and to Lombardy, and persuaded three hundred and thirty-five of his countrymen to make the long voyage to Townsville which, being 1600 kilometres north of Brisbane, was to them an outpost of a remote continent. Most of these labourers brought their wives and families with them. One hundred and nine Italians settled in Wide Bay in December the following year, and chain migration from their home towns began. The lure was high wages: Herbert and Lower Burdekin planters were paying 15 shillings a week, on top of keep. The climate was enervating to British-born immigrants, but for that kind of money an Italian would toil all day in the fields uncomplainingly, in temperatures that did not distress him. For reasons that no doubt had some connection with a distrust of swarthy-skinned foreigners, it had been assumed that they would not be able to handle the work. In many Piedmont villages every family lost at least one member to the north Queensland canefields, where the newcomers soon

showed they were anything but work-shy. Employers found them honest, thrifty, and very systematic.

Unfortunately, the old Australian suspicion that immigrants took jobs from Australians was revived during the Depression of the 1890s. In the decade 1881-90 Australia had a net gain of 382 741 immigrants, much the highest figure since the gold rushes, but in the ten years after that, the gain was only 24 879, the smallest gain since the 1860s. The proportion of females to males in the 1890s was, however, more even than it had been in the 1880s, and in widely scattered Italian villages there were families who knew that when the good times returned, north Queensland was a place they could go to, find well-paid jobs and be among their own people. So that although there was never Italian emigration, on the scale of the waves after World War II, the Queensland schemes ensured that there was a sporadic stream. By 1923 there were 1900 Italians in Ingham, for example, less than a third of them bachelors, and almost all of them from northern Italy. There were two hundred and eighty-eight Italian families whose descendants would be Australians, working with Australians, accepted by Australians of other stock. Intermarriage with Anglo-Saxon Australians was rare among Italian immigrant communities, but the Italians, being family-orientated, sent back to Italy for brides. And they were pioneers as much as any of the native-born Australians who opened up Queensland and made it the prosperous State it is today.

By 1988 the so-called Italian community in Australia will number 1 750 000; Italians are now the largest group of non-British immigrants, and more than one million Australians were born in Italy or have at least one parent who was born there.

Queensland was not the sole beneficiary of the Italian flow that speeded up in

Immigrants arriving in Queensland in the 1880s. The benefits of welcoming Italian and German migrants were that they brought their families with them and often began chain immigration from their districts of origin.

the 1870s. Nineteenth-century Italians from Messina took up fishing in Western Australia, some from Veneto transformed themselves into farmers in New South Wales and South Australia, and families from Vicenza province, in the Veneto, went to Victoria to mine and farm. There was always a livelihood to be sawn out of timber in southern New South Wales, or hewed out of silver and lead at Broken Hill, or built up in market gardens near the big cities.

They ran into problems in Boulder and Kalgoorlie, however, because of the low wages they accepted as contract miners. There were two commissions of inquiry in Western Australia after the turn of the century, and eventually the contract system was abolished. If Italians lived in sub-standard houses, the old cry went up about immigrants lowering living standards. Australians had got used to high wages, good conditions by the standards of the early twentieth century (when the living standard was estimated to be the fourth-highest in the world) but nobody had adequately addressed the problem of how to develop the country without increasing immigration, because there was no answer.

Eventually the Queensland canefield jobs went to Italians by default, because Australian workers did not want them, and the trade unions decided that was permissible provided they could induce Italians to join unions. Italians in the Murrumbidgee Irrigation Area of New South Wales had to bear the resentment of soldier-settlers who went there after World War I and found they could not

Queensland canecutters pose for the photographer. Some of the men pictured came from Russia. (Macleay Museum, University of Sydney)

adapt to farm life. It is worth recalling that the first Italian at Griffith, in the heart of the MIA, went there as early as 1913. Francesco Bicego came from Reviso province in northern Italy, and after the war – in which he and several other Italians fought – migration chains began that eventually increased the Griffith area's population by more than 1600 in just over half a century. Almost two-thirds of these people can trace their ancestry back to Bicego's native region, and many others came from Calabria. It has been estimated that three in every four Griffith area properties are owned by people with Italian names. Italians in the MIA had to struggle against discrimination, and it was at the official level. Because of strong feelings that soldier settlements should not be transferred to anybody who was not born in Australia, and because of resentment of the more efficient Italians, attempts to keep the Italian farmers at bay eventually had to be squashed in court.

The Amending Immigration Act of 1925 was a blatant blow at intending Italian immigrants and other foreigners with non-British customs and traditions. It aimed to refuse entry to anybody who did not seem likely to become assimilated, and thus ignored the fact that the immigrant can scarcely be expected to assimilate fully even if he does manage to cope with conditions in his strange new land. On top of that, Australia did not have – and to an extent still lacks – the facilities to help immigrants assimilate, and the Anglo-Saxon community for the most part did not show much willingness in this regard. Other restrictions discriminated against poor emigrants.

The 1920s were prosperous years in Australia, and immigration restrictions in the United States which curtailed the flood of southern, central and eastern Europeans presented Australia with a great opportunity to secure its future by bringing some of the would-be emigrants

Italian labourers visiting a friend's fruit farm. (John Oxley Library)

to our land. Australia would have needed to take only a small proportion of them, so great had been that flood across the Atlantic, for between 1891 and 1920 the United States had absorbed 7.8 million people from central and eastern Europe, and 4.4 million from southern Europe: of 15 924 400 immigrants who made the voyage to America during that period, 12 364 100 had come from the central, eastern and southern countries of the Continent. That was why Congress had stopped the flood, of course – a fear that America was being overrun by people who were not from north-western Europe, which was where earlier immigrants had come from. Instead of pausing to consider all the facts and put them in the proper perspective, Australia simply echoed the American sentiment, to its cost. America was a developed country, with a population of more than one hundred million, compared with six million in Australia; it was not only the richest nation on earth, but was challenging Britain's position as the most powerful nation on earth. Above all, it was largely self-sufficient in resources, and had sufficient people to ensure that by natural increase alone, if need be, it would retain its position, economically and by virtue of numbers, as a fortress. But Australian leaders heard only the American voices wailing that the influx of Italians and Hungarians, Russians and Poles, Greeks and Romanians

Italian canecutters in Ingham, Queensland, in about 1912. (John Oxley Library)

and all the others had gone on too long, so that the United States had been in danger of losing its racial purity, that is to say, as a race of super Anglo-Saxons. It had also become obvious that the melting pot had not done its job in the big cities, which contained ghettoes of foreigners packed as thickly as all but the worst European slums.

Fear of communism was one factor in the rush to slam America's door on Europe's huddled masses, and the unions, as in Australia, were worried about cheap labour. There was also a lot of talk about mysterious organisations such as the Black Hand and the Mafia. In America, the most concerted violence was done by the Ku Klux Klan, which in 1924 had about 4.5 million members, all white Gentiles, and much larger than any gang that the likes of Al Capone could muster.

Fears of the Black Hand had free rein in Australia, too, but there was little to fear.

Accusations of Mafia activity in fruit and vegetable markets in the big cities surfaced in the 1960s, but no links were established, though some Italian-Australians did not help clear suspicions by their refusal to discuss the matter with police and community leaders, no doubt because of a fear of 'becoming involved'. Some native-born Australians of British ancestry took this attitude to indicate that there was a cover-up, or that some Italians were not showing sufficient respect for their adopted country, with its British rule of law.

Of more recent and much more intense concern has been an apparent Italian connection in the Griffith area with marijuana growing and distribution. The murder of the anti-drugs campaigner

Donald Mackay and the long, sometimes puzzling delay in clearing up that case, fuelled suspicion. Bearing in mind the number of Italian-Australian farmers in the MIA, however, or, for that matter, the enormous number of Italian-descended folk throughout Australia, the number of Italians involved in investigations has been proportionately very small. A number of police in different parts of Australia have been dismissed for involvement in the drug trade, and most of them undoubtedly are of old Australian Anglo-Saxon stock. The attraction of a quick illegal fortune is not associated with genetics or national origins. If the Italian-Australian community had to be categorised in a few short words, they would probably be 'law-abiding, hard-working and honest'.

Every immigration programme involves risks. The United States' successive Administrations under a score of Presidents and thousands of different Congressmen understood that in the one hundred years between 1820 and 1920 when the gates were wide open. The old Australian exhortation 'Have a Go!' is often observed more in the breach than in any willingness to practise it; in the United States it has been a plank of the so-called American Way. America, built on risk capital and cheap labour and the invitation to the foreign hordes to come over the oceans and 'Have a Go!' was, to be sure, always intent in the nineteenth century on preserving its north-western European origins. Only when it appeared that that predominance of north-western Europeans was actually being challenged, or would be later on, was the door closed. We have to remember, too, that by 1920,

Italian canecutters at their Annual Picnic Day in the Babinda district, Queensland, on Christmas Day 1929. (John Oxley Library)

there was an awareness in America that there had been a high cost, in human terms, of importing factory fodder and leaving the mass of newcomers to fend for themselves. It had been estimated in 1904 that somewhere between ten and twenty million Americans were living in poverty; the tenement slums were bulging, and immigration that decade reached one million a year. Industrial accidents had cost tens of thousands of lives, injuries on the shop floor had reached hundreds of thousands a year: the sweated labour system was brutal, safeguards few, and the illiterate foreigner took his life in his hands. But America, which a century earlier had felt itself hemmed in on all sides, had got all the people it needed to exploit its resources and make it impregnable.

The continent at the other end of the Pacific, roughly the same size as the continental United States, had neglected the business of people-building. It could boast a high standard of living, but it was anything but self-sufficient, relied on complementary trade with its mother country, and was extremely vulnerable. Every expression of the latter fact only served to increase the Australian's xenophobia. Not until the degree of that vulnerability was demonstrated by direct attack on Australia, thus proving that distance was no deterrent, did Australia feel forced to change its mind about immigration, and non-British immmigration most of all. Even then, that change would have to be made with great delicacy.

After Federation, Australia, a nation at last, settled into cosy complacency. It was intent on conserving what it had got: a very large piece of the world's real estate, with adequate land under cultivation to produce exports for the benefit, ultimately, of all.

A German tradesman with his family, Gympie, Queensland c. 1871. (John Oxley Library)

The German Glee Club which was founded in Brisbane by Ferdinand Rosentengel in 1880. Members participated in many civic concerts and receptions. (John Oxley Library)

Australians, now united, could feel themselves important in the world. They were more prosperous than most of the peoples on earth. What the powerful countries such as Britain and the United States had – homes for most citizens, cars, the material evidence of abundance – Australia had too. And Australia's participation in World War I, so willing and loyal, had given her a seat at the table of the mighty (with William Morris Hughes as her representative), alongside the greats, Woodrow Wilson of the United States, Lloyd George of Britain, Georges Clemenceau of France.

A more realistic appraisal might have been that Australia was a grown-up colony, largely dependent on Britain, which most Australians still saw as a mother with an umbrella to keep out the rain. Above all, there was no scorching need to go out and build up the country with people to develop rich resources that were still untapped because nobody had bothered to go out and find them. There was no bugle blast summoning men to Valley Forge or New Orleans or the Alamo; the only bugle sounds had faded on the cliffs of Gallipoli and Flanders fields, and they were half a world away. Australia was one, and it had arrived. A long snooze began.

CHAPTER 9

No Way to Build a Nation

IT MUST SEEM STRANGE to modern Australians that many of their ancestors were lukewarm about Federation, or were opposed to it (more than a quarter of those who bothered to vote on the issue, in fact). 'Tyranny of distance' was a term that applied not only to the vast geographical gulf between Australia and the Old World, but to the separate Australian colonies themselves. They clung to their identities. Nothing demonstrated that so dramatically as the farce that led to each colony insisting on deciding which railway gauge it would use, when all logic dictated a uniform gauge. (In the end, there were three gauges. New South Wales, after originally deciding on the 5 feet 3 inches [1.6 metres] 'Irish' gauge, opted for the 'British' gauge of 4 feet 8½ inches [1.4 metres]. Victoria went for the Irish gauge, while Western Australia and Queensland selected the narrow gauge of

Woolclassers at work in New South Wales.

3 feet 6 inches [1.1 metres]. South Australia and Tasmania each had two gauges: the former started laying track with the wide gauge and then switched to narrow, while the latter began with the intermediate width and then swung to narrow.)

Australia in the last decades of the nineteenth century was a nation in waiting, but not in the making, judged on the efforts made to foster immigration. In the forty years after 1860, the net gain in immigration was 766 000, of whom 45.7 per cent were assisted. The worst decade for immigration was the Depression-ridden 1890s, during which Australia's migration gain was just 24 800, a pitiful figure. Moreover, some of the colonies did little or nothing to assist with passage money. Victoria's programme petered out after 1880 and did not revive until 1907. New South Wales threw in the towel in the 1890s, and its programme did not recommence until 1906. There is a gap be-

Left and opposite page: *Streetlife for the young late last century. The Depression of the 1890s made immigration less of an issue than survival at home.*

tween 1885 and 1911 in South Australia's assisted programme, and Tasmania's gap was almost as long, extending from 1891 to 1913. Even Queensland, which had persisted with immigration programmes and attracted Germans, Italians and Scandinavians, suspended assisted immigration from 1893 until 1899. Only Western Australia had a continuous programme between the mid-1880s and the turn of the century, and it was so meagre as to be meaningless, as the annual figure sometimes fell below one hundred, and rarely got past two hundred. It is a truism that a big country cannot be fully developed without a lot of people, and Australia's lack of regard for people-building no doubt is one reason why Australians languished in blissful ignorance of the extent of the nation's natural resources for so long.

Almost half of the immigration gain was in the form of assisted passages, so it follows that Australia, whatever pride she held in herself as an emerging nation, was not regarded in Europe as a gold passport to prosperity for emigrants. America was the big attraction. Historians usually attribute the difference in appeal of the two countries to the relative closeness of the United States to Europe, but that is not the whole story. America was rich, both in natural resources and in people, and had gathered an unstoppable momentum. To a great agrarian economy had been added a mighty industrial one, and it was a supremely innovative nation. It was both questing and thrusting. Unlike Americans, Australians had no overriding need to look to themselves for every aspect of their future: even after Federation, much of that future was bound up in mother England. But even if we acknowledge that, it is hard to understand why some of the American drive to attract immigrants to help expand and build the United States did not at least seep into the Australian consciousness. Australia's suspicion that immigrants were people who competed in the market place for jobs was equalled, if not exceeded, by its fear of invasion. The average Australian never paused to consider that this was a contradiction in terms, or that fear of invasion might pass if there were sufficient Australians to justify sole occupancy of the continent and sufficient to defend it. American immigration agents roamed Europe broadcasting the virtues and blessings of the United States. Australia for the most part looked not at all to Continental Europe and to Britain only for a trickle of new blood. In the 1890s, about 96 per cent of the population rise in Australia was from natural increase. The 4 per cent from immigration can scarcely be said to constitute an immigration programme at all.

His Social Joys

A typical Subject

Occupation

A Favorite Pastime

Relaxation

Australia by then had attained one of the highest standards of living in the world. But one reason for opposition to immigration was a resistance to sharing our wealth with any hordes of new arrivals. Britain was on top of the world, militarily and industrially; Australia, at the bottom of the world, geographically and militarily and industrially, was happy to depend on Britain.

So our immigration policy was essentially a negative one, and thus had negative results: in 1892-93 and 1898-1900, economic recession resulted in more people leaving Australia than sailed in.

All of this explains why Australia's population in 1900 was only 3.1 million, or slightly more than one person for every square mile (2.7 square kilometres) of the entire continent.

The immigration programme was still dormant in the first decade of the twentieth century, and between 1902 and 1906 total departures again outstripped total arrivals. All political parties embraced the White Australia Policy, which excluded non-Europeans. The Immigration Restriction Act of 1901 provided a so-called dictation test. It was designed to exclude any immigrant who because of his colour might dilute the white strain. (This was one of the few measures in which Australia can be said to have led the United States, which in 1917 imposed a literary test on those seeking to settle. Congress imposed it over the last of a number of Presidential vetoes by Woodrow Wilson, but it did not stop almost a million immigrants arriving in 1921. Although emigration to America dropped remarkably in the 1890s, it became a tidal wave after 1900, and at its peak up to 15 000 immigrants were arriving in New York each *day*.) Australia, of course, could not take nearly as many as 15 000 a day, because it did not have the means to support such numbers, but the American figure illustrates how far Australia had to go. Australia's average net gain per day in immigrants in the first decade of this century was 32. Not all of the immigrants who went to America stayed, of course, and during bad times immigration fell off in both countries, but 15 000 compared with 32 cannot be explained away by theories about the tyranny of distance, or the fact that America was so rich in resources, or had an economic base to support a large inflow. (The economic base had been developed in no small part because of a

Houses like these could be had by those migrants who were fortunate enough to be accepted. They were unlikely to be large or luxurious but were functional and dry.

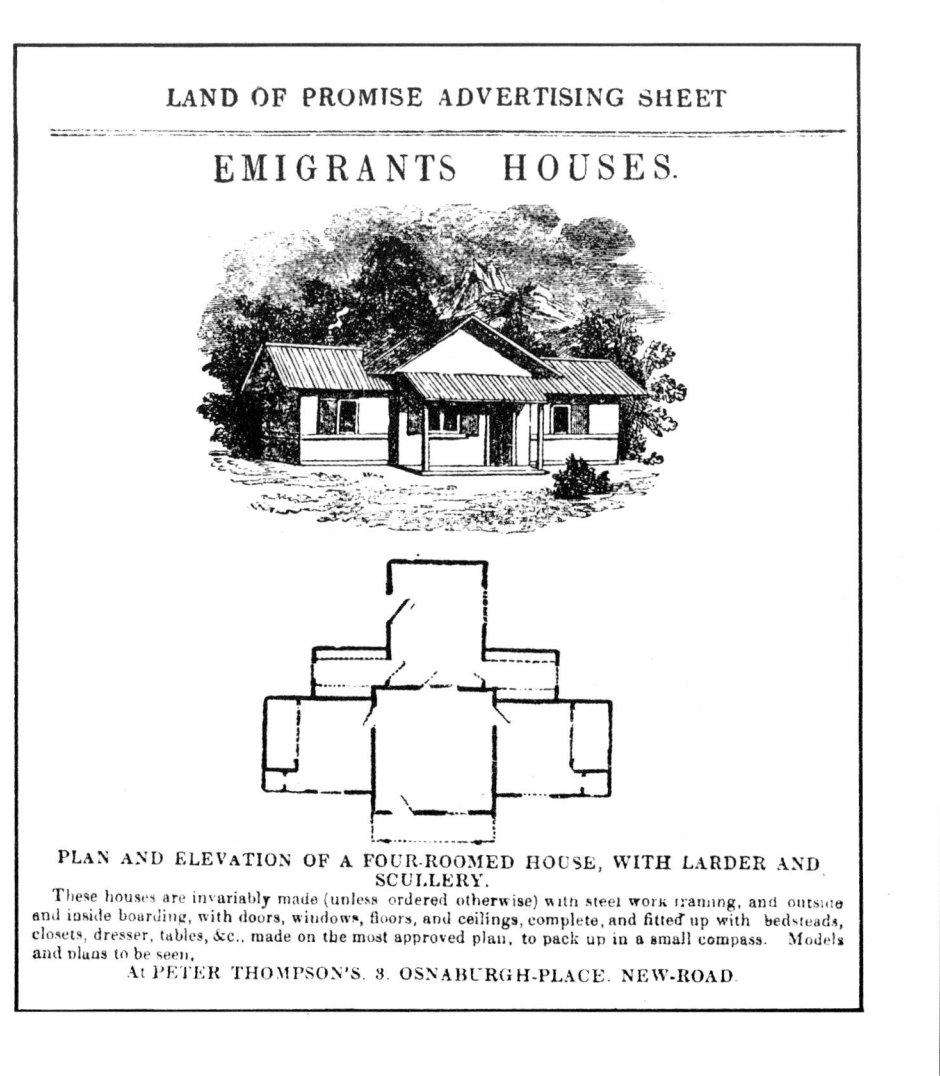

LAND OF PROMISE ADVERTISING SHEET

EMIGRANTS HOUSES.

PLAN AND ELEVATION OF A FOUR-ROOMED HOUSE, WITH LARDER AND SCULLERY.

These houses are invariably made (unless ordered otherwise) with steel work framing, and outside and inside boarding, with doors, windows, floors, and ceilings, complete, and fitted up with bedsteads, closets, dresser, tables, &c., made on the most approved plan, to pack up in a small compass. Models and plans to be seen,

At PETER THOMPSON'S. 3. OSNABURGH-PLACE. NEW-ROAD.

Migrant workers at Mount Morgan mines in Queensland.

positive attitude to immigration over the previous century.) Australia had a net loss of migrants in some years because it did nothing to replenish, and it did nothing to replenish because of a fear that new arrivals would take the jobs of Australians. This, in such a large continent, was sowing the wind ...

When all the pros and cons are sifted, and tyranny of distance and economic base weighed against what might have been possible to achieve, one fact remains: the United States welcomed the immigrant throughout most of the entire period that brought it, in the last twenty years of the nineteenth century, to the front rank of nations. There was antipathy in America to new arrivals in the first part of this century, and we should not forget that. It found its target in the poor and dispossessed of southern and central Europe, many of whom were illiterate and thought unlikely to be able to assimilate – that is, to become 100 per cent Americans with the super-Anglo-Saxon mission of carving out an empire in the New World, and who would be wedded to democracy and the other ideals of the Great Republic. But it is arguable that by the time this antipathy surfaced, America had taken sufficient immigrants anyway to ensure that, with natural increase, it had secured its future and position in the world. Early this century the flood was so high that only one person in three in America had parents who were

The Comino Brothers' Cafe, in Childers, Queensland, c. 1920. The business was begun by the five Greek brothers in about 1907. During the cutting season the town was usually flooded with at least a thousand cutters: the Greeks among them haunting the Cafe. (John Oxley Library)

both native-born Americans, an astonishing proportion. Two in every three people in America were either foreign born, or were the offspring of immigrants.

The chief difference between the two countries was one of attitude. Australia did not see the need for immigrants as clearly as did the United States, and yet that need should have been obvious, given, especially, Australia's fear of invasion. But then Australians had much less positive attitudes about where their country was headed than did Americans. The optimism of Americans, their dedication, discipline and willingness to work towards a common goal, all these qualities had been clear on the goldfields. America, in terms of immigration, was positive and unafraid. Australia was negative and fearful. That was the essential difference between the two countries.

Emigration to Australia ceased during World War I. The war cost the lives of 59 000 Australians; at the end of it, of the 270 000 men who had to be brought home from Britain, France and the Middle East, about one-third were wounded or incapacitated. Australian industry had been built up during the war, which, because of the numbers of Australians fighting, their gallantry, and the influence William Morris Hughes had exerted at the Versailles Peace Conference, brought Australia to the attention of world leaders.

Quite apart from the loss of manpower, the war produced in Australia a need for fresh manpower for the new industries, and also an awakening that fresh manpower was needed for defence. 'Billy' Hughes saw this as coming from Britain, and thus strengthening Australia's ties with Britain. There was talk of Australia's population reaching 100 million, or even double that figure, which was indeed fanciful: there were 5.4 million souls in Australia in 1920, and the plans for assisted immigration, though significant compared with what had been proposed in the past – which was little – were scarcely

Beer being given to unemployed men during the depression of 1902.

Below: *The isolation of the bush encouraged strong bonds of mateship among men. These four are feasting on melons and billy tea.*

Promotion for emigration to Australia in England in about 1913. This huge poster was situated in the Strand and was said to be the largest in London.

large scale. One spur to Australia's acceptance of the post World War I Empire settlement plan was fear of Japan, which had been an ally of the British during the war, but had revealed expansionist tendencies.

The principles of the migration agreements were thrashed out at the Imperial Conference of 1921. Assistance was provided under the Empire Settlement Act of 1922 and the so-called '£34 million agreement' of 1925. The Federal Government took responsibility for immigrant selection in 1920, and took control of Australian immigration operations in Britain in 1921 – a milestone, and the virtual end of individual immigration programmes organised by the States.

The outcome was that more than 300 000 immigrants arrived from Britain in the 1920s. However, the scheme proved largely that – a scheme. There was a lot of big talk, but not enough action. Only a quarter of the money allocated to the scheme was ever spent on it. If the Japanese 'threat' was ever going to be a spur to Australian immigration, it would have to materialise much closer to Australian shores than it ever looked like doing in the 1920s. Australian fears were

assuaged in 1922 when Japan agreed that Britain and the United States had a right to larger navies than Japan because they did not operate only in the Pacific. There was also an agreement to limit the size of navies. In addition, Britain strengthened Singapore, its sentinel on the tip of South-East Asia.

So people-building did not take on an urgency for Australia. The Empire settlement scheme was a solution to a British problem. There was no outcry in Australia when the scheme failed to reach full flower. Australia had shed its blood for Britain, had shown its mettle, shown its support, and that support would always be mutual … that was the sentiment. Japan could be checked by the Royal Navy if the need ever arose.

At the end of the 1920s the forty-year cycle of boom-and-bust brought depression again, and this time it was horrific. With a third of the workforce unemployed, immigration slowed, stopped, and once again Australia suffered a net loss of immigrants. (This occurred during the first three years of the 1930s.) Assisted immigration was abandoned in 1931, and the Empire Settlement Act was not brought out of its dusty pigeonhole until 1938. By then, Europe was again preparing for a war that would decide the balance of world power. Australia was taking immigrants again, but once again it was a case of too little, too late.

Britain declared war on Germany on 3 September 1939, and emigration to Australia again came to a halt. Australia's immigration record in the 1930s, which began in the Depression and concluded in World War II in a quarter-century, was a sorry one. We had gained 30 000 people – about what the New York immigration officers had regarded as a hard two day's work forty years before.

There had, however, been a significant departure from the Australian practice of taking British only in 1938 and 1939. There was a migration agreement with

HRH the Prince of Wales and Mrs Barnardo farewell a party of children in 1929. Under the Barnardo Scheme 2600 children were resettled in Australia between 1921 and 1954.

Holland in 1938, though it was not productive. Several thousand refugees from other European countries were admitted. They did not have assisted passages, and Australia would have continued to rely almost exclusively on British immigrants even if more Dutch had come.

Two factors changed Australia's views on immigration, views that had been held throughout most of the period of white settlement: Pearl Harbor, and Winston Churchill's obstinate insistence that Australian fighting men continue in the role to which both they and the British were accustomed, which is to say, defending Britain's immediate interests. But the attack on Pearl Harbor and Japan's great southward thrust negated the latter factor, because suddenly Australia was

alone, except for the one power that had recognised, one hundred and fifty years earlier, that you cannot develop and defend a large land mass without a lot of manpower, no matter who your friends are. The French had been friendly towards the Americans when America had decided that its responsibility for its security, and therefore its future, lay with Americans. Recognition of that responsibility had been thrust on the American people, and they had responded. Now it was about to be thrust on the Australian people. But how to get them to respond? That story is one of the most interesting in Australian history. It is as much a political story as a sociological one. The key figure in the drama would be a man of American extraction.

Success on the goldfields was largely a matter of luck. Technical know-how was scarcely used despite the example of some American teams.

Folk dancing at the Barossa Festival in South Australia. The settlers of German-origin in South Australia have contributed enormously to the growth of the Australian wine industry. (Australian Picture Library)

CHAPTER 10

Origins of the Big Push

IT IS ARGUABLE that the promotion of large-scale immigration after World War II was the most eventful and beneficial change of course in Australia since Federation.

Not even the politicians who, immediately after the war, were busy organising the immigration programme realised the nature of the flood it would produce. Certainly they did not know it would have a much stronger component from Continental Europe than they had ever envisaged. They were about to usher in the biggest immigration programme in Australian history. More than that, the number of immigrants, as a proportion of the Australian population, would come to rival the largest influxes elsewhere in the world over the past one hundred and fifty

The Prime Minister, Joseph Benedict Chifley, and the Minister for Immigration, Arthur Calwell, welcome the first group of British workers to migrate to Australia under the post-war scheme. (Department of Immigration and Ethnic Affairs)

years. About 4 million immigrants have arrived in Australia since 1947. Not all of them stayed, of course, but between January 1947, and mid-1985, Australia had a net gain of 3.2 million immigrants. In the same period this nation helped 2.2 million immigrants to start a new life by providing them with assisted passages. The numbers of those who came do not compare with the huge and prolonged migration to the United States, which in the early years of this country was attracting more than one million people a year, and which absorbed 16 million between 1891 and 1920 (thus increasing its population, through immigration and natural growth, from 64 million to 106 million in three decades). Canada had 5 million immigrants between 1942 and 1981, 76 per cent of them non-British, and that wave rivals, proportionately, Australia's. It is the orchestration of the Australian programme, through assisted passages and other inducements, and sharp rever-

By the 1930s, department stores, like David Jones, above and top, were a familiar part of life. (David Jones)

sal of Australian attitudes to immigration which made the programme possible, that sets it apart from the great flows elsewhere on the globe.

The programme has been, by and large, well organised and run. It had to be. Had it been handled with less delicacy by the politicians and public servants who con-

ceived it and brought it to fruition, the results might have been very different. Because the first Minister for Immigration, the late Arthur Augustus Calwell, 'sold' the programme to the public partly by emphasising that the British component he and his Federal Labor Government were counting on would be much the biggest group. No fewer than ten in eleven, and later, three in four new arrivals were to be British; that was the Labor plan.

As things turned out, in the first three years of the programme after it actually began to produce immigrants, the ratio was close to the reverse of what the Government had initially aimed at: Continental Europeans made up more than 60 per cent of new arrivals. The British, who had settled the country and given it its traditions and customs, took second place, and continued to do so until after the point had been reached where there was much doubt about the value of non-British immigration. There was a little bit of luck and a lot of good management in this.

Today, any native-born Australian, of whatever age, accepts that among his neighbours he is likely to count an Italian or a Greek, a Yugoslav or a German, a Hungarian or a second- or third-generation descendant of the Balts – the Lithuanians, Latvians and Estonians who were in the vanguard of the big immigration push. It seems natural now, but it did not seem natural to a lot of Australians thirty-five years ago. Australian attitudes were very different from those of today. They were changed because they had to be changed.

It is illuminating to remind ourselves that although Australians for many years regarded their domain as the Lucky Country, it was always a country that had not done enough to justify continued exclusive tenure of its vast area. There was a large element of selfishness in this. In some quarters, most notably the labour movement, there was a tradition of posi-

The slower pace of life allowed more time for a chat in the sun with a mate.

tive opposition to immigration. The unions had fought long and hard to establish working conditions and wages that were the envy of most of the world. Unions feared that the immigrant, in his headlong rush to acquire some of the fruits of his new, bountiful homeland, would undoubtedly be willing to work harder and longer and for less money than the native-born Aussie, thus undermining him financially, endangering his job prospects, and striking at the basis of his relaxed lifestyle. The main fear was non-British immigration. The British assimilated. Other peoples were risky prospects. Some of them had no proper understanding of British traditions, one of which was the discipline of trade unionism, which wrought improvements in wages and working conditions. Undermine that, and Australia would lose one of its greatest traditions, one it had helped pioneer for other nations to emulate.

When World War II removed the last traces of the Great Depression, Australia looked back on a decade, the 1930s, in which there had been a net *fall* in migra-

tion. Assisted immigration virtually ceased between 1931 and 1937, and the Empire Settlement Act, reactivated in 1938, was curtailed by the outbreak of the conflict in Europe. Similarly, an immigration agreement with the Netherlands in 1938 failed to bring an influx, because all able Dutch males were required for the war effort. The Australian mission to Europe which nurtured this agreement was also interested in luring Swiss from their snow-clad fastnesses to the beauties of the wide brown land. The Dutch and the Swiss fell readily within the category of what was known by the pleasant euphemism of 'the right class of people' for immigration – meaning those of north-western European stock. They were the right class because it was presumed that they had the same values and ideals as native Australians – or were capable of identifying with them.

In contrast to the bleakness of the Depression years, the 1920s had been a relatively fruitful period of immigration. The Federal Government had accepted responsibility for migrant selection in

Life in the 1920s and 1930s was simpler than today: budget priced variety stores like Woolworths (which sold just about everything except food and groceries), were revolutionary. These two pictures were taken on the opening day of the Fremantle, Western Australia store in 1929. (Woolworths)

1920, and the following year took from the States control of all Australian migration operations in Britain. As we have seen, more than 300 000 immigrants arrived in Australia during that decade, two-thirds of them assisted under the Empire Settlement Act of 1922, and the £34 million agreement of 1925. The motivation of this programme was a perceived need for a redistribution of the white population of the Empire, rather than an all-out attempt to fill the vast Australian void. The Federal Department of Labour and Immigration, in a review of immigration from 1788 to 1975, noted that from the programme 'few viable plans for development emerged, and only a quarter of the money available was used'.

Australia had some taste of refugee settlement following the Evian Conference of July 1938, called by President Franklin D. Roosevelt to consider ways of helping large numbers of people who were being persecuted in Europe. American opinion had been roused by the problem, which was one basically of anti-Semitism, and was not confined to Germany and Austria. So representatives of many nations gathered in France to consider solutions. It is interesting to reflect on the Australian attitude at the time.

It was estimated in America that 660 900 people in Germany and Austria would require resettlement; the American plan was to get them all out in five years, at the rate of about 134 000 a year. The United States, which despite a long tradition of sympathy for refugees was hamstrung by its own immigration restrictions (quotas, established in the 1920s, to stop the deluge from southern and central Europe) agreed to take 17 000 emigrants from Germany for permanent residence in 1938. The figure was to be raised by 27 370 the following year.

The Australian Minister for the Interior, John McEwen (later Sir John, Deputy Prime Minister and Leader of the Country Party), announced his Government's offer in the House of Representatives on 1 December 1938. They would take 15 000 refugees – over three years.

'In arriving at the figure,' he said, 'the Government has been influenced by the necessity that the existing standards of living should not be disturbed and for reconciling with the interests of refugees, the interests of Australia's population and of the people of the British race who desire to establish themselves in Australia.

With a fine sense of the superiority of

David Jones' fleet of delivery vans waiting to go. (David Jones)

David Jones' barber shop. (David Jones)

his own race – which among other things had managed to establish an undisputed tenancy of the Australian continent while simultaneously leaving most of it vacant – the Minister went on to say that 'special consideration' would be given to individuals with the capital and experience to establish industries not already catered for, particularly those industries that would produce for export as well as for domestic consumption.

Anybody reading his history objectively would have been tempted to the conclusion that the ingenuity of the race from which Australia was about to absorb a trickle had been demonstrated for centuries past. In fairness to McEwen, a tough, shrewd and immensely capable politician who could later have had the leadership of the country had he been willing to desert his own party for the Liberals, he was not being any more shortsighted or racist than his contemporaries, including those on the floor of Parliament as well as on shop floors across the land. For McEwen had expressed himself

mildly compared with the views put forward by the likes of A. E. Green, the Labor member for Kalgoorlie, who told the House in forthright fashion that his opposition was 'far stronger' than it would have been if the immigrants 'were of the Nordic race, and came from northern European countries, from the north of Italy or from Yugoslavia. People from these places would help to develop Australia …we have enough exploiters among our own people, but these other people are the kings of exploiters.' And in the NSW Legislative Council, the Hon. Graham Prattan let it be known that the hordes of homeless who were clamouring at the gates for admission must be regarded as foreigners, whether they be German, Austrian, Italian, Czech, 'they are just as foreign to our Jewish community as they are to us …a real anti-Semitic movement is already evident.'

(The Jewish community was reportedly ambivalent about the arrival of refugees. It had been a characteristic of the very small number of Jewish folk who had come to Australia that until about thirty years before World War II they had been almost entirely from England, so that they had British birth on their side, or had become Anglicised before emigrating. There had never been in Australia a ghetto or separate Jewish quarter of towns, as had sprouted in Europe and America.)

Australians who came into contact with the refugees after they did arrive were somewhat puzzled. They had assumed that the refugees would be destitute. 'There was some bewilderment and resentment on the part of certain Australians that some of the refugees had managed to bring considerable funds with them, which they promptly invested,' says a retired senior officer of the Immigration Department. There was local sensitivity to the occasional unguarded criticism which newcomers made of Australians and things Australian, for this seemed to smack of ingratitude, and there was 'an immediate antagonism towards those who admitted that they intended only marking time in Australia until an opportunity arose to move on to greener pastures'. The few Jews who had arrived in previous generations tended to 'slip in almost unnoticed, and once here, sought absorption as quickly and unobtrusively as possible, endeavouring to re-find their lost peace and security in grey anonymity,' he said.

Those who came post-Evian were reportedly disappointed not to have been given a warmer welcome, since the usual community attitude towards them was felt to be one of indifference; individual Australians seldom went out of their way to offer friendship, or to show much interest in what they had been through, or their resettlement difficulties. Since most of them were accustomed to the indifference of Gentiles, however, they were only thankful that the attitude of Australians was not hostile.

The Evian Plan would be judged a fai-

Two dining rooms in David Jones' department stores. The Grand Restaurant, at the Elizabeth Street store, top, was very much in vogue during the 1930s and 1940s and was one of the best restaurants in which to lunch in Sydney. (David Jones)

lure, mercifully to be half-forgotten and half-excused as the Empire summoned up all its own ingenuity and force to strike back at the refugees' oppressors. Australia could, however, claim that it had been generous compared with other nations which had taken part in the conference, and our own intake was, proportionately, much higher than that of the United States, which had called the conference. Australia's quota for the first year was filled in the nine months that remained before of the declaration of war.

Australia was still very much British, not just in terms of its stock, but in the way it perceived the non-British world. Australians might well view them-selves, *within* the context of the Empire on which the sun never set, as very different from the class-conscious Englishman with his superior airs. (Those airs, just one of many distinguishing characteris-tics, were practised on colonials as much as on the lesser breeds who populated the planet.) Australia and Britain were virtu-ally complementary countries, in climate, culture, and a host of other ways. The former colonies would provide the raw materials from which Britain produced manufactures. Everything interlocked, but Australia was the small child of the relationship. But in their attitude to the outside world – the one outside the Empire – Britain and Australia were united by an unbreakable bond of kinship and tradition, and they never doubted the supremacy of it. Even Americans, who spoke the same language, or something approximating it, could not be considered any closer than cousins of the British fam-ily, so much had they diluted their tradi-tions and modified their directions. (They had also diversified their racial stock to

Woolworths' cafeteria at their Kings Cross store was heavily patronised by servicemen and women during World War II. During the war the cafe was largely staffed by volunteers. (Woolworths)

The Greek School in South Brisbane, Queensland, set up by the migrant community to preserve its cultural identity in the new generation. (John Oxley Library)

the point where, outside the South, only one person in four could claim to be of wholly English ancestry. The magnitude of this change had never been fully comprehended in England or Australia.)

So the trickle of refugees from the Continent would arrive in Australia in the late 1930s to a muted welcome, although public opinion was, in the main, sympathetic. There was a determined effort to ensure that they were distributed as widely as possible throughout the country, and with no undue aggregation in any particular towns or centres. McEwen said for the record that it was hoped that they would become 'patriots of their new home, without this action disturbing *industrial conditions* [emphasis added] in Australia'. McEwen need not have feared any opposition to his sentiments from Her Majesty's Opposition, whose leader, John Curtin, would reply for Hansard:

I think I can say unhesitatingly that the principles involved will be acceptable to the people of Australia. The Opposi-

tion feels, and I believe the country feels, that Australia is a place where lovers of liberty should be welcome, and where those suffering from the infliction of despotic authority should be given an opportunity to live which will enable them to realise their own highest and best future, 'and at the same time [help] in the building of Australia into a great democratic power' and a centre of civilisation in its best cultural sense.

But to the full-blown rhetoric of this lofty statement he added a rider that, whatever reason he had for it, could not have been calculated to put him at any risk with a xenophobic Anglophile electorate. 'I believe that the Government is anxious that, in accepting these refugees, there will not be involved any deterioration of economic or social standards in Australia,' Curtin said. 'The quota suggested by the Minister seems to be a reasonable one. I feel also that the vigilance exercised by the Government over these people will

The Paragon Cafe in Queensland provided a high standard of food and service and a contact point for members of the Greek community. (John Oxley Library)

be sufficient to prevent the formation of racial colonies in Australia. The imposition of conditions under which refugees will be permitted to land in Australia conforming generally to the practice followed with respect to the admittance of white aliens, is a perfectly sound arrangement.'

Curtin was having a quid each way. Australia, great and noble, felt for the 'huddled masses yearning to breathe free' (to borrow from Emma Lazarus' thunderous five lines which are inscribed on the Statue of Liberty) but would take a limited number and keep a close eye on them because they were 'the wretched refuse of your teeming shore' (to borrow from Lazarus again). The shore was non-British, and suspect therefore. Curtin would, as Prime Minister during the war, exhibit statesmanlike qualities. Obviously, a lot would be required to change

Australian thinking about large-scale immigration, particularly non-British immigration. It would take a thunderbolt.

Just such a jolt was being prepared, for other reasons, far to Australia's north.

Almost one hundred and fifty two years after the first white settlers raised their flag on the shores of Sydney Harbour, Australia was once again preparing to help defend England. This was to be the fourth war in just over half a century in which Australians had taken up arms on behalf of the motherland. The navies of New South Wales and Victoria had even lent a hand during the Boxer Rebellion, but we did not count that as a war. The 1939-45 conflict, however, would be the first in which Australia was directly threatened.

In mid-May of 1940, when the Nazi thrust across western Europe was at its peak, the Australian Government moved the second reading of the Immigration Bill which provided, among other things, for the deportation of any non-British person convicted of a crime of violence against a person or of extortion by force or threat. The Minister for the Interior, Senator Foll, made no bones in Parliament about the Bill's target: the Black Hand had emerged in areas Italians had helped settle in the Queensland sugar-cane belt. Abhorrence of things Italian could perhaps be understood in the atmosphere of the time, since Italy was part of the Axis. It is the attitudes that honourable MPs displayed towards

Right: *John McEwen, the Minister for the Interior who, in 1938, accepted 15 000 Jewish refugees into Australia.*

Below: *John Curtin, Prime Minister of Australia during World War II walking in Canberra with J. B. (Ben) Chifley. (Australian Information Service)*

immigration – attitudes by no means out of step with public opinion – that illustrate how much Australians were out of touch with the country's destiny. Senator Collings spoke for the Labor Party, and his ambivalence and muddle-headed approach to the subject were quickly apparent. But views such as his were much more likely to be greeted with a chorus of 'hear, hear!' than boos in the Upper House in 1940.

'Australia should profit by the experience of other countries, particularly America, and the greatest care should be taken to ensure that we do not build up in this country a racial problem similar to that with which the older countries have had to grapple owing to lax migration policies,' the Senator said. 'The Opposition does not harbour any racial animosity, but we must take care that our feelings do not carry us to extremes.' If the good Senator had been more honest, he might have said that good Australian blood could be diluted, but not too much without ill effect. He went on to admit the need for greater population – he even said it was one of Australia's most urgent problems. But Labor's 'social service' policy stressed the urgency of improving the lot of breadwinners, because the ALP believed in the encouragement of 'the natural tendency of young people to marriage and family life'. Here, the Senator was acknowledging that in a Depression couples are less likely to produce large families, as the 1930s had shown – the natural increase (excess of births over deaths) had been 8.24 per cent, compared with 14.35 per cent the previous decade, a figure that would never be reached again. Australia was moving towards zero population growth. The Senator went on to say that new settlers should be, as nearly as possible, in tune with Australia's ideals, should adjust to our social conditions. tions. As if that was not enough, he said Labor would 'object to the introduction of people from other countries if there were

in Australia one individual fit and willing to work but unable to find employment'. In other words, one of Australia's most urgent problems, acknowledged and easily defined – the need for more Australians – would have to be solved by getting the native-born population to devote more of its energies to procreation, because immigrants threatened jobs and were unlikely to assimilate if they were foreign-born.

The Senator ignored a gloomy prediction that had been made in 1936 by a man named Wolstenholme, who said that the population would rise by only 254 000 in the twenty years between 1943 and 1963 if the trends of the mid-1930s prevailed. That meant the country would go into the seventh decade of the twentieth century with a population of only 7.3 or 7.4 million.

As Hitler's hordes overran Europe, some MPs wondered out loud in the immigration debate whether Australia might not benefit from the tide of Norwegians, Dutch and Belgians who would be looking for somewhere safer to live. 'They will be people of our own race and of Nordic descent … no more desirable class of people can be brought here than the Norwegians,' Senator McLachlan reminded his colleagues.

France fell in June; the British, with no ally in Europe left, were turning to the United States for assistance.

What if Britain should lose the war? John McEwen summed it up in a debate on the Budget when he said the fundamental issues at stake were 'whether we shall retain the ownership of this country, whether those children attending school today shall grow up to be bound or free, and whether the government in power after the last shot has been fired shall be backed by enough authority to determine the immigration policy of Australia.'

Defeat, he said, would mean the loss of the right that had been enjoyed to regulate the number of foreigners who came here. 'If we were to lose that right there would be an influx of southern Europeans which in one decade would change the whole composition of the Australian people. At the worst there might be an influx of Asiatics which would cause the loss for ever of everything for which we have struggled.'

His worst fears were the fears of his countrymen, too. It is not too difficult now – in the light of what Australian leaders were saying forty years ago – to imagine the mood of the Australian people after the Japanese entered the war. The Japanese followed the attack on Pearl Harbor, on 7 December 1941, by sweeping deep, deep to the south, and in a matter of months took Burma, invaded New Guinea, and began making hit-and-run attacks on the Australian mainland.

England not only would fail to come to Australia's aid, but insist that Australian fighting men remain in the Middle East. The audacity and force of the Japanese thrust, however, was more than enough to extinguish any feeling in Australia that the defence of the motherland was more important than the immediate preservation of Australia from the yellows. To hell with what Churchill might pretend about re-taking Australia from the Japanese after England had prevailed – eventually – elsewhere.

Australia would go much further than that, too, reaching out to the United States for assistance because the United States, though a foreign country, was the only one that could help, and was now an ally. The power of the United States had been built not least on the kind of 'lax' immigration policy that Australia had disdained. The assistance Australia sought would be freely given and lead to events that, ultimately, would bring Australia into a new economic and defence relationship, doing much to weaken the old bonds with Britain. Australia, going into conflict against Japan with a population that, after one-and-a-half centuries of

Arthur Calwell, who argued that Australia should accept great numbers of European migrants to build up the population.

white civilisation, had reached just seven million, was about to cast aside prejudice because of a stronger emotion: self-survival. This was made possible because of the need for new policies, and these were evolved by a new federal government.

The first Curtin Government was sworn in on 7 October 1941, exactly two months before Japan entered the war. Arthur Calwell, who had entered Parliament in 1940, was not elected to the Labor Ministry, but it was already apparent to his colleagues that Calwell, a forceful politician and rugged debater, was on the way up the party pyramid. In May 1942, when the fate of the British Empire hung in the balance, Calwell made his first significant contribution to the cause of immigration. It was a remarkable effort, given the confused thinking that had permeated so much of the debate on non-Anglo-Saxon immigration over the years. Australia, he said, must open its doors, and quickly, to whites whether they were British or not, otherwise the day of the white race in Australia would be finished.

'Honourable members opposite have overlooked one vital point,' he said.

'There are 7 million people in Australia, which is an area almost as great as the United States of America. There are 130 million people in the United States of America. If the whole of manhood of this country were to be conscripted and sent overseas, the contribution in point of numbers would not be very great. It would not be sufficient to determine the issue of a major battle in the Pacific, the Atlantic or elsewhere, but if Australia were denuded of its manpower, the future of the nation would be dark indeed.

'It will be dark enough, even if we win the war. Europe may be quiet in another twenty-five years, but while Australia remains an outpost of white civilisation and insists upon the maintenance of the White Australia policy and while we have very few people in this country, we shall naturally excite the avarice and covetousness of our coloured neighbours to the north.'

Calwell said flatly that Australia must bring its numbers up to 20 or 30 million within a generation or so, or else there would no longer be a white Australia. No sensible man could honestly object to the

Arthur Calwell, Australia's first Minister for Immigration with his private secretary, R. E. Armstrong, at Australia House in London, June 1947. (Department of Immigration and Ethnic Affairs)

immigration of whites under proper conditions and provided that they were not sent here to relieve their native countries of unemployment. He would welcome the arrival of 'many hundreds of thousands of white people from the other side of the world' if industrial development depended on immigration. If necessary, development works, including water conservation, must be undertaken to give the new citizens the opportunity to live in the standards of decency that Australia desired to maintain. (It is noticeable how far the line had been moved, and how quickly: a panicky Australia was now being exhorted to actually provide a home worthy of non-Anglo-Saxon newcomers.)

Calwell invoked the human powerhouse of America by way of example. 'When I see the splendid specimens of American manhood walking the streets of Australian cities and recollect that America has been, for more than a generation, a melting pot for European nations, I am satisfied with the result of the amalgamation,' he said. (This could scarcely have been imagined coming from an Australian leader two years previously.) Now Calwell revealed the proposal that was forming into policy. 'We should lose nothing by adopting a similar policy,' he said. 'It would be far better for us to have in Australia 20 million or 30 million people of 100 per cent white extraction than to continue the narrow policy of having a population of 7 million who are 98 per cent British.' The alternative, he said, was no future for Australia, because Australia must have a population prepared to defend it when a militarised Asia moved south – when that time came Europe would probably have settled into peace, and America might be disinclined to further assist Australia. McEwen echoed Calwell's fears. Australia, McEwen said, was 'confronted with grimmer possibilities in defeat than any of our allies' because it would cease to be a British nation.

Later that same year, W. D. Forsyth reinforced the Wolstenholme view; in his book *The Myth of Open Spaces*, which analysed Australian, British and world trends of population and migration, he predicted that the growth of the Australian population would cease, and that by 1970 or 1980 would actually decline.

Forsyth added that large-scale immigration from Britain would be a thing of the past if there was a revival of world trade. There might be a wave of British immigrants if there was a fall in Britain's living standards, or people just wanted to get away from Europe, or there was a deliberate policy of reducing Britain's population for strategic reasons (he thought this unlikely). The same remarks applied to north-western Europe as a source of immigrants, he said.

That left southern and eastern Europe; numbers of emigrants from there would be low if the post-war period was prosperous, and if it were not, nations like Australia wouldn't be able to absorb immigrants easily anyway.

It was a dismal picture, but punctuated with insights – Australia would be able to promote moderate immigration from southern and eastern Europe over a long period if this country could develop its secondary and tertiary industries, Forsyth said.

He overlooked the possibility that Europe might have to endure an immediate post-war period of unemployment while Australia suffered from lack of manpower.

Hitler and Stalin were implementing policies that while despicable, would produce a ready-made answer to a great Australian problem.

The European war was over and the conflict with Japan was only weeks from finality when the Labor Government established the Immigration Department in July 1945. It was a momentous month. John Curtin, his span shortened by the

Joseph Benedict Chifley, Prime Minister of Australia 1945–49.

severe strain of leading the nation for almost four years of the war, died. The new Prime Minister, Joseph Benedict Chifley, lost little time – Curtin had told his Cabinet the previous year that he intended setting up a department for immigration after the war.

Arthur Calwell had been severely disappointed not to have been elected by the Labor Caucus as a minister in 1941. But he reached the ministry in 1943, and in the Information portfolio had displayed a strong hand – when he was not wielding a mace.

Information relating to the conduct of the war, how the Australian forces were faring, and anything which might be construed as touching, however vaguely, on national security – or even relations with our Allies – was doctored before it was allowed to be purveyed to the public. Years later, when the archives in Canberra were opened to scrutiny, this censorship would be seen, when it had been exercised in the extreme, as ludicrous and paranoid.

Calwell was so strict that he wound up in a long battle with newspapers that led,

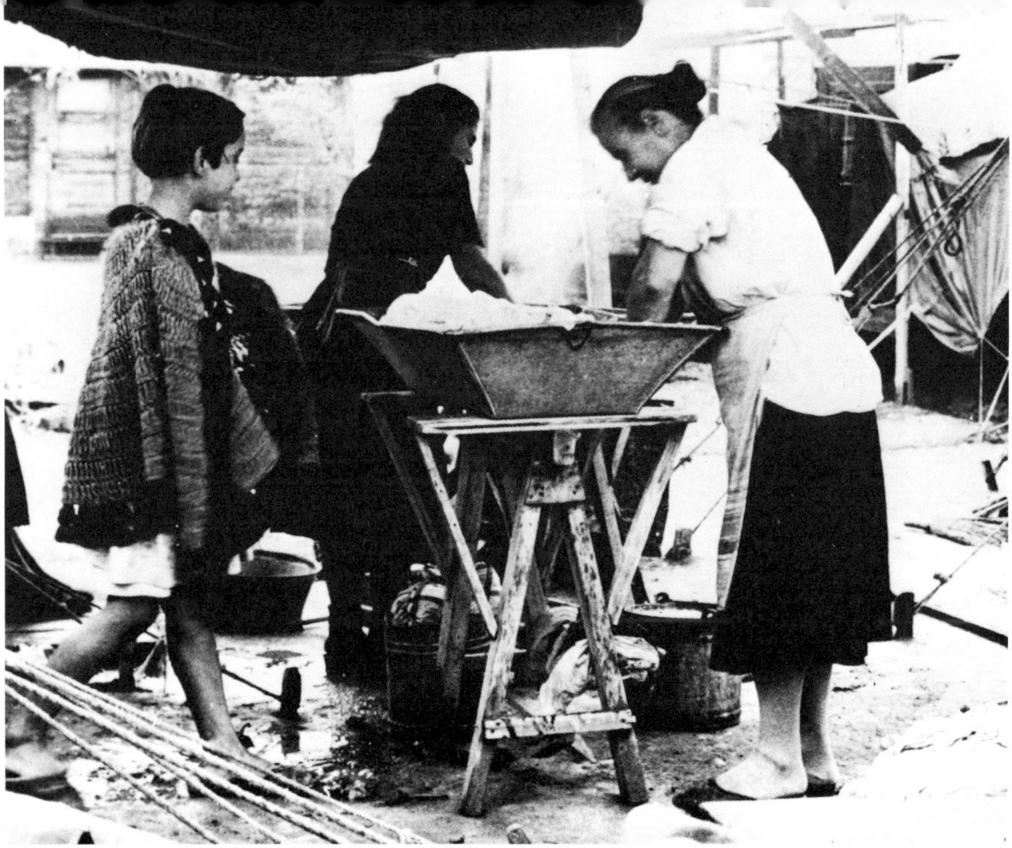

A scene in a post World War II refugee camp. (Department of Immigration and Ethnic Affairs)

John Albert Beasley, Minister for Defence in the Curtin Government, who opposed Information Minister Calwell's policy on censorship.

in 1944, to a High Court case on censorship. He reportedly called for the sacking of the Bench after the case. It got to the point where the Minister for Defence, Calwell's colleague John Beasley, supported criticism by the Opposition of the administration of censorship after the Japanese had surrendered. Calwell was unmoved. (I recall finding a copy in the archives of a letter of condolence sent to Mrs Curtin by the Cabinet on the death of her husband. It was unremarkable, except for the fact that it was stamped 'Secret'.)

Calwell was extremely sensitive about what friendly nations might think of Australia. He also had an inordinate distrust of the press. It was also demonstrable that he did not have full regard for the native intelligence of ordinary Australians to receive information and judge for themselves ...he was, after all, a socialist in the old sense of the term as used by the ALP in those years – big government was best, and knew what was best for the people.

Croat national dress is dramatic in its colour, suiting a people whose history has been so turbulent.
(Australian Picture Library)

School children from the multicultural Cabramatta Primary School in Sydney, New South Wales on an outing. (J. Wood)

This Jewish family was one of the many who immigrated to Australia in the immediate post-war period.

Calwell's heavy-handed approach to censorship, which could not have continued as long as it did without the support of his government colleagues and 1200 censors who vetted postal and telegraph communications, show just how panicky the atmosphere became while Australia was under direct threat. But as Information Minister he learned the skills that were necessary to sweeten, for public consumption, news that might be potentially unsettling.

The Labor Government's decision in 1945 to launch a programme of population expansion by immigration was supported by all political parties. Calwell was appointed first Minister for Immigration. To him would fall the ultimate responsibility of ensuring the success of the policy. If it failed, his political future would be in doubt. Much more importantly, Australia's future would also be in doubt.

He said Australia must populate or perish. He envisaged that 75 per cent of the intake would come from Britain. Twenty-five per cent non-British was a lot to expect Australians to accept, but fear of extinction was strong too. At the end of the war Australia's 7 700 000 square kilometres of territory were occupied by a population that had struggled, snail-like, to just 7 391 000.

The war, however, had put such a strain on services that the nation had a backlog of about 250 000 dwellings to be constructed. There was a shortage of schools and hospitals, blackouts were common because of power shortages, and coal and steel production, which had risen during the war, was now in decline – steel output was down by almost one-third. The railways were in a mess. Transport services, overall, were run-down and suffering from severe manpower shortages.

Concentration camp life had left deep mental scars as well as physical ones, particularly in young children, many of whom had experienced no other way of life. (Department of Immigration and Ethnic Affairs)

Calwell told the House on 2 August 1945, that any expanding country could be expected to absorb an annual population increase of only about 2 per cent. Since the natural increase in Australia was about one per cent, the immigration programme should be set at about one per cent. This meant just on 74 000 initially, but increasing with population, which would put Australia on target for the 20 or 30 million people who, he had said back in 1942, Australia must have 'within a generation or so'.

As part of the necessary infrastructure to cope with these numbers, the Government decided to create a nationwide employment service to provide details of the labour market and to put people in jobs. The Immigration Department would use this information to recruit the numbers and types of immigrant workers Australia needed.

Australia had the need particularly for heavy manual labour. To head off the anticipated outcry from the trade union movement, a skilful 'information' programme would be required. The unions were told that their members would be 'the bosses' – foreman material under whom the new arrivals would work.

An assisted passage scheme for wartime civilians in Britain was announced in 1946. British ex-servicemen and their families, much sought-after by the Australian Government, were to be paid from the British Government's purse to emigrate to Australia. In August 1946, the State premiers agreed with Chifley that the States would be responsible for the reception, welfare and after-care of the British. Inquiries from prospective British emigrants had been pouring into Australia House in the Strand, London, since October 1945.

But for two years after the war, Australia's new immigration programme produced no results. Embarrassingly, in the year 1945-46 there was a net *loss* of 9764 people, and the following year it happened again – fewer were leaving, but 6443 did, nonetheless.

Servicemen who had fought for the Allies were high on the Government's priority list of prospective immigrants. Calwell's chagrin can be imagined when, for example, he invited American GIs who were marrying Australian women to settle down in Australia. He was virtually ignored. About 10 000 GIs wed local women. According to a retired head of the Immigration Department, 'we got a few back as migrants, but not a very large number I would think'. The Americans not only failed to stay, but were taking Australian women with them when they went home. The reason they did not stay was not hard to find, though some Australians might not have accepted it. Couples could be expected to set up home where the husband wanted to work, and the breadwinner was naturally looking to his homeland for his job. Besides which, the United States – whatever the prevailing mood in Australia about 'Yanks' – was a more prosperous country than Australia, and in many way an exciting prospect for young, untravelled Australian women.

Britain, Australia's traditional source of immigrants, faced all kinds of difficulties of post-war reconstruction (and despite American aid under the gigantic Marshall Plan). This made her recovery so much more protracted. There was no rush from anywhere to Australia, not least because of the lack of ships. Much of the English merchant navy was at the bottom of the sea.

One of Calwell's first actions as Immigration Minister was to appoint as his private secretary R. E. (Bob) Armstrong, a career public servant from New South Wales who had served in the Army and been involved with the Australian security service in the internment of aliens during the war. The Department of Immigration fascinated him, as it did so many officers who served in it: they grew to feel that they were playing an important role in securing Australia's future and in the shaping of the population that would do that. Armstrong and Calwell had met when Calwell was chairman of the Aliens Classification Advisory Committee. About 6000 aliens had been interned, but politicians and public servants had come to feel that there had been a lack of sensitivity in pulling so many people out of the mainstream of Australian life and depriving them of their rights. After all, hadn't the local councils in some parts of Queensland, which immigrants from Italy had helped to prosper, continued the practice of issuing rate notices in Italian? In South Australia, with more than a century of beneficial experience of German immigrants, it was traditional to recruit Lutheran pastors

State Premiers and State and Federal Ministers for Immigration meeting in Canberra to discuss Australia's immigration programme in 1946. (Department of Immigration and Ethnic Affairs)

from Germany, and sermons had been preached in German. Australian authorities considered the loyalty of such people would be to the fatherland, not mother England, and some of the pastors were interned.

Of Australia's aliens, welcomed to these shores in peace, but suspect in war because of Australian fears, Armstrong was to say: 'We realised we had never made any real effort to integrate these people.' Calwell, realising the need for non-Anglo-Saxons if the distant population target was to be achieved, decided he could use this man. He also decided to moderate his ratio of non-British-to-British immigrants: in November 1946, Calwell was still talking of one 'foreign' immigrant for every ten from the United Kingdom. But by the following March he had stopped talking about ratios.

Calwell, his wife and Armstrong set off on an overseas mission in June 1947, to try to solve the immigration problem. They had three aims. The first was to get Britain's Labour Government to help arrange transport to Australia for British emigrants. Australia did not have the means. Second, to broadcast, as widely as possible, the news that Australia was going into the nation-peopling business in a big way. Calwell and Armstrong went to twenty-three countries in twelve weeks, concentrating solely on Europe and the United States.

Their third aim was to contact the International Refugee Organisation and work out whether some of the 25 per cent non-British immigrants Australia was prepared to countenance could be found among Europe's 'displaced persons' – a euphemism for refugees.

About seven million people in Europe fell under this classification at the end of the war – people who had been forced into Germany as heavy labour to assist the Nazis' war machine, or who were anti-communist and had fled their countries before the Iron Curtain came down.

Eighteen months after the war about 900 000 of these people still remained to be repatriated; 712 000 of them came under the jurisdiction of the IRO, and they were making it clear that they would never return home. Most of them came from eastern Europe, which was not in the bull's eye that the Australian Government had marked out on its target.

The Australian Cabinet had reacted indifferently to pressure from the IRO to do its part in relieving the suffering of these people. But Chifley agreed that Calwell should check the prospects. The feeling in Cabinet was that these folk, alien to the Anglo-Saxon tradition, were tarnished losers, presenting an image of races that had been broken in spirit. They were not the kind of people that Australia, strong, proud, free and victorious, and with a proven record of defence of its traditions, wanted as a plank for the new Australia. But some at least might be useful.

The Calwell party had an arduous mission. It was as a last resort that they went to the Continent. Calwell, industrious, firm-minded, did not spare himself. Shipping was scarce, he was told time and again, but American Liberty-style transports were available if Australia was desperate. They were rudimentary, but would do the job, and refugees probably would not quibble anyway. They would have put up with cramped quarters on the long voyage if they sincerely desired a new start.

What Calwell found in Germany was confirmed later by others who went there; men like George Kiddle, who was to spend the rest of his working life in the Australian Immigration Department. He had served in England with the RAAF during the war, and was awaiting repatriation when he grasped the chance to join the infant department. He was to become one of a very small group of Australians responsible for selecting 'reffos' for Australia.

It must have been a shock to Calwell,

Evatt and Calwell talking to colleagues.

and others who followed when they arrived at the refugee camps. They were full of 'displaced persons' all right. Tempest tossed. The wretched refuse of a teeming shore. Huddled, yearning to breathe free.

They certainly fitted the lines inscribed on the Statue of Liberty. Calwell, a descendent of Americans, might have recalled those lines.

The displaced persons, many of whom had only the vaguest notion of what Australia was like, were for the most part tall, upright, and from their manner and bearing, their dress and nutrition, little different from the defeated Germans all around them. Not a few had professional qualifications. The pick of them, despite the deprivations of the long war, including loss of their homelands, appeared unbroken. Naturally they were apprehensive about the future – they had been waiting for years, in some cases, for a solution to that. And immigration officers from Australia, like Kiddle, became very enthusiastic when they noticed how many of these people were blond and blue-eyed.

That may seem a little strange today, but Australia was different then. Many of these people had come from an area that, many centuries before, was the birthplace of the tribes from which the Anglo-Saxon race developed.

The term 'displaced persons' never caught on in Australia, though 'reffo' with its old connotations did not die for a decade. But the word 'Balts', which referred to people from the Baltic States – Lithuanians, Latvians and Estonians – would come into general usage. It would also be a term used approvingly, and its meaning widened to encompass people of neighbouring nationalities who helped build Australia in the 1940s and 1950s.

The first 'Balts' were carefully screened before they were put on a ship for Australia. Kiddle and others knew how important the approval of the Australian public would be.

Looking back now, over thirty-five years, immigration officers still say: 'They were absolutely the finest immigrants we ever chose for this country.'

CHAPTER 11

The Country They Came To

NATIVE-BORN AUSTRALIANS of Anglo-Scots-Irish descent had little understanding of the national characteristics of other peoples who would come to make such a large contribution to Australia's wealth and dynamic.

This lack of understanding was chiefly attributable to distance from Europe and the fact that, from 1788 to the Suez crisis of 1956, Britain – principally, England – was pre-eminent in world affairs. The Anglo-Saxon, in his own eyes and in the eyes of most of the world, was at the top of the tree. He had the knack of stable, enduring government and a rule of law that was the envy of other nations. His ingenuity, commonsense, discipline and

At the time not everyone appreciated what Calwell's immigration scheme was meant to achieve. Mr Justice Barry presiding at the first naturalisation ceremony in 1948. (Australian Consolidated Press)

sense of duty and destiny had allowed him to prosper while bringing civilisation to lesser peoples on far-flung continents. There was scarcely a facet of human endeavour in which he did not excel, and many in which he was predominant. Militarily, he was certainly dominant. The only nation that he had failed to conquer was peopled by his own offspring, and they, the Americans, regarded themselves anyway as super Anglo-Saxons.

The people of Anglo-Scots-Irish descent who developed Australia in the nineteenth century took a long time to grasp the idea that this was a new nation. Their idea of Australia was of a country that in many ways complemented Britain (in trade, climate, geography, lifestyle) but was firmly British nonetheless. The white Australian, from 1788 right up to the 1970s, believed that it was the duty of the immigrant to assimilate, to conform as far as possible with the Australian way of things.

The drabness of a Woolworths store of the 1930s, a style which didn't begin to change much until the early 1950s. (Woolworths)

It was assumed, as it had been in the United States, that kindred peoples such as Germans and Scandinavians would assimilate much better than the southern and central Europeans, while the 'lesser breeds' with yellow or black skins would not be capable of assimilating at all, because they had only the vaguest notion, at best, of Anglo-Saxon ideals and culture; their standards were simply too low in too many fields, from hygiene to respect for Australian trade unionism which had helped raise living standards.

The relatively small numbers of immigrants of non-Anglo-Saxon stock who arrived before 1947 generally made all haste to 'fit in' or else departed these shores forever. Jewish folk even changed their religion, and were careful not to incite suspicion that they were creatures from another planet. Converting from Judaism to Anglicanism was no mean feat, but people who had been persecuted for centuries by Gentiles generally found the decision to convert a little easier because they at least had some choice in the change. The German Gentiles, espe-

cially when congregated in their own towns in South Australia and Queensland, evoked admiration for their practice of Anglo-Saxon virtues of discipline, hard work, thrift and industry. They not only kept their traditions, they celebrated them in festival and song, passed down from the *Deutsche kultur* from generation to generation, and even managed to get members of the British-descended ruling classes to celebrate with them.

Italians, in north Queensland and elsewhere, generally had a harder time of it, because they were thought to be susceptible to reversion to the old ways – clannish Italians at their worst, the Anglo-Saxons believed, might kindle the Black Hand or resort to medieval behaviour that would threaten the good, well-ordered community that had been set up by rational, disciplined and forward-thinking Protestants.

The British Protestant supremacy did have one potential problem to deal with – the Irish Catholic, who spoke English, was familiar, through centuries of English domination, with the Anglo-Saxon way, and yet for the most part stubbornly refused to yield his Celtic heritage. The Irish were in a difficult position – they respected the British, were willing to live under the British Crown in order to share in the benefits of the British supremacy, but they were haunted, periodically, by the spectre of the suppression that their ancestors had endured for hundreds of years. And they came in large numbers, particularly to New South Wales. In time, they would have influence enough to change the course of Australian history, and each time that change would be attributed to their adherence to their religion and their ancient distrust of the British.

The Eureka Stockade was but one expression of dislike of Anglo-Saxon overlords. In the World War I conscription referendums it was the Irish Catholic vote that tipped the scales against the call-up, and this led to the defection of the Labor Prime Minister, W. M. (Billy) Hughes. With the 'no' vote and the loss of Hughes and others, the Labor Party came under the dominance of the Irish Catholics, and remained in the political wilderness for most of the next half-century, until the ascendancy of the fresher, intellectual approach of men such as Edward Gough Whitlam and Robert James Lee Hawke, both of British Protestant stock. The Irish Catholics also entered a titanic struggle in the trade unions, in the immediate post-World War II period, against communists and Labor Party left-wingers, which produced 'the Split' in the ALP; the resultant Democratic Labor Party hived off, and its predominantly Catholic membership, while retaining the old Labor concern for the socially deprived and indigent, allied itself firmly with the conservative Liberal-Country Party coalition on foreign policy,

Many of the immigrants from Continental Europe tended to be self-employed. The owner of this cafe was probably working behind the counter. (Macleay Museum, University of Sydney)

State aid to schools and most issues in which communism or religion were a factor. But the DLP withered and died after the Vietnam War, the loss of which failed to unleash the Yellow Peril whose spectre had been hanging, cliff-like, over Australia ever since the gold rushes. All that descended on us was a few leaking boats carrying a trickle of refugees from Vietnam, Kampuchea and Laos. Their countrymen, like the Chinese, had only the vaguest notions of Australia, it transpired.

What did the motley collection of non Anglo-Saxon emigrants to Australia over the past two centuries expect to find here, to contribute to the country and get from it? Well, the Irish mostly expected higher living standards than in their poverty-blighted homeland. The Germans sought religious freedom, reward for hard work, freedom of expression, and the kinship of a cousinly race whose royal line had intermarried with the German royals. The Anglos and the Germans had a lot in common.

The Scandinavians, with whom the Teutons felt in harmony, were escaping poverty, and longed for living space.

The southern and central Europeans were different. They clung to what northern Europeans regarded as quaint notions: strict loyalty to family no matter what the circumstances. They had a tendency to suspect, sometimes fear, the community outside the family. In that kind of tight-knit family unit, the voice of the *pater familias* was law, and if he raised it at all, the rest of the family had better be quiet and listen. Sometimes this rule of the family unit might be deemed to supersede any abstract Anglo-Saxon rules about the law. The native-born Anglo-Saxon did not express alarm provided that the allegations of Mafia-style standover men operating in the big city vegetable markets, or Croats and Serbs fighting out old scores that should have been left behind in Yugoslavia, did not directly touch him. All of that kind of nuisance helped shore up the Anglo-Saxon's image of himself as superior to other breeds.

The refugees, whether from Hungary or Lithuania, Estonia, Latvia, Czechos-

Louis' Cafe reflected the continental influence which began to develop during the 1940s. (Macleay Museum, University of Sydney)

A cartoon satire on Arthur Calwell's preferred immigrant type. Calwell had to take what he could get.
(Australian Consolidated Press)

lovakia, or South-East Asia, in many cases knew little more of Australia than that it was a great, open, freedom-loving, law-abiding land (but not necessarily God-fearing anymore). Particularly after World War II, a lot of refugees came here because it was as far as one could get from Europe and still be in a democratic country with European traditions. European or, later, Asian, they all came to share a common experience: the struggle to reorganise their life into a tidy existence, save for a home, provide their children with a better life and a brighter future than they could expect in the old country. Some, including not a few who came to Australia in the late 1940s as refugees, did not look on the new country as their homeland, but rather as a staging post for a second move, to a more 'civilised' existence – wherever that might be – but wound up staying here anyway. It gradually dawned on them that *terra australis* offered at least an abundance of material possessions, security, freedom, a relaxed lifestyle, free schooling, good health care, stable government and equality before the law. There would be no midnight knock on the door.

What did Australians expect of the newcomers? It ought to be acknowledged at the outset that the native-born Australian of Anglo-Scots-Welsh-Irish stock usually thought he was doing the non-English-speaking immigrant a favour by allowing him to set foot across the portals of the wide brown land. That the newcomer's fare should be subsidised was the height of generosity, verging on gross indulgence. The immigrant would be expected to start on the bottom rung in the workforce (foreign qualifications counted for little or nothing).

He would be expected to acknowledge and respect the standards of the Anglo-Saxon Australian, even if he could not attain them himself. The Old Australian was ever-watchful. Not until the immigrant population had swelled to a tide in the 1960s did the immigrant come to exert his own right to exist more or less by his own standards provided these were within the law. (Some of these, including those relating in some instances to hygiene, were more relaxed than official Australian standards – and occasionally it was the Australian who relented. Some Continental foods – the kind that made the native-born Australian salivate at the sight of them – could not be made without using the hands to knead and mould. And if the lavatory at an el cheapo Italian or Greek restaurant was more like a dunny than the official by-laws demanded – well, who cared, the food was what mattered, wasn't it? Australians began to learn from the newcomers. One of the things they learned was when to look the other way.)

In public, the immigrant was no longer furtive, self-deprecating. He could speak up for himself, even if only to ask for street directions. I like to recall a scene at the Sydney Cricket Ground in the middle of that decade. Australia that Saturday was doing battle in its favourite fashion – on the field, against its old friend-and-foe, England. Some of the most intense clashes were reserved for Rugby League. At the rear of the Paddington Hill a clutch of pommy immigrants, half-drunk like not a few of the native-born Australian spectators, were uproariously cheering their team to victory. The crowd, irritable as always when Australia is not faring well against the poms, let them be. But when a couple of swarthy Italians, who had taken the trouble to dress up in collars, ties and jackets (not the usual dress on the Hill) stood up to watch a try in a game they may have scarcely understood, drunken Aussie louts behind shouted 'Sit down, you bloody wogs!' The nearest Italian removed his hands from his pockets, meaningfully, and, red-faced with fury, shouted back: 'Don't you call me a wog, mate!' There was no rejoinder, and that section of the crowd fell silent for a short time. Something had been learned since the years when all foreigners were 'reffos'.

Silver, lead and zinc mining at Broken Hill.

In the late 1940s Australia, at the start of the Big Immigration, was a country with some misconceptions of itself and its place in the world. The wane of British influence, not only in Australia but around the globe, coincided with much-increased American interest in Australia – meaning American business and government, which were not unrelated.

To Australians, the United States was a big, populous, highly productive and highly commercialised country whose people, however friendly, were Anglo-Saxons gone wrong. They dressed loudly, spoke loudly, and were at once mystifyingly olde-worlde courteous and New World rude. They were relaxed, easy-going but also frenetically commercial and given to fads. What is today known as 'hype' seemed to permeate everything in

their lives, from religious observance to promotion of cola soft drinks. 'Hype' was not in the lexicon in the 1940s, but there was a recurrent, down-to-earth Aussie phrase: 'Yankee bullshit'. If an American mentioned, however innocently, that something was 'as big as Texas' (say, the potential of his business for expansion) he was, to Australian ears, immodest, and worse, guilty of 'Yankee bullshit'. The American never hid his light under a bushel, and always seemed to be reaching out for something bigger and grander. That irritated Old Aussies, the overwhelming majority of whom had not come to understand that Australia was a country afflicted with a cultural cringe (a phrase that would gain currency later) and which too-readily accepted near-enough-is-good-enough standards in the

Open cut mining. Mineral discoveries helped switch Australia from being an agricultural primary producer to a mineral primary producer.

workforce, in politics, in fact, across the social spectrum. A lot of the new immigrants were not like that.

There were other misconceptions. Australians saw themselves as pioneer stock, tough, resilient, individualistic, basically rural-living (since that's where the export income and the country's international reputation had been earned). They regarded themselves as hard-working. But however true this might have been, big changes were occurring. In the 1950s and 1960s young people from the rural areas were forced to seek their livelihood in the burgeoning cities. As the new, sometimes superficial affluence rolled over the nation, the old-style pioneer seemed to be receding into the pages of Lawson and Paterson.

Overseas capital was freely available for new industries, and lots of nice minerals had been discovered to exploit as a hedge against drought and the loss of any markets overseas for rural produce. The nation had never been so prosperous: it was just a matter of exporting raw mat-

erials, and divvying up the spoils. Shear the sheep, reap the wheat, load the beef, dig up the ore and ship it out. It all seemed so simple.

The immigrant fleeing a homeland that was poverty-stricken, which discriminated against his religion, or was riddled with class distinction, often suspected that many native-born Australians did not understand just how fortunate they were. The better-educated immigrant sometimes wondered if it would all last: those in big business worried about the prevalence of short-gap, quick-fix decisions made by politicians who were too near-sighted to embark on long-term national policies to safeguard Australia's future. World War II had shown just how vulnerable Australia was to a new, rising power such as Japan; the aftermath, with the decline of Britain's power, ought to have led to a redoubling of efforts to make the future secure. Australians, however, were happy to acquiesce in short-term policies that bolstered pay-packets and kept virtually every able-bodied wage-

De-wheeling a train at Chullora railway workshops in Sydney. Migrants were desperately needed by Australia to help in heavy industry.

earner in a job. In a democracy, politicians who do not give the public what they want are usually soon out of a job. In Australia, the prevailing mood was

she'll be right, mate, everything is jake.

Australia was lucky to find minerals in abundance just when Common Market protectionism was denying us markets for agricultural produce. The idea that Australia could manufacture for export was never seriously considered. The Americans, who developed a motor vehicle manufacturing industry in Australia (first by General Motors-Holden's in 1948, and later by Ford and Chrysler), used Australia as an export base to the Pacific, Asia and even Southern Africa – but this languished later on, when it became cheaper to manufacture in countries with lower wage scales. Australians were notoriously loath to invest their savings on the share market (except in speculative ventures with high profit potential). The old them-and-us ethos did not fade on the production floor. The attitude of union leaders was that the worker should grab all he could get, since Australia was never going to be able to compete in traditional manufacturing industries against other established nations (or rising ones with lower wage structures). Preserving the Australian standard of living was the chief catchcry of the unions. Conservative management philosophies did little to alter the image overseas of Australia as a hedonistic, self-centred economic colony of America that was, for lack of a more serious-minded approach to its future, guilty of not a little irresponsibility.

If Australia paid insufficient regard to manufacturing, it paid virtually none to opportunities for innovation in the high-technology fields. A lot of tough decisions that should have been made in the 1960s were pigeon-holed. In that decade Australia was ranked in the first half-dozen nations in the world in living standards but thereafter it slipped. One measure of building for the future is the proportion of gross national product devoted to education: in the 1960s Australia ranked about sixteenth in the world. Tertiary education was expensive, and entry to it was limited, with the result that relatively few people

A boot repairer of the late 1940s: humble beginnings but a secure future. (Department of Immigration and Ethnic Affairs)

from families on average incomes found it within reach. The proportion of school children completing secondary school was drastically low compared with that in the United States. The proportion of seventeen-year-olds still receiving secondary education in 1987 in Australia was barely 50 per cent – compared with about 90 per cent of seventeen-year-olds in Japan and the United States. The youth unemployment figure, 23 per cent, was the worst of any developed nation except Britain. The Whitlam Labor Government made tertiary education free in the 1970s, and between 1950 and 1980 the proportion of the Australian workforce with tertiary qualifications doubled, to 7 per cent. In the same period it rose in Japan from one per cent to 39 per cent.

The immigrant played a big part in changing Australian attitudes, or at least forcing a reappraisal of them. For a start, he may have been brought to Australia as factory fodder (the Australian view) but he saw himself as much more than that. He was highly resistant to them-and-us attitudes on the factory floor if he had been forced to flee a less fortunate Continental land, and he was sceptical, if not downright ornery, when it came to heavy-handed attempts to organise his support for some of the wilder schemes of militant union leaders. Bread-and-butter issues he understood – ideological aims and theories flavoured with '-isms' of any kind turned him off.

Although a high proportion of immigrants were factory fodder, a surprising proportion scrimped and saved to join the ranks of the self-employed. Moreover, within a generation their offspring were competing for and winning places in universities and colleges in large numbers. A casual perusal of university graduation lists shows just how strong this drive for education has been.

And in business – including big business – the effect of the immigrant has

Greeks enjoying a convivial dinner at a Greek restaurant. Note the picture of the Parthenon alongside the photograph of Queen Elizabeth II. (Department of Immigration and Ethnic Affairs)

A supermarket opening in 1957. The crowds are livelier and the merchandising more emphatic than earlier years. (Woolworths)

cant proportion of them had business skills. Since their recent past had been perilously insecure – and some had lost most of their relatives – they redoubled their efforts to make their own futures secure. The Budapest Jew who had escaped the fate ordained for him in Hitler's death camps, the German trades-man, the small-scale businessman from Birmingham, all found Australia indeed a land of opportunity – but only if it was grasped. The immigrant had a need to prove his decision to come here was cor-rect. And because it was harder in a new country, he had the incentive to excel. Not everything was harder – in business the cut-throat competition he had known in Europe might make Australia seem easy pickings by comparison – and here the sky was the limit, and he could reach for it.

I once asked an east European immig-rant who had made a fortune out of real estate development whether he was now a multi-millionaire. He had started from scratch, but with not a little capital, and had made it, all the way. 'Yes, that's true,' he said, 'but then my brothers-in-law in Florida made $93 million.' He hadn't measured his efforts or his performance by Australian standards: in time, Austra-lia began to measure its standards by his. This kind of osmosis, achieved not always according to the accepted practices in business, has nevertheless had a benefi-cial effect. It could never have occurred without the immigrant – in particular, the non-Anglo-Saxon immigrant – who brought to this country fresh approaches, big ideas, big aspirations. He was a man in a hurry: go-slow, them-and-us attitudes were anathema to him. But to succeed, he would have to overcome those attitudes in others that could be traced all the way back to the original convicts and which were still dictating the pace and sub-stance of much that remained in the Australian psyche.

It is puzzling that so many Australians,

been extraordinary. In a little more than one generation the proportion of immig-rants and sons of immigrants of non-Anglo-Saxon stock at the top of big busi-ness organisations has risen to a level directly commensurate with the propor-tion of immigrants in the community. He also made his mark in the arts, and his influence spread throughout the spec-trum of social endeavour – including, eventually, those curiously Anglo-Saxon sports, cricket, Australian Rules and the Rugby football codes.

The effect of the immigrant has been extraordinary, but it is less surprising to him than it may be to native-born Austra-lians. He has had to overcome a certain amount of discrimination and intoler-ance, and to live with (and sometimes overcome) curiously Australian charac-teristics. The immigrants flooding into Australia from Europe were mostly unskilled, but a small and highly signifi-

The production line at Chrysler Australia Ltd in Adelaide, South Australia, during the 1960s.

native-born, had continued to tolerate those attitudes. Perhaps they did not fully understand how deeply rooted those attitudes were. It was as if the country had been lulled, all too easily, by its apparent prosperity. There were others who understood us better than we understood ourselves. Author Donald Horne it was who described Australia as the Lucky Country, and it was.

The nearest, readily understandable model Australia had at any time, if it had been in any doubt about large-scale immigration, was the United States. The benefits that it had produced there were undeniable. Among other things, it produced the manpower and materials that would win the war against Japan. Our understanding of America, after that war, was clouded, even though we had been host to a friendly invasion by almost one million GIs between Pearl Harbor and VJ Day. An American academic, Dixon Wecter, wrote in 1946 that before American servicemen set foot on Australian soil, 'the average American seldom thought of that land save as a large blank continent with a zoological sense of humour. Concerning us, the Australians had a knowledge of sorts. Thanks to his press – which maintains a battery of New York and Hollywood columnists, with an eye to the more lurid and lunatic aspects of life in America – and to the movies, magazines and canned music, the Australian reacts constantly to the vibrations of American life.' Wecter, a PhD from Yale and a Rhodes scholar, had lectured at Sydney University the year the war ended, and got it right when he wrote that Americans' ignorance of 'our cousins down under' was tinged with smugness, while Australians' ignorance of Americans was 'accompanied by keen interest and some anxiety'. Writing in the *Atlantic* he said: 'No officious Congressman need remind them – these few English-speaking settlers of a big continent lying upon the perimeter of a restless Asia – that in their darkest hour the armed forces of America did for them what the Royal Navy was helpless to do.'

He noted that American enterprise built the first telegraph lines and cable cars in Australia, broke records with clipper ships and set up the famous Cobb & Co. stagecoach services. When the Australian colonies federated, they turned frankly to the United States for their political and judicial model. Yet he could write: 'However puzzling colonialism may be to the American mind, however strong the suspicion that Australia has given Britain – in resources, war manpower, and export of her best brains – more than Britain has given Australia, the fact remains for one's admiration that a mother country and race can inspire such tenacious loyalty. No nation save England has ever been able to gain it.'

Wecter may not have fully understood how much Britain had given to Australia in terms of stable government and rule of law, but he did home in unerringly on troubling aspects of Australian life: 'near enough' standards of comfort and education and culture, a long-rooted programme of social planning that was of keener real interest than matters of foreign policy, a go-slow policy that put a ceiling on the unionist's efforts and had raised production costs out of line with world parity prices. 'It is one reason why Australia will never become a highly industrialised nation, but must continue to count upon the world's buying her raw wool and unprocessed steel,' he said. Australia, he noted, had sought to insulate her demi-paradise against poverty, competition and external pressure – and these were still the concerns nearest her heart. He wrote all that four decades ago! So much of it is still true.

Americans had long enjoyed the largest manufacturing base in the world, and had one of the largest populations – Wecter,

Classes in English being held on board the liner Fairsea *en route to Australia in 1962.*

Workers at the Ford motor works at Geelong, Victoria, in 1956. Fifty-four per cent of the 4500 workers employed there at the time were migrants. (Department of Immigration and Ethnic Affairs)

no fortune-teller, could not know how readily Australia would clamber under the American umbrella for security. But in considering how America developed that manufacturing base, it is important to recall some of the reasons why the United States built its population so quickly. Just as Australia had fears in 1942, the United States had them in the late eighteenth century – and they were a dramatic spur to immigration policies. The Australian view of history was, of course, distilled through British eyes, and the British failed twice in armed struggle against the Americans. The feeling that Australia might have to take positive steps to justify sole occupation of this continent came very late. The United States had appeared besieged after the War of Independence (which led directly to the white settlement of Australia). The War of 1812-14 had the Indians assisting the British; there was the ever-present threat of Spanish Florida, French Louisiana, as well as Mexican designs on Texas, the rest of the south-west and California. The Americans had to increase their numbers and expand their borders as quickly as possible. After they moved in force over the Mississippi they gained, by purchase, annexation and arms, whatever they wanted. They even invaded and captured Mexico City at one stage, to make a point. ('I do not think there was ever a more wicked war than that waged by the United States in Mexico,' a young lieutenant said – and he was Ulysses S. Grant, later commander of all Union forces in the Civil War, and two-term President of the United States.)

Because of some national inertia that has never been properly explained, Australia, for most of its formative years, and even when feverish with xenophobia, failed to overcome a short-sightedness towards national planning and policy, not least towards immigration. We should have learned the lessons of American history: in 1790, fourteen years after the Declaration of Independence, it had only four million inhabitants, but in just over-sixty years from 1783 the United States more than trebled its area, and from 1820 its population almost doubled every twenty years. Australia had no need of geographical expansion, only to inhabit the land.

The Americans were energetic, adaptable. They would also, long after populating their country, reveal themselves as short-sighted in some respects, but they redressed the error. As William Manchester recalled in his great work, *The Glory and the Dream*, in 1938 General George C. Marshall had testified that American armed forces were too weak to repel an invasion of the country. (Invasion of such a vast land, well-populated and well-developed, had been unthinkable.) To put things in perspective, Hitler's blitzkrieg in Europe had been supported by 3034 aircraft, 4000 trucks, 10 000 artillery pieces and 2580 tanks. In the following five years America turned out 296 429 aircraft, 2.4 million trucks, 87 620 ships, 5425 cargo ships, 102 351 tanks, and 372 431 artillery pieces. This was a phenomenal effort. It saved the Allies. The key was people. They provided the base – and the manufacturing base, when it changed gears for for civilian needs after the war, dominated the western hemisphere. Bigger than Texas was correct. This is not to assert that Australia was ever going to be in the same league, but it highlighted a lesson our ancestors had refused to learn.

In 1984, Maximilian Walsh, writing in *Australian Business*, said Australia had been slipping down the international growth league for years with no discernable effect on the fate of the government of the day.

We, as a nation, do not have high expectations of economic growth. That has been bred out of us by decades of poor performance ... It is at last beginning to sink into the collective psyche of Canberra that the free rise on the coat-tails of Japan's super growth has come to a halt. At best, we can hope to hold our share of a much slower growing market for our resource exports. Even that is unlikely, given Japanese investment in Canadian coal and Brazilian iron ore. In Asia we face tougher competition for our resources from lesser developed countries that are hungry for foreign exchange.

Agricultural income is not going to grow strongly and we have an entirely inappropriate industrial base for the closing decades of the twentieth century. Even in the good times Australia has not been a strong performer in the international growth stakes. The difference between positive and negative economic growth is probably slimmer in prospective terms than it has ever been.

A chilling forecast. Who would have thought that Australia, after four decades of unprecedented development, could find itself in such a position?

The *Economist*, the influential British journal, noted in 1984 that back in 1870 the white population of Australia had been the richest in the world, with a per capita income 25 per cent higher than Americans enjoyed. By 1980 Australia had dropped to eleventh place, and within a generation will be overtaken by Singapore, Malaysia, Taiwan and South Korea.

It would be misleading to pretend that Australians would ever have been able to control all of the factors responsible for the slide. Nevertheless, it is beyond doubt that part of the problem lay in a continuing habit of throwing up our hands and insisting that we could never get into the big economic league or be a self-supporting economy because our population was too small. Sweden, with a much smaller population than Australia, managed to overcome that obstacle, and is both economically strong and secure, despite high wage scales. The United States chose a different path: it built its infrastructure on low wages and cheap power, then when it was secure achieved high standards of living for the wage-earner. By the 1980s, Australian labour had priced Australia out of many export markets. Australia, because of its lack of ingenuity in secondary and tertiary industries, was hampered in its search for fresh export markets and it lacked economy of scale in domestic markets. Put simply, Sweden, though resource-poor and people-poor, had the ingenuity to main-

Two English migrants at the steelworks at Whyalla.

tain its living standards by exporting; the United States had a home-grown market for its high-priced goods, and Australia was losing its overseas markets and did not have a large domestic market. We had put off too many vital decisions for too long.

Australia seems eerily alone again, and at the mercy of larger, potentially overwhelming forces. Our associations with the United States – economically and politically – no longer seem the sure-fire guarantee that they have been in previous decades. Australia has indeed been riding on coat-tails – and not just Japan's. But the attention of our major mentor, the United States, has been diverted to more urgent needs and different directions, some of them on the USA's doorstep. Australia was associated with the United States in three major wars in a quarter-century, but was finally forced to reconsider its international image – and particularly its image in the United States, where it still counts for little with the average citizen. I think this began to dawn on the Australian conscience when President Richard Nixon leaned over to Prime Minister William McMahon at an official gathering to ask whether the Australian's name was pronounced 'McMaan' or 'McMann'. Malcolm Fraser was referred to once in America as Prime Minister John Fraser – because John is his first name.

Riding on the coat-tails ... we have been content to import our technology, and much else that we need to sustain ourselves now in our daily lives. Australia's failure in post-secondary education (surely a pre-requisite for any big move in secondary and high-tech industries) is, in the words of Justice Michael Donald Kirby, then chairman of the Australian Law Reform Commission and vice-chancellor of Newcastle University, 'shocking, unless the word be perilous'. We rank in this area with Turkey and Greece.

The proportion of Australians in full-time higher education in the early 1980s actually declined. It declined by almost one-fifth between 1975 (the last year of the Whitlam Labor Government) and 1982. Justice Kirby said:

Why, when all the nations with whom we compete are increasing both the quantity and quality of the education of their people is this country falling behind? Where will this lead? We can see the answer in the relative decline of the Australian standard of living in the course of this century, from being one of the top four at the beginning to barely making the top twenty now [in 1982].

We have ridden on the sheep's back. We have tried to clamber on the band waggon of the mineral boom that never was. We have imported technology and manpower. And we have gone to the beach and taken it easy. We have deprived advanced education and begrudged investment in it.

We have lampooned 'intellectuals' and 'academics'. We have mocked excellence.

Our theme song and our national obsession are 'Come on Aussie' and 'I feel like a Tooheys'.

And he went on to paint a dismal picture of Australians becoming the 'poor whites' of the Asian region unless there was a big change in our attitudes in the decades ahead.

To put it another way, the judge was saying Australians were in danger of being forced to pay for decades of neglect, for taking the soft options. Perhaps we could have made a start toward solving more problems if we had imported a lot more manpower much earlier: the result might have been a boost in confidence that comes with size, greater competition internally and thus a greater incentive to solve our problems, instead of pigeon-holing them or importing solutions. Australia presents a puzzling countenance to some thinking foreigners in the 1980s: it had embraced the consumer economy with a vengeance before the nation had been properly developed, instead of afterward, as America has done.

There was a plethora of examples of our folly. To take but one; the cities were littered with service stations (whose owners struggled to make a living because of over-competition) and we had no fewer than five car-makers producing locally (some unprofitably) but Australian lives were being wasted on the roads and millions of litres of precious fuel wasted each week because we had never made anything approaching a proper investment in roads. There was over-competition in many service industries, long before we had built up a lasting infrastructure in secondary industries. We had aped affluence, and thus revealed that we did not understand the true basis of enduring affluence.

In one week in March 1984, there were official warnings that Australia's poor export performance was attributable to reliance on low processed commodities such as agriculture and minerals, and that Australia's scientific discoveries rarely achieved commercial exploitation. (The former was issued by John Menadue, secretary of the Federal Trade Department, and the latter by Barry Jones, Federal Minister for Science and Technology.) Australia's penetration of most overseas markets including South-East Asia had declined, Mr Menadue said, and our share of world exports had fallen from 1.7 per cent in 1970 to 1.3 per cent in 1982. Mr Jones noted that Australia had produced four Nobel Prize winners in the sciences – the same number as Japan. Mr Menadue said there was a clear connection between exports, employment and education – and all were vital to Australia's economic future.

It had become clear that what Wecter had said was correct. But in Australia, not even relatively high immigration rates had kept wage rates at realistic levels – which was not true in the United States in the nineteenth and early twentieth centuries.

It may not be too late to redress the situation. The task, which includes continuing to attract large numbers of immigrants, is much more difficult than it was for the United States in the eighteenth and nineteenth centuries. America, less than a week's journey by sea from Europe, beckoned much more strongly than Australia ever did. Perhaps that pull is declining in an era that threatens nuclear annihilation. A reorientation of national priorities at base level in Australia is both essential and unlikely, but it is not inconceivable that a gradual change will occur. One thing seems certain: we chance little if we increase our immigration target once relatively full employment is restored in this country. Living standards in Australia have increased, but relative to other wealthy nations will continue to fall in the short term in any event: long-term planning, including long-term immigration, is the only way to reverse that trend.

CHAPTER 12

What the Big Push Has Achieved

IT IS A CURIOUS PARADOX that when the Immigration Department was established after World War II its purpose was to foster immigration to a country that had always feared invasion by foreign legions, but which had hitherto been considered relatively unattractive by tens of millions of peaceful people who had been forced to cast around for a country to emigrate to. In other words, Australia had been seen by Australians as attractive to invaders but had been relatively unattractive to peaceful settlers, the people we really needed even if we did not really desire them. If you had told the average Australian in 1945 that most Asians, those supposedly primitive souls who represented the amorphous Yellow Peril, scarcely knew where Australia was, let alone harboured a malevolent desire to attack and overwhelm it, you would have been regarded as naive, or even as a lunatic. Japan's leaders had turned envious eyes southwards, of course, but even when their forces reached Australia's doorstep, they did little more than rattle the door-knocker, rather than rush in where all but the Aborigines and a few million Britons and Irish had dared to tread. Some doubt has been expressed in recent years about what Australia took for granted during the war and for decades afterwards – that the Japanese had been hell-bent on conquering Australia. Even now, you can find university-educated Japanese who are not aware that Japan attacked Darwin and Sydney. (Much later, after the Vietnam War, it emerged that only Australia had ever seen participation by her fighting men in that war as necessary to stem the Yellow Peril: the Americans fought in the name of democracy, or thought they did, and the 45 000-

In 1955 Australia welcomed the one-millionth post-war immigrant, Mrs Barbara Ann Porritt and her husband Dennis, an electrical fitter. (Department of Immigration and Ethnic Affairs)

Greeks in the community continue to express their heritage. The Greeks maintain cultural awareness with lessons in Greek language, history and the arts. (Department of Immigration and Ethnic Affairs)

strong South Korean force was there because South Korea was militantly anti-communist. The Vietnamese invasion of Australia manifested itself in a few leaky boats that made it, with their wasted human cargo, to our northern shores after hostilities ceased in Vietnam. These people were anti-communist to the last man.)

Still, we should not quibble now about the paucity of Australian logic in 1945. The fact was that Australia had feared the Yellow Peril within her boundaries during the gold rushes, and had feared it from without her boundaries ever since the Russo-Japanese War of 1905, when the Russians sailed three-quarters of the way

around the globe to receive a thrashing. It was the first occasion in modern history when a white power had been defeated by a 'coloured' one in a major conflict, and it scared the daylights out of Australians, who a few decades previously had been afraid of a Russian naval invasion. Our fighting men were fearless overseas, and gave a great account of themselves, but everybody assumed we would always lose a war on our own soil, even though the defender has advantages: there were simply too few of us, and too many of 'them', no matter who 'them' was.

(To put the matter in perspective, it has long been recognised that the only means by which a foreign power using conventional weapons could attack Australia would involve air power or naval forces, or both, or else a 'strategic lodgment' of its army on Australian soil to prepare a sweep on the major cities. The only Asian nations with anything like the capacity to mount an attack of such proportions are Japan and Indonesia, and neither possesses either the air or naval forces for that. These nations with the 'perceived potential' would have to spend years and a great deal of national treasure to build up their forces to the size and status required, and Australia would have plenty of warning that this was occurring. I write this not to suggest that Australia's defences are sufficient – though sophisticated advances are being made or are planned – but to emphasise that Australia, because of its size and remoteness, is no sitting duck, and never has been. As for the Chinese, who now number one billion,

they do not seem to have been considered a threat since the United States lost in Vietnam and Australia recognised the People's Republic: no doubt psychologists will explain this phenomenal change in the Australian attitude one day, though that is not necessary.)

Australia's pre-World War II immigration agreement with the Dutch was renewed after the war, but it could never yield all the manpower Australia hungered for. The Netherlands had about the same population as Australia, too small by itself for a big emigration base. The Immigration Department was keen to get all the Dutch it could, however – the Dutch were blond, big, orderly, disciplined, and they had a history of quick assimilation in Anglo-Saxon countries. They did not congregate in big population centres, nor did they huddle in ghettoes. They were excellent farmers, made

Welcoming the first group of refugees to arrive in Australia following the 1956 Hungarian uprising. (Department of Immigration and Ethnic Affairs)

great tradesmen and craftsmen. Unlike the French, who never forgave the British for bombing targets on their soil during World War II, the Dutch considered the damage to their ports part of the price of liberation. They were pro-British.

It must have been galling to Arthur Calwell in the immediate post-war years as the reality became more and more obvious: the British weren't coming in a flood, and the Americans, all those servicemen who had grown used to the Australian way of life, were leaving – and what's more, taking Australian wives with them.

That put paid to the idealistic notion that almost all the immigrants would be English-speaking. And with each year that passed, as Britain and the countries of Continental Europe began to rebuild their economies, emigration would become less attractive. Even the millions of displaced persons in Europe were going back to their homelands. Only the hard core remained in Germany. Australia, even when it opened its gates, was missing its opportunity – again. Calwell, whose grandfather had lived in the United States when immigrants in that country were proving that a British background was not a prime requisite, or even a requisite at all, of nation-building, quietly revised his ethnic table. He had been saying that ten out of eleven immigrants would be British. He marked that down to 75 per cent Britons. Calwell was merely being pragmatic. And just as well, otherwise his immigration programme would never have been the success that it was. It is important to consider just how much the programme might have suffered if he and his Government had stuck firmly by the 10:1 or even the 75:25 formulae. Just on 1.25 million people from Britain and British colonies arrived in Australia between October 1945 and June 1981, intending to settle permanently or remain here long term. That is, 23 per cent of the 5.3 million people who arrived to settle or to stay for a long period. It is safe to assume that the number who made the decision to leave Britain might have been smaller than it was, had there not been so many non-British immigrants, particularly in the 1940s and 1950s, to help build the economy and make the country more attractive as a strong haven or a place where people could indeed make a new start.

The worth of those non-British immigrants, in the workplace and elsewhere, was reflected in the ever-widening scope of the assisted passage scheme, which by 1981 had been extended to a total of forty non-British nations, as well as eight nations that had links with Britain, such as Malaysia, Sri Lanka and Eire. We may have wound up with fewer than one million immigrants in that quarter-century if we had relied solely on Britain and her colonies. We do know that without the big push in immigration, Australia's population now would be only about 10 million, instead of 15 million: it would have been one-third smaller than it is now. Moreover, Australia would not have reached its present level of development, and culturally and socially it would be much less diverse, and thus so much weaker. It might even have continued to be a nation dependent on pies and fish 'n' chips for a night out on the town, red meat and two veges boiled twice over for Sunday dinner, and a much restricted choice of restaurants. It has long been fashionable to stress the change in Australian eating habits by way of emphasising the contribution non-British immigrants have made. We should emphasise instead a massive infusion to the arts, including notably, music and painting; to most sports; and not least to business, large and small, the professions, commerce and academe.

Two Melbourne economists produced a report in June 1985 that showed that immigrants improve the job prospects of unemployed Australians, increase the nation's growth rate, earn more and

Language lessons accompanied assisted passages for migrants. Orientation and counselling sessions were also included in the education programmes which were designed to enable the New Australian to cope with the new environment. (Department of Immigration and Ethnic Affairs)

spend more than the average Australian, and work harder.

The study was made over three years by Dr Neville Norman and Kathryn Meikle, and was sponsored by the Immigration Department and the Committee for Economic Development of Australia, an independent organisation of business leaders and academics. The report contradicted the notion – which dates back to the nineteenth century – that immigrants are a drain on welfare and education resources, take jobs from native-born Australians, and are not as productive in the work force. Immigrants who are not refugees arrive with an average of about $32 000 per family, which amounted to $777 million in 1983-84. They tend to buy their own homes relatively quickly, and spend more on food, clothing and housing

costs than native-born Australians. Their households typically are larger, and have more members working. According to employers, they work longer and harder, are less interested in unions, do not cause problems with management and do not create as many additional costs to employers. They are more mobile in their search for jobs, and take jobs others shun.

When Australia sent its national soccer team over the oceans in 1974 to do battle with the best teams in the world for the World Cup, having reached the finals for the first time, British newspapers (which have always felt free to be disparaging about us) noted that most of the players had been born in Europe, and the coach, Rale Rasic, was a Yugoslav. That missed the point, which is that so many of the people who have made a first-class con-

A group of Hungarians on their way to Australia in the 1960s. A significant proportion of migrants arrived here with substantial assets and many were highly skilled. (Macleay Museum, University of Sydney)

tribution to Australia over the past four decades were born outside Australia, or are the sons and daughters of immigrants. It is also true that an Australian representative soccer team is likely to be much less dominated by players of European birth than previously was the case, which is to say that immigrants of both British and other stock built the code in Australia and presented it in a refurbished and greatly strengthened form to all Australians. On the other hand, if we look at Australian Rules, the only uniquely Australian sport, and Rugby League and Rugby Union, which we imported from Britain, we cannot fail to notice that these codes have claimed the attention of immigrants and sons of immigrants. George Peponis, one of the most respected of players to captain

the Australian Rugby League team, is of Greek stock (and managed to qualify as a medical practitioner while working his way up the League ladder, no mean feat given the rugged competitiveness of his sport and the study and work hours demanded by his profession). Eric Grothe, who has been classed as the world's greatest Rugby League winger, is of German blood, though that is of no importance to a League fan, who rightly judges any player on his performance, on what he gives to the game . That is the way it should be in any field of endeavour, of course – but was not, during the long years of xenophobia. Reg Gasnier was captain of Australia's XIII and rated one of the greatest Rugby League players of all time: his name, a household word wherever the game is played, never prompted Old Australians to puzzle over his French ancestry, just as no Victorian Football League fans raised eyebrows at names such as Barassi, Jesaulenko, Kekovich. Karen Krantzke and Dianne Fromholtz (tennis), Jon and Ilsa Konrads (swimming) and Robert de Castella (marathon) are Australians, as much as a Brown, Smith or O'Flaherty whose ancestors arrived rattling chains. When I was a boy, we couldn't correctly pronounce the name of an up-and-coming cricketer who went on to become one of the the best captains Australia has produced: it was, we discovered, Richie 'Benno', not 'Ben-ord' as Australians unfamiliar with French would be tempted to pronounce the name Benaud.

Continental European names now surface from every page of football programmes in Sydney, Melbourne and elsewhere, so that we find a Brett Lobb playing alongside a Ben Gonzales, a Peter Burgmann and a Joe Vitanza in Penrith's first grade Rugby League team, while elsewhere Paul Grob, Carl Frommel, Wayne Jensen and Gerry de la Cruz line up against Bronco Djura, Arthur Kitinas, Joe Fenech and Geoff Cheung – which goes to show that Asians may lose nothing on a football field to Anglo-Saxons (or 'Anglomorphs', as Professor Frank Knopfelmacher, perceptive social commentator, prefers to term Anglo-Saxons and Anglo-Celts). Sports are great levellers, even if the fans stumble over names such as Katsogiannis, Fahd, Fyvie and Khalifeh, Manguso, Ghosn and Psaltis, all playing grade Rugby League on the same afternoon at North Sydney Oval. It has taken a generation or so for young men and women with strange-sounding names to make the grade, as it were, but they have done so as Australians – not as Yugoslav-Australians, Greek-Australians or Italian-Australians. If it is that way on the sporting field, which consumes relatively little time, why should it not be so in the workplace, which consumes half of each worker's waking hours? There is a lesson for advocates of multiculturalism in this.

It is natural that so many fine Australians who have distinguished themselves – and thus their adopted country – in the arts, should hail from Continental Europe. The painters, from Hans Heysen (German-born) to Judy Cassab and the late Desiderius Orban (both Hungarian-born) have been outstanding. Philippe Mora, the film director, is the son of a French immigrant ... the list could go on forever. It is not confined to the modern era, of course (for example, Henry Lawson's forebears were named Larsen; they came from Norway, seedbed of not a few darkly pessimistic and highly renowned exponents of the arts). If we look at photography and television, we find that immigrants and their offspring are very well represented.

The contribution of immigrants to science is well known, and is testament to the great interest in education that so

The factory of Emmco Pty Ltd in 1958: an inspector giving finished refrigerators their final check. At that time the company employed 450 migrants out of its total workforce of 1200 people. (Department of Immigration and Ethnic Affairs)

In Italy, bocce is traditionally a man's game, but in Australia the codes of behaviour loosened with assimilation and before long a women's bocce club was formed—probably the first in the world. (Department of Immigration and Ethnic Affairs)

many have shown, especially for their children. Two Australian scientists, for example, are assisting American experiments in space. Dr Joseph Hoh has experiments scheduled to fly in the NASA Life Sciences programme on Spacelab IV in 1986. Dr Leopold Dintenfass' experiment, taking micro-photographs of blood in space, went aloft in a Space Shuttle. American scientists queue for opportunities like these.

Ralph Sarich, of Yugoslav stock, plugged away in his workshop in Perth, trying to perfect his revolutionary orbital engine. Australian companies, as usual, were slow to realise the potential of the design, and it was not until the French company Renault showed positive interest that BHP got behind it, and stayed there, pumping in millions of dollars. Sarich's design, a small, light-weight engine, promised great power and was fuel-efficient. After more than a decade it has not been perfected for commercial application, but along the way Sarich and his assistants built a novel fuel injection system that does stand a real chance of worldwide application.

All those people have made it to the top, and by being there, as well as by their contribution to scientific thought and progress, have helped squash the racist notion that, in an unequal world, the pinnacle belongs to the Anglo-Saxon. It may very well be true that the English, for example, managed over many centuries to organise themselves as a nation so that they were pre-eminent in many fields (battlefields were not the least of them, and success there led, historically, to increased wealth). But that is not to say that the individual Briton was superior to, say, a Scandinavian, Frenchman, Spaniard, Italian or Chinese with the same advantages and opportunities, including to name a few, good nutrition, good schooling, medical care and parents or guardians with the nouse to guide him or her to a successful career and life. Perhaps Australians of Anglo-Saxon stock have traded too long on the Anglo-Saxon inheritance, which gave us the basis for stable government, peaceful existence within our own territorial boundaries, and directed us to growth and prosperity. Australian Anglo-Saxons have tended to take all that for granted, as a birthright, and thus, no doubt, do not value it sufficiently, and pay lip-service to it. The struggling immigrant families from less fortunate nations value these things highly because they provide the ground for a decent existence: the children of such families often feel, therefore, that the gates have opened for them and hence a way to the top in whatever career they choose. Hardly surprising, then, that they make the extra effort which, so often, is most of what is required to actually reach the top.

This brings us to the broad field where it is so obvious that immigrants, or their offspring, have reached the top rung: business. Obvious, because success in business – especially big business – quickly becomes known to the entire community, which is fascinated by success stories that can be shown in words and pictures, and through television and radio. Wealth, power and their trappings make for news. What is apparent is that in just a little more than one generation, immigrants and their families have reached the apex in big business in pleasantly large numbers, to the point where, proportionate to the total number of immigrants in the community, they have caught up with the Anglo-Celt (as represented by the number of top Anglo-Celtic businessmen

proportionate to the number of Anglo-Celts in the community). Eleven of the top sixty-five businessmen in the country, as categorised by the magazine *Australian Business* are of non-Anglo-Celtic stock: which is near enough to one-sixth. The magazine's list did not include members of the 'old-money' Establishment, whose success could not be gauged because their companies are private ones, and thus so are their incomes.

A list of top businessmen would include such men as Sir Peter Abeles, managing director of TNT Transport, the company that was built up by (Sir) Ken Thomas, and which Abeles enlarged greatly before taking control (with Mr Rupert Murdoch) of Ansett Airlines. Sir Peter is Hungarian-born. Sir Tristan Antico, chairman and managing director of Pioneer, the concrete giant, is from Italy. The list goes on to Sir Arvi Parbo, chairman and managing director of Western Mining Corporation Ltd, chairman of

The 50 000th Dutch immigrant to Australia, Mrs Frank Zindler, nee Maria Scholte, who joined a cooking class of trainee nurses as part of her introduction to her new hometown of Melbourne. (Department of Immigration and Ethnic Affairs)

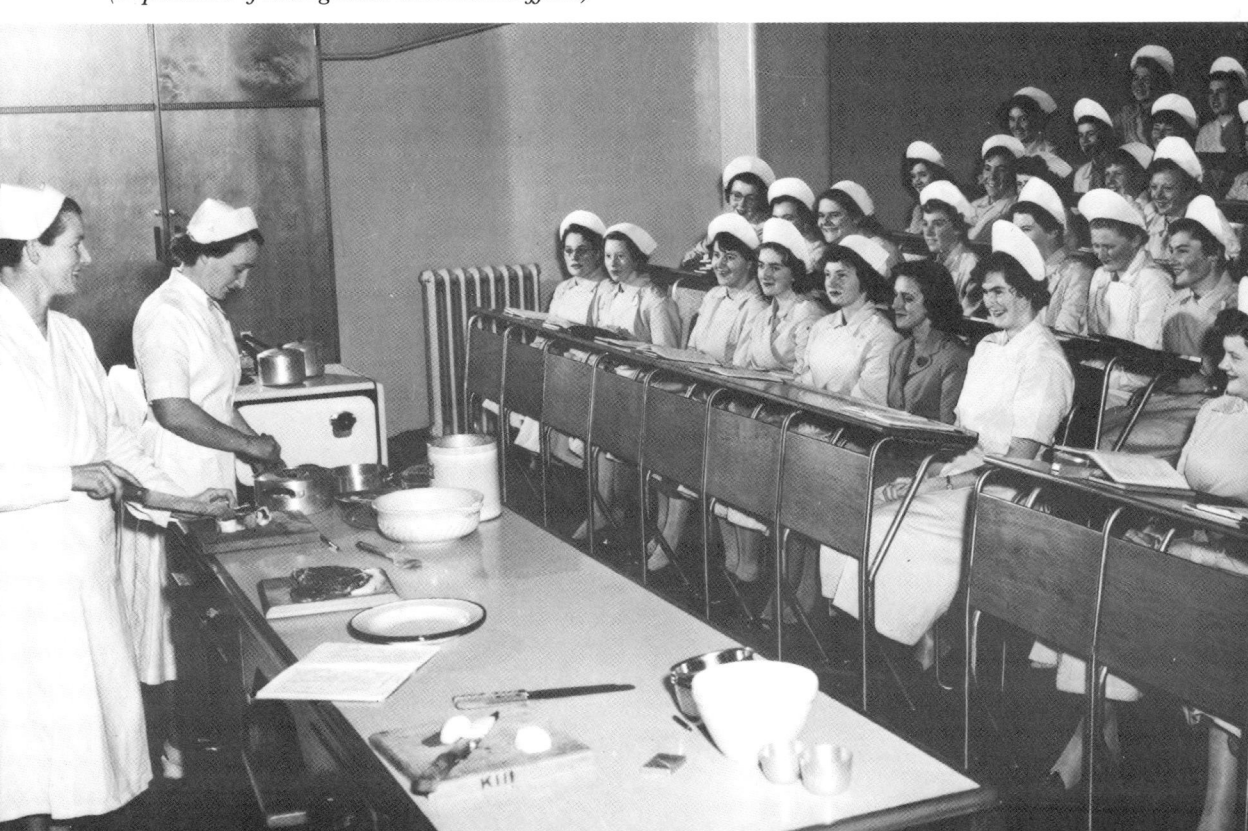

Alcoa of Australia Ltd, and chairman of B. H. South Ltd, to John Spalvins, managing director of Adelaide Steamship, which has had a remarkable rise, through takeovers, in recent years. Then there's Alex Morokoff, chairman of Energy Resources of Australia, a mining company; Bill Kocass, general manager of Concrete Constructions; Tony Berg, deputy managing director of Hill Samuel Australia, the merchant bank; John Utz, executive chairman of Wormald International; David Elsum, managing director of Renison Goldfields, Lloyd Zampatti, managing director of Castlemaine Tooheys; and John Uhrig, managing director of Simpson Holdings, the whitegoods manufacturer. A longer-than-top-sixty-five list would include Robert Strauss, managing director of Bridge Oil; Michael Strauss, chairman of FCB/Spasm, the advertising agency; Olev Rahn, a key executive at BT Australia, merchant bankers; and Peter Steigrad,

Ann Plotke, MA, LLB Hons., left Germany as a child. She came to Australia where she became the first woman to sit on the Council of the Law Society of New South Wales. (Law Society of New South Wales)

managing director of John Clemenger NSW, the advertising agency.

Immigrants are among those tycoons who are not only self-made, but have virtually run their own show, and they include G. J. Dusseldorp, the Dutchman who built up Civil and Civic Constructions and Lend Lease, and who is one of the greatest living examples of the immigrant-made-good – good beyond the dreams of the average Australian. They are all worthy representatives of the peoples who came from non-English-speaking countries, who outnumber those who came from English-speaking countries during the same period and who, with their children, number almost one-fifth of Australia's population.

For every big success story, of course, there have been tens of thousands of ordinary successes that do not make it into print or on to the tube, the kind that will nevertheless be related by grandchildren around the dinner table years from now. For many immigrants, to settle and partially assimilate has been the mark of success, and who would deny the truth of that? But it must be said also that at least until recent years, Old Australians have been ignorant of the problems non-Anglo-Saxon immigrants faced in settling in Australia. Too many native-born Australians simply didn't care to know the nature and extent of those problems. To say that Australians regarded the newcomers as factory fodder is perhaps being too severe: the Old Australian did bare his racism as soon as he was reminded that not all peoples on the planet were precisely like him in taste, style or speech, but usually he has respected anybody who does a fair day's work for a fair day's pay. He does not look down on people who work in factories. How could he? So much of the old Australian ethos was only a step away from its blue-collar origins.

The derogatory term 'factory fodder' relates more to the tendency of some immigrants to resist entreaties to join or

Judy Cassab, the Hungarian migrant whose contribution to Australian art has been outstanding. (John Fairfax & Sons Ltd)

automatically abide by decisions of trade unions. It is useless to paint this scenario in black and white. No doubt many immigrants failed to adequately understand the contribution of trade unions to the Australian community at large, in terms of safety on the shop floor, health, and distribution of the national wealth. On the other hand, the immigrant, if he had come here because his native country had been taken over by communists, might volubly resist the more harebrained decisions of his trade union, especially when he stood to lose wages needlessly. Occasionally such maverick immigrants made the news pages, and nothing irritates union officials more than one of their own members (or non-members) standing up to call them to account. It is like being fired on by their own platoons when the enemy is supposed to be the managers, big companies, multina-

tionals and, even, the Arbitration Commission. Put concisely, the immigrant did not come here to foster a them-and-us attitude on the shop floor. He was in too much of a hurry to put up with too much of that. And if managers and companies were ignorant of the need for industrial relations befitting the late-twentieth century, many an immigrant was not fussed about that, either – not until he had established his family and home, anyway. Fortunately, Australian companies are putting more effort and resources into the creation and maintenance of good industrial relations than they did in the past.

About 60 per cent of the immigrants who have arrived since 1947 have come from countries other than Britain – more than one hundred different countries, in fact. Of those non-English-speaking countries, Italy, Greece, Yugoslavia, Germany and the Netherlands have been the main single contributors of immigrants. The Germans and the Dutch came in relatively large numbers in the early years of the immigration programme before the revival of the west European economies and the growth of the European Economic Community. They had much less difficulty adjusting to Australia than did the southern Europeans.

The Italians
The strong pull of Australia on Italians is demonstrated in the numbers who have immigrated without assisted passages as well as the overall number who have come here. In the first two decades of the immigration programme, 86 per cent of British immigrants received assisted passages, while only 17 per cent of Italians did.

Italians began emigrating on a huge scale in the late nineteenth century, to the United States and South America, chiefly Argentina, Brazil and Venezuela. (Australia, with the exception notably of South Australia and Queensland, was simply not interested in promoting non-British immigration in that period. Italians have

Latvian born twins John and Ilsa Konrads brought Olympic fame to Australia with their swimming successes.

gone to Australia, Canada and the United States since World War II. The chief regions from which Italians have emigrated to Australia in the past four decades are Sicily, Calabria, Campagnia and Abruzzi in the south, and Veneto and Venezia-Giulia in the north-east. Many more have emigrated from the north than many Australians seem to acknowledge.

To understand the Italians who came here, it is necessary to have much more than the tourist's-eye view of Italy, which swivels from Roman ruins to chic fashions and expensive, sporty cars, takes in the pleasing sights and galleries of Venice and Florence, and dwells fleetingly if at all on the vast numbers of Italians who, by Australian standards, were simply not well-off. It has been estimated that the average person in Italy at the height of the immigration programme consumed only one-third as much as an Australian, and even less in southern Italy, where potential immigrants were predominantly rural workers, used to villages, and who lived on a simple diet, with a lot of bread, pasta and vegetables. (Veal and pork, the meats they preferred, they found expensive in Australia, while lamb, which is inexpensive here, they do not like.) Secondary schooling was free of charge, but not compulsory until the 1970s, so the vast majority of Italian immigrants arrived here with nothing more than primary schooling behind them, and six half-days a week at that.

What they did bring of considerable worth was a very strong sense of the nuclear family and extended family, an ordered home existence of mutual depen-

Ernest Kirby, who won the University of Vienna medal in Law in 1933. He emigrated to Australia in 1938 and gained his Australian law degree while serving with the Australian Army in World War II. (Monte Luke Pty Ltd)

dence. That, and the enormous asset of being self-starters – they made do for themselves. And, last but not least, strong backs – they were energetic, and no shirkers. According to one study in Melbourne, half of the Italians who had been in Australia fewer than six years lived with relatives. But other figures show that in the same city, 82 per cent of Italians who could be classified as the titular head of their household owned or were paying off their own home, which was a higher percentage than for Australian-born heads of households. Renovating dilapidated housing stock in near-city suburbs became an Italian trademark. These houses were sold and left for a new owner's enjoyment when the former owner moved to the more spacious, airy

outer suburbs. Few Italians live in flats or are a drain on public housing resources. That, and their deep-seated desire for independence, as evidenced by the numbers of them who have started small businesses, plus their energy and optimism, has vindicated fully the decision of governments of various complexions to keep the door open to them over the years.

By the mid-1950s they had come in such numbers that they had established themselves across the entire spectrum of such businesses as the growing, distribution and wholesaling of vegetables and fruit. An Italian who had lived with relatives for the first few years after he got off the ship could save enough to put a deposit on a few hectares – sometimes less – and often he worked from a fibro-cement cottage that he put up with the help of, again, his relatives. Chain migration played a large part in the Italian success story in Australia. There were always relatives to support and assist the newly arrived and those getting established in business of one kind or another. So with a few simple tools, sometimes a rotary hoe, our Italian set to work growing vegetables, often just beyond the outskirts of a growing metropolis, where the land was still inexpensive, but would appreciate in value. There were Italians in the markets, scads of Italian fruit and vegetable shops:

thus the Italians became a highly visible and readily identifiable part of the Australian community.

In addition, Italians have tended to make good, law-abiding citizens, people with a sense of their own worth. This doubtless stems in part from their innate desire for respect, which is so important to families in Italy. Because of the Italian family structure, in which cohesiveness is all so evident, and male and female roles so clearly defined, some Italian families have found the prevailing Australian social climate cool and loose, especially when they have teenage children to worry

A small town English boy who made good in Australia, Alan Bond is now the head of a multi-million dollar Australian company. Pride in his adopted country led him to build the successful challenger for the America's Cup in 1983. (Department of Immigration and Ethnic Affairs)

about, while native-born Anglo-Saxon Australians have found the Italian social climate too close for comfort. In an era in which children are questioning and challenging parents' cherished notions of what is good and proper, it's not surprising that the Italian papa and mama are suspicious of 'loose' values that strike at the heart of their basic concepts of what a good Italian boy and girl should be brought up to believe. But then, there are quite a few middle-class Australian parents of Anglo-Saxon stock who are worried, too. If Italians have had their problems adapting, so have others, because there is a revolution going on in relations between young and old Australians, and nobody is immune from it. The breakdown in the extended family, and now, the nuclear family, has affected Australians of most ethnic backgrounds. The Italian concept of a cohesive family unit is built to weather most of the storms.

The Greeks

The people, or rather peoples, from the world's oldest democracy have an extraordinary history in Australia. The first Greek is believed to have arrived during the great Victorian gold rush: he jumped ship, stayed twenty years, and made enough money to buy a house on his return to his native Ithiki, and retire there. He really started something, because large numbers of his relatives and friends, hearing the good news about the wealth in the Great South Land, queued up to crew Pacific-bound ships so they too could jump ship in Australia. The first man from Ithiki was Andreas Lakatsos. Some of the relatives who followed him, and whose descendants continue to live here, now go under the name of Lucas.

Greece's modern history has been one of confusion. It was part of the Turkish Empire before gaining its independence in 1832. The Greek economy picked up when Greek wine exports replaced those of France in the 1870s and 1880s, after phylloxera had killed the French vines. In time, the French wine industry revived, and the Greeks found it tiresome to grub out vines and go back to the cultivation of olive trees, so their big emigration began. The Graeco-Turkish War in the early 1920s persuaded many Greeks that it was time to seek a new homeland, and the American immigration restrictions of that decade, aimed at southern and eastern Europeans, should have been enough to awaken Australian politicians and public servants to the opportunity to attract some immigrants. That, of course, did not happen to any worthwhile extent.

There were fewer than five hundred Greeks in Australia when the 1891 census was taken; in the period 1921-28 Australia had a net gain of 5444 Greeks, well below 1000 a year, to help populate the country. At the rate Australia was taking them in the prosperous 1920s, the Greek arrivals were, individually, helping populate Australia at the rate of one Greek for every 2700 square kilometres of country: a paltry effort by the Australian authorities. They had been influenced by American fears of a dilution of America's Anglo-Saxon stock by waves of southern and eastern Europeans. They should have paused to consider that the United States had populated itself with immigrants of various ethnic stock *before* introducing restrictions.

But after the shock Australia received in World War II, Greeks found themselves welcome in increasing numbers. Melbourne now has the second or third largest Greek-speaking population in the world. That has been achieved – and an achievement it is – in four decades. If it had been attempted earlier, the results would be so much the greater now.

The Greeks are clannish. The way in which Greeks from different areas and islands of their homeland have gravitated to different Australian cities is fascinating to review. (It is also entirely natural, given

Sir Arvi Parbo, an Estonian born Australian who is now the Chairman and Managing Director of Western Mining Corporation. At the time this photograph was taken he had just been appointed General Manager. Sir Arvi came here as a post-war refugee and still sees Australia as a land of opportunity. (Department of Immigration and Ethnic Affairs)

the complex geographical nature of Greece.) Ithicans were drawn to Melbourne, Kythenans to Sydney, Kastellori-zons to Perth, while Spartans congregated in Brunswick in Melbourne in the early post-war years, Messenians in Prahran, Pontians in Yarra Valley and Macedonians in Fitzroy and Collingwood. In Sydney, the inner suburb of Surry Hills became host to Mytileneans, while Redfern, an old working-class suburb that unlike some of its neighbours will probably never make it up the social register, was the starting point for many Cretans and Peloponnesians.

Greeks, of course, came well within the ambit of the insulting description of 'wogs' used in the 1950s by the more coarse and insensitive Anglo-Saxon Australians. The word was applied chiefly to immigrants from southern Europe with swarthy complexions. It was many years before 'wogs' were accepted as first-class citizens, but only the most crass of people use the term now. With this acceptance, and as governments began to take a closer look at the lot of the non-English-speaking immigrant, some surprising facts emerged. The Great South Land was, to Greeks and others, a great place to make money, but in other respects it fell far short of expectations. The Greeks had a tough time getting used to Australia – and many never did.

The heart of the problem lay in the difference between the Greek family structure and the native-born Australian's family structure, in the way families related to the outside community. The Greeks, it appears, found it harder to adapt to Australia than Italians. There was a similar emphasis on honour and self-respect (*phitotimo*), but Greeks placed more emphasis on preserving a knowledge of Greek culture and the language. By the end of the 1970s there were about three hundred and fifty Greek ethnic schools in Australia, used after normal school hours for instruction in Greek culture, origins, religion and values. The relationship between the sexes is very different in Greece from Australia. The Greek father, who often works at two or even three jobs to fulfil his role as provider, is king of the household, and if he wishes to spend his nights with friends at the local Greek coffee house, that is his business. The mother accepts her role. Problems sometimes arise, however, when their children begin to see and feel the difference between their own protected upbringing and that of native-born Australian families. All the peer pressure, the influence of television and the changing nature of Australian life bring traditional Greek concepts of what is right and what is wrong under a severe spotlight. This is unfortunate, but it is inescapable; it creates confusion, but then Western values are being re-examined in every country populated by peoples of European origin.

The Yugoslavs

Few countries which have contributed to Australia's immigration programme have a history as turbulent as Yugoslavia's, and few people are as diverse in their cultural heritage, religious beliefs and outlook as the Yugoslavs. For a start, the country has two writing scripts. The Croats and Slovenes use Roman letters, but the Serbs and others from the south use the Cyrillic alphabet. One-third of Yugoslavs are Roman Catholics but about two-fifths are Orthodox, and one-eight are Moslems. Over the centuries the Russians, Turks, Hungarians and Austrians have all managed to grab control of parts of what is now Yugoslavia (which may be translated as 'South Slavia').

Yugoslavia was formed in 1918 from diverse units, the Croats, Serbs and Slovenes. It was under a royal dictatorship in 1929, but the King was assassinated when he was on a visit to France in 1934. For Yugoslavia, World War II was a three-cornered slaughter-chamber; about half of the 1.75 million inhabitants who were killed died at the hands of their countrymen. The Germans and the Ustashi under Ante Pavelic, the Fascist

In 1963, the Minister for Immigration in the Menzies Government, Mr Downer, presented the 250 000th Italian migrant to Australia Mrs Antonia Bellomarino and her family with a gift of an Australian made canteen of cutlery. The occasion was widely reported in the press and on television. (Department of Immigration and Ethnic Affairs)

British migrants take their first look at Sydney, Australia, from the Fairsea *in 1968.*

puppet, were in one corner. The Chetniks, also anti-communist, were in another. The Partisans, under Tito, were in the third. The Germans and the Ustashi fought both the other groups, and killed Jews and Moslems as well. The Chetniks fought the Partisans, Ustashi, Croats and Moslems. The Partisans fought the Ustashi, Germans and Chetniks. Even after the war, the dispute over national boundaries, the political turmoil and uncertainty as Tito struggled to keep the Soviet Union at bay, and the economic difficulties of existence in a country not richly endowed with natural resources, convinced many Yugoslavs that it was time to look elsewhere.

Life for Yugoslav immigrants in Aus-

tralia was difficult from the outset. Many had had little schooling, were not skilled, had no English, and even ordinary white-collar jobs were not within their reach. Almost two-thirds of them wound up in manufacturing or construction jobs: they were factory hands, or worked on buildings. Australia's manufacturing industry expanded greatly in the 1960s, and with it came the need for a virtual sub-class of assembly line workers, men and women. There was nothing attractive about the work, which was simple, repetitive, and mind-numbing – nothing, that is, except the prospect of a regular wage, modest by Australian standards, but a handy prospect for an immigrant from the backblocks of Yugoslavia, which were impoverished. Most Australians have never seen an assembly line, except on television. Many of the one hundred and forty different peoples who came to Australia during the Big Push were no strangers to these lines: they could go to them virtually from the ship, there to piece together cars or can fruit.

Eleven years ago, in 1974, an assembler at a car plant started work at $72 per week. I joined just such a production line once, for a newspaper article. My editor had been prompted to assign the story because the Federal Minister for Labour and Immigration Mr Clyde Cameron, a member of the Whitlam Government of the day, had described assembly line jobs as rotten, soul-destroying and dehumanising. I spent a day on the production line of a family-sized sedan, with workers from as far afield as Chile, Greece and Portugal. There was a complete turnover in the production line force each year at this plant, testimony to the monotony of the jobs, but those who could put up with the work – for the overtime or the opportunity of promotion – stayed for years. I was bored rigid before lunchtime. Cameron, a former shearer who knew drudgery, was right, and it was easy for me to imagine that anybody who could adapt to the assembly line and stick at it for years might wind up cocooned in boredom, and lack the imagination or strength to break out of it. My 'tutor' on the line was a Yugoslav, Ilija Latinovic, who had been in Australia just one year, and spent all his working hours on the line. He spoke hardly a word of English. His lot was the lot of countless thousands of immigrants. When the knock-off whistle blew they all left the floor at a high speed – a sure sign of how they felt.

The Yugoslavs had other things to worry about in Australia. Some Croats were Ustashi sympathisers, and opposition to them from other Yugoslav groups, notably the Serbs, led to violence, including bombings, in the 1960s. There was consternation in Federal Parliament and in the Australian security forces, and much debate about whether or to what extent Yugoslavs were being trained on Australian soil for terrorist plots in their native land. Age-old differences among Yugoslav factions surfaced, with Croats taking to the streets to parade their beliefs in placard, song and flag. Politicians could not ignore atrocities or condone a struggle that should have been allowed to rest when immigrants reached Australia. In time, things settled down. Now, the children and grandchildren of Yugoslav immigrants take their place in the Australian community on an equal footing with the average Australian of nineteenth-century Anglo-Saxon stock.

The Hungarians

Few immigrants have been as successful as the Hungarians when the numbers who have made a mark on Australia are compared with Hungary's population, which was only about the same as Australia's when the Big Push began. The performance of some Hungarian businessmen, notably Sir Peter Abeles, the transport magnate, has been spectacular, but Hungarians have also been outstanding in the arts (with Judy Cassab, the Archibald Prize-winning portraitist perhaps the best known of them all). Some, being Jewish, were lucky to survive Hitler's concentration camps; and even when they arrived in Australia with money, they often found they had to start in a new occupation because their Hungarian qualifications were not recognised. Sir Paul Strasser was an example; he had a law degree that was useless in Australia. He had a few thousand dollars when he arrived in 1948, and that was a considerable sum, although he had been forced to leave a fortune behind when he fled. He had spent two-and-a-half years in forced labour at Kiev during World War II, and only barely survived. He worked for eight years in Australia without much success

Vietnamese immigrants arrive at Canberra Airport in 1979. The 'Yellow Peril' has not descended on Australia, even though the Vietnam War was lost, but some refugees have come.

as an accountant, was an importer and exporter and later was with a small finance company before moving into land development with Robert Ryko. Their company, Parkes Developments, got 30 000 Australians into their own homes, and Strasser's empire spread to office and shopping centre construction, oil and minerals exploration, motels, liquor sales, travel goods, publishing and restaurants. Strasser became a millionaire, though his business later failed. Sir Paul believed the most successful Hungarians had come to Australia first because they had stood to lose most under communism: that was why Hunga-

rians in Australia had done well.

There were, in fact, three waves of Hungarian immigration, the first of them just before World War II, the second in the late 1940s, and the third after the Hungarian uprising in 1956. Strasser and his wife Veronica arrived in 1948. Ervin Graf, who arrived in 1950, is another success story. He borrowed his fare for the voyage and was almost penniless when he got here. He had been a university lecturer in building structure in Budapest, but wrote down his occupation as 'bricklayer' on the forms provided by the Australian immigration authorities. Eventually he became managing director of Stocks and Holdings Ltd, home, office and shopping centre builders. Graf's start was in industrial construction (after a year spent as an architect) and his lucky stroke was in meeting Albert Scheinberg and his brother John Hammond (who had changed his name). Graf went into business with them. Scheinberg, himself an immigrant, had a superb flair for fostering talent and helping bankroll it.

Julius Charody, who became executive director of Silverton Industries, another prominent development company, had been manager of a Hungarian engineering company before starting life again in Australia – as a diesel mechanic. But eventually he got a job as manager of a bakery – whose directors included Albert Scheinberg, who later helped Charody to became personal assistant to Ervin Graf at Stocks and Holdings. Julius Charody's brother, John, became an associate director at Parkes Developments, Sir Paul Strasser's company ... Julius Charody became fond of telling the story of how he waited outside an Immigration Minister's office for three days in 1951 so he could get his name changed from Csaroday, because Australians did not know how to pronounce it (and if nobody knows your name, how can you ever become successful?). The Minister who chose Charody (pronounced 'Sha-road-ee') was Harold Holt, later a Liberal Prime Minister. The Charody family had been wealthy in Hungary, and had known Judy Cassab there (her name was originaly Kaszab), and five of his old classmates emigrated to Australia. Australia was a stroke of luck for Julius Charody – like a lot of other immigrants, he applied for migration permits to other countries as well (including the United States). Australia responded first.

A Hungarian immigrant who made millions in business once told me that in a way it was easier for a newcomer to make it to the top in Australia, because starting all over again provided the immigrant with a fresh perspective, 'like looking down on a town from a hillside'. Perception is a necessary ingredient of success: Sir Paul Strasser forecast more than a decade ago that Australia, 'the best democracy in the world,' as he put it, would face only one long-term problem, and that was poor industrial relations, with a consequent lack of productivity. John Kaldor, a very successful Hungarian fabric maker, said most immigrants from eastern Europe had no choice but to make good in Australia, because they could not go back, unlike the English, Dutch or Germans. Kaldor virtually echoed Strasser in the early 1970s when he said his adopted nation was 'a terrific country' but was in danger of becoming spoilt. 'You can be a lucky country for so long – after that you have to pull your finger out,' he said bluntly.

The Hungarians, whose country fought with Hitler's Germany and was overpowered by the Soviet Union, were a natural source of immigrants who were resourceful, talented, hard working and highly motivated. For many central and eastern European immigrants the decision to leave their homelands was a desperate one, and stories of Czechs, Romanians, Bulgarians, Poles and East Germans would serve as well. They had to be bold to jump the moat. After the Hungarian uprising Australia had to wait twelve years for another opportunity like that one, and it came in Czechoslovakia, in similar circumstances – and again, we got a wealth of talent. (Among those who came was Anton Cermak, who had represented Czechoslovakia as an Olympic rower and youth soccer player: his reputation in Australia is as a newspaper photographer of international renown.)

Two of my favourite immigrants are Austrian-born Mr Ernest Joseph Kirby and German-born Ann Plotke, both solicitors. He won the University of Vienna medal in law in 1933, the year the Nazis came to power in Germany, and was an assistant lecturer in political science before he became a prosecutor in criminal courts of German terrorists bent on destabilising Austria. He and his wife, Anne, left in 1938 as German soldiers marched into Vienna. He was among the first refugees here to volunteer for the Army, continued his law studies while on active service and wrote his examination papers on an ammunition box, graduating with honours in 1945 before the war with Japan was over.

While continuing his legal practice he became chairman of seventeen companies which were subsidiaries of corporations in Austria, Germany and Switzerland. His efforts for the advancement of international understanding, goodwill and peace have been acknowledged in Europe, and he holds distinguished awards from Austria and West Germany. He has assisted with everything from Rotary (which made him a Paul Harris fellow in 1981) to the establishment of the Australian Association of the Sovereign Military Order of Malta, the oldest Order of Chivalry in existence – it was founded during the crusades in AD 1099. It runs a hospital in Brisbane, looks after two hospices, and has bus services for the needy. Mrs Anne Kirby (they changed their surname) gained a Bachelor of Economics degree in Australia, and wrote several books on labour relations, a topic that is also close to Mr Kirby's heart. When I first met him he was seventy-two and still putting in a full day.

Ann Plotke was ten when she arrived in Australia in 1939 soon after war broke out in Europe. She took an honours degree in law and a master's in arts, and eventually became the first woman ever to sit on the Council of the Law Society of New South Wales, which is the solicitors' self-regulatory body in that State. She became a partner with Mr Kirby in his firm in 1959 and was still there after a quarter-century with him. Mr Kirby was Catholic, Miss Plotke Jewish – both left Europe for the same reason. In achievement and stand-

ing in the community they have set a marvellous example for others.

As Australia spread its immigration net, the diversity of the intake increased. In 1971-72, for example, only one nation – Britain – contributed more than 6 per cent of the intake of permanent and long-term arrivals, and that was just under 33 per cent. The United States, Yugoslavia and New Zealand were equal-second, on 6 per cent, and Greece and Italy each contributed just 3 per cent. Countless other nations were the homelands of 42 per cent of arrivals. Undoubtedly, the American figure rose because of dissent in the United States over the Vietnam War, and civil unrest in America. The American immigrants never came in really large numbers, and the flow did not continue, but those who did come were usually well-qualified in the workplace, including the professions and academe. Many preferred the pace of Australian life, which even in the larger cities was slower than in American cities. Most complaints seemed to centre on what was seen as the cultural aridity of Australian life and the passive attitudes of Australians to national and community problems. Some returned home. A relatively high porportion of those who have stayed earn their living as academics or business executives because their qualifications were so often held in high esteem.

The widening source of immigrants caused controversy and attracted criticism in the late 1960s and early 1970s when Lebanese and Turks arrived in visible force. Lebanon is a divided country – some commentators do not regard it as a nation, but rather as a collection of different peoples, separated by religion and civil turmoil. Turkish immigration touched Anglo-Saxon sensitivities because of lack of education in hygiene (some Turkish children in Melbourne were reported to know so little about it that they used the playgrounds as

Children at play on a Sydney beach, 1985. They are brothers, sisters and first cousins of English, Scots, Irish, German, and Indian stock.

Bavarian costume adds colour to this festive occasion. (Australian Picture Library)

lavatories). The Lebanese have been in Australia a long time, and they have a reputation as tough, unforgiving and unyielding businessmen. To some Australians of Anglo-Saxon stock, it seemed that the Turks must have a poorer prospect of adapting to Australia, let alone assimilating, because of their background of poverty in the homeland, and their attitudes, not least towards women.

The controversy arose when Australia seemed at last to be becoming aware of its long-ignored cultural deprivation, lack of attention to education, and lack of recognition of women's rights (all three of which received attention from the Whitlam Labor Government in 1973, 1974 and 1975). If pumping money into arts grants, schools and universities, and moving towards legislation to give women equal rights in the workforce was a sign of sophistication, why were all these ignorant peasants being admitted to the Great South Land? That was the way the argument went. Especially when there seemed a concerted effort by less scrupulous groups of them to grab everything they could from private and public welfare systems, taking handouts or going after workers' compensation for non-existent ailments such as the mysterious, difficult-to-diagnose 'Lebanese back'. This argument conveniently ignored the fact that for every Polish or Yugoslav steelworker who was only too eager to work double-shifts at Port Kembla, Newcastle or Whyalla for the chance of a lifetime, there was a Lebanese shopkeeper who would keep his doors open from 8.00 a.m. until 8.00 p.m., and work seven days a week, serving Anglo-Saxon Australians and others, just as the Italians and Greeks were eager to do. It has long been recognised in the United States that there are limits to assimilation in the first generation, the generation that gets off the ship or airliner, and limits to the degree of assimilation of the second generation too.

It may take up to thirty years before the arrival of the third generation, which is wholly indigenous; and the future that awaits them, and is provided by their parents, is often superior in many respects to that provided for children of much older Australian stock. Immigration programmes are building blocks for the future.

Thousands of South Americans arrived in Australia in the 1970s and 1980s, victims of oppression and lack of economic opportunity. Surely the most poignant story of all in the recent history of the Big Push has been that of Indo-China. The Vietnam War divided America, but it rent the entire social fabric of the land where it was fought, and the shock-waves of that era reverberated through neighbouring Kampuchea and Laos. The refugees who arrived on the northern shores of Australia in their leaky, unseaworthy boats fuelled yet another immigration controversy: if Australia welcomed them too openly, the trickle might become a stream, but to turn them away would invite international ostracism. The Vietnamese are a people of fierce tenacity, and Australians, whose news media had been saturated with reports of the war over a period of a decade, were fully aware of the deep wells of stamina in a people who had resisted the Chinese, French, and finally, the Americans. Assimilation, for them, would be difficult: some of those who came here might well have felt that the United States, and by extension its ally Australia, which fought in the war, had let them down. As refugees, it was natural that they clung together, and thus became a visible minority. Their ability to exist on next-to-nothing became apparent during that war: their ability to survive, and go about their daily tasks, is legendary.

I recall that once, during the mid-1970s when I was a newspaper feature writer, being assigned to cover the arrival in Sydney of a group of Vietnamese refugees who had, incredibly it seemed, sailed in their rotting, overloaded boat all the way to Australia. It was so overcrowded they slept on the open decks. There were no lavatories. A mechanic nursed the ancient, ailing engine. The water ran out, there was little food, and at least one of the elders was suffering from advanced tuberculosis, a disease that itself died out in Australia decades ago. A countryman journeyed all the way from Brisbane to Sydney on a motor scooter to greet them. Looking for leads for a colour article, I knocked on the door of a flat occupied by one of his friends, at 7.00 a.m. It was what the English term a bed-sitter, a single room in Darlinghurst with not much more than the bed, a small locker, and a gas stove from another age. Breakfast for the two occupants was noodles and tea. They worked in factories, dressed in tattered fatigues and shirts that were reminiscent of the early synthetics, which is to say nylons, and they were pale and weary. But they went out there, to the North Head quarantine station; at the barrier on the road that leads to all those spare, antiseptic-looking huts, they announced themselves, and lent their moral support.

It was one of the most touching scenes for me in a quarter-century of journalism during which I had 'covered' (in journalistic parlance) the activities and utterances of monarchs and presidents, prime ministers and all manner of the rich and mighty, decision-makers and society-shakers. A couple of scantily clad Vietnamese on that spluttering motor scooter, standing there in the chill on the road as the breeze swept in over the breakers through the Heads and the sun rose up on a new life for their compatriots; clean, free, a land of opportunity for people of even the most humble origins. The ancient Heads seemed as symbolic as the Statue of Liberty had been for millions before that morning. The Vietnamese visitors were not allowed past the barrier, but the Anglo-Saxon journalist got in. You have not seen despair, uncertainty,

controlled fear until you have looked into the face of the refugee who is surrounded by medicos and officials and cameras, his face, and the faces of his adult sons and daughters, and the dulled, half-knowing faces of their children. Safe at last – perhaps. If they got this far, they can survive anything, I thought, and they will beyond any doubt adapt to the wide brown land and its people.

I wrote my article and went home that night to my comfortable North Shore middle-class house, surrounded by trees and articles of prosperity, and felt not shame – nobody should feel that way, it would be illogical – but a deep sense that what I saw and heard that day was important, to me, and to this country, and that something should be learned from it. It was still the Lucky Country in the mid-1970s, but did we really know what we had? Did we care enough, about ourselves, and those less fortunate who only asked the chance to make a go of it? Would we work for our future, as they would work for theirs, those refugees? Would we learn from *them*?

I began to forget about that in the peak-hour traffic next morning, but the thought kept re-surfacing: elephants and ants, elephants and ants. The admirable ant. In the species *Homo sapiens*, the ant can become as big as an elephant, that distinguishes the species from all others, and is the *raison d'être* of our economic system. The ant is small, and immensely strong and resourceful: he is no flea, or rat, or parasite. He rests seldom, and is never soft.

Americans already knew this, well over a century ago. Lance Morrow, a senior writer for *Time* magazine, summed it up well in a fine piece of journalism which appeared in July 1985. America had offered a prize – its wealth, its freedom and promise – and then, Darwinian, had dared those strong enough and bold enough to make the leap. He wrote:

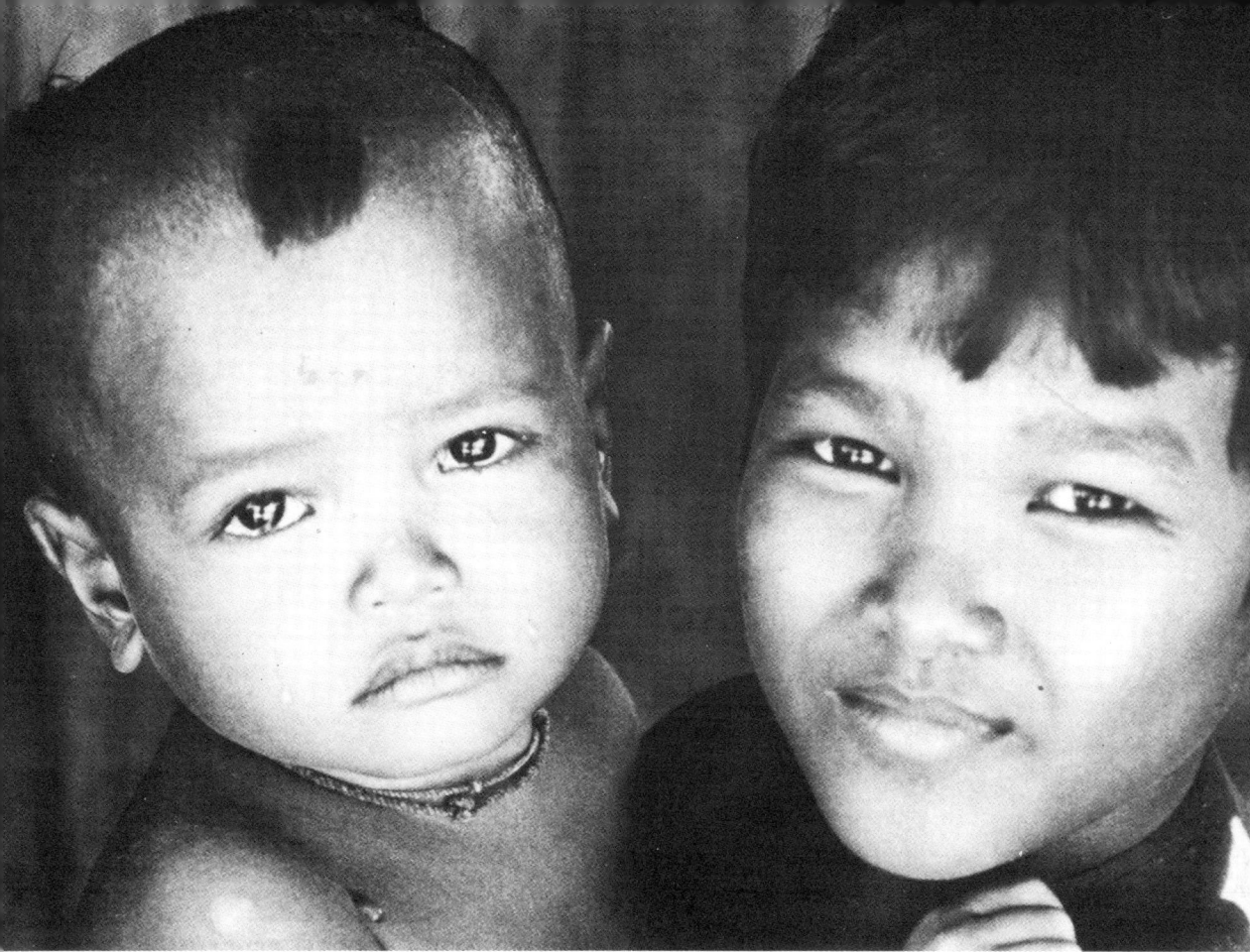

Refugee children from Kampuchea at the Ban Mai Rut camp in Thailand. The recent upheavals in Asia have created a new style of migrant. (Department of Immigration and Ethnic Affairs)

It was America, really, that got the prize: the enormous energy unleashed by the immigrant dislocations. Being utterly at risk, moving into a new and dangerous land, makes the immigrant alert and quick to learn. It livens reflexes, pumps adrenaline. The immigrant, uprooted, cannot take traditional sustenance from the permanence of home, of place, from an arrangement that existed before he existed and would persist after he died. Everyone is an immigrant in time, voyaging into the future. The immigrant who travels in both time and geographical space achieves a neat existential alertness. The dimensions of time and space collaborate. America, a place, becomes a time: the future.

What holds true for America holds for Australia, too.

CHAPTER 13

Multiculturalism: Myth or Reality?

'THE DECISION TO MIGRATE is, on the whole, taken by people with superior character to an average Australian: that's the nature of migrants as a worldwide phenomenon. It is always a major and difficult decision; striking roots in a new country is a very difficult and painful process.' – Professor Jerzy Zubrzycki, of the sociology department at the Australian National University, Canberra, who is chairman of the Australian Ethnic Affairs Council and a staunch proponent of multiculturalism.

It is difficult to come to grips with the debate on multiculturalism and the extent to which promotion of a multicultural Australia is desirable or not. The term did not come into use until relatively recently, during Al Grassby's term as Immigration Minister in the Whitlam

In the late 1940s a Canberra concert given by an all New Australian cast was an outstanding success. (Dept of Immigration and Ethnic Affairs)

years. Put simply, multiculturalism is the belief that Australia is, culturally, a pluralist society, that this should be recognised, and fostered to an extent by various means, including the use of government funds. As an example of what multiculturalism means to some people, proponents of it have claimed that a truly multicultural society would make provision for the use of all languages in everyday affairs, including official transactions. The preservation of cultural links with the Old Country, including the use of the native language, is seen as valuable to the immigrant and his children, while the diversity of cultures would strengthen and enrich Australia. Thoughtful advocates of multiculturalism have been careful to frame suggested policies that recognise and assist minority cultures within the Australian community while stressing that this should not be at the expense of the core culture... teaching of minority languages should not be at the expense of English, and so on.

The debate on multiculturalism – and it is fair to say the topic has not excited the nation, nor enlivened many dinner parties – has thrown up some strong advocates, including the voluble and compassionate Mr Grassby, and some strong opponents, including Professor Frank Knopfelmacher, who came to public prominence in Australian intellectual affairs two decades ago as a controversial anti-communist speaker and writer. Mr Grassby is an amusing debunker of myths and superstitions who, it might be said, can get Australians to re-examine their attitudes after they have stopped laughing about them, and that is valuable. Professor Zubrzycki is, broadly speaking, in the Grassby camp, and Professor Lauchlan Chipman, whose skills are in philosophy (at Wollongong University) and jurisprudence (Sydney University) has spoken against multiculturalism, but in milder tones than Professor Knopfelmacher.

Knopfelmacher, uncompromisingly anti-multiculturist, says bluntly that anglomorph societies are superior to all others that exist (from his own political and moral standpoint) and that the assimilation of ethnics in anglomorph Australia 'has been one of our success stories'. Noting that early this decade about 3.1 million Australians (21-22 per cent of the population) were ethnic, or non-anglomorph Australians, he says the future of stable anglomorphy in Australia depends largely on the total integration, without significant residual disprivilege, of the second-generation ethnics. Non-anglomorphs should have 'absolutely open access' to all levels of Australian society 'without the gratuitous benefit of patronising sermons', he said.

In Canberra, in 1954, two prefects elected at Canberra High School were from ethnic backgrounds: Miss Bondien van Wely from Holland and Uldis Jekabs Sterns from Latvia. (Department of Immigration and Ethnic Affairs)

In the 1960s, assistance in teaching migrants came from a variety of sources. Here the Puerto Rican born wife of a visiting United States Air Force NCO teaches some newly arrived Spanish migrant children. (Department of Immigration and Ethnic Affairs)

Just in case anybody should be in any doubt about what he is driving at, Knopfelmacher says the aim should be to assimilate non-anglomorphs into the prevailing culture, which is, historically, English. 'The objective is not to fuel a melting pot brewing a nondescript Australian of the future, but to dissolve and transform non-anglomorph kinship lines in such a way that their issue will be anglomorph,' he said.

Major alterations in the balance of power, the growing economic downturn in the world, and even a local disaster (for example, a new regime hostile to us in Indonesia) may, he says, confront us with dangerous problems beyond our power to tackle or to evade. 'Yet, whatever happens externally, it is better to face it, like the Poles, as a culturally unified nation, capable also of drawing on the resources of the greatest of modern civilisations of which we are a part, the fount and origin of which is in the British Isles, rather than as a banana republic of squabbling and mutually resentful expatriated mini-cultures, each with its own separate bunch of ethnic (or, conversely, Anglo-racist) führers, and widely open to internal subversion.'

With all these 'professional' viewpoints, it is difficult to determine where this leaves the Australian public. The debate erupts, if that is the word for it, only occasionally. It is a separate issue from the much more volatile national debate on Asian immigration and the extent to which the Asian intake should be encouraged or cut. When Chifley's Cabinet was nervously considering in late 1946 and early 1947 whether Australia should take large numbers of displaced persons (opponents of the policy thought DPs presented the image of broken races) policies aimed at multiculturalism instead of total assimilation would have been considered lunatic. Just as, until the 1970s, ethnic radio and television stations would have been considered divisive and economically wasteful. Few people believe that now (besides, the world news programme on SBS TV, formerly known as Channel 0/28, is one of the best in the world, and that channel's motion picture presentations have moistened the wasteland of Australian television, dominated as it so often is by productions that are arid and unappetising).

The pro-multicultural lobby claims there is a need for social cohesion, cultural identity and equality of opportunity and access. The demand for social cohesion limits the extent to which groups should develop their separate identities in isolation from the rest of the Australian community, and a truly cohesive society can be achieved only through a commitment to certain common ideals by all members of society, irrespective of their backgrounds.

Multiculturalism means different things to different people. 'Hard' multiculturalism includes the notion that tribal Aborigines should perhaps on some matters be able to operate with their own traditional concept of what is legal and what is not – in other words, the established, British-derived concepts of law and justice would not necessarily in all respects apply to them. As Professor Chipman has pointed out, if that concept is allowed to flourish, why not include all ethnic groups? 'Are we to say that sexism and honour killing are all right if you are a Calabrian but not if you are Welsh?' he asks. 'The answer will be no...'.

Polyethnic Australia has only partially resolved the problems and tensions sadly associated with mixed communities, he believes. 'However, the new hard multiculturalism, which is particularly influencing State educational administrations, is of doubtful theoretical validity, is confused and confusing in its application, is backward looking, and could well be itself a source of new tensions as it rides in to influence through denigration and de-legitimation what there is of a "mainstream" Australian culture.'

An obsession among a portion of the public with roots and origins has led some critics to describe multiculturalism as dangerous, and the 'group pluralism' which is at the root of hard multiculturalism as worrying, because it lumps people involuntarily into groups, rather than treating them as individuals.

On balance, it is hard not to side with those who question the more assertive proposals designed to promote multiculturalism. That there should be laws to prevent discrimination on the grounds of race, religion or culture is easy enough to understand. That immigrants from non-English-speaking countries will have a tougher time adapting to Australia, all other things being equal, than English-speaking immigrants, at least in the early years, is apparent. The Australian Council on Population and Ethnic Affairs says it is established beyond doubt that people lacking fluent English or coming from a non-English-speaking background are handicapped and cannot compete on an equal footing in Australian society. The Council, which is pro-multiculturalism, also says that the preservation of cultural heritages entails the retention of minority languages, though it notes that the teaching of minority languages should not be at the expense of English. 'Clearly, multiculturalism will not work unless there is a government commitment to it, and a set of government policies and programmes to give effect to that commitment,' the Council says in its 1982 policy discussion paper, *Multiculturalism For All Australians*, sub-titled *Our Developing Nationhood*. The paper was prepared for the Minister for Immigration, at that time Mr Ian Macphee (Liberal, Victoria). The paper was presented to the Minister by Professor Zubrzycki, and says that the government approach can range from: a *laissez-faire* tolerance of initiatives by individuals and groups; to the use of moral persuasion on society, exhorting people to adopt views and follow practices consistent with multiculturalism; to the allocation of public resources to provide services and facilities that enhance the development of a multicultural society; and finally to the use of coercive or regulatory powers to require certain forms of behaviour or to prohibit others. It also notes that in practice, responsibility for multiculturalism will fall upon the individual members of society.

Well, given the realities of human nature and the prevailing economic climate, it is not easy to imagine the broad mass of native-born Australians support-

European festivals in Australia: German born revellers at a 1970s Oktoberfest *in Canberra. (Department of Immigration and Ethnic Affairs)*

Harold Holt, Minister for Immigration in one of the Menzies Governments, poses with migrant children.

ing the use of more than token amounts of taxpayers' money to promote multiculturalism. Use of taxes for English classes for immigrants makes sense, just as teaching foreign languages does if it is part of a balanced curriculum. The public feeling is likely to be that if an immigrant suffers because of lack of English, then the sooner he learns to speak it the better for him and everybody else; he can scarcely expect to relate to the mainstream culture unless he is at least willing to undertake that much. If he does not wish to do that (and there are such immigrants who do not make the effort) then nobody except those who rely on communication with him, such as his foreman, accountant, his children's school teacher, and so on, need quibble, provided the numbers of such folk do not become a community problem. In other words, it is up to him.

There has been a great move in recent years away from the philosophy that throwing money at problems (particularly taxpayers' money) is a panacea, and the motive for that shift in opinion should be clearly understood. It is this: if there is not enough money in the pot to go around for all the causes that special-interest groups espouse (and there never is enough) then governments must decide how to apportion what money they have, and borrow the rest. But they cannot go on borrowing indefinitely without putting back into the pot (at least that is the concern of Western economists of the past decade).

To argue on a different plane, if the immigrant has, on the whole, a superior character to the average Australian, as Professor Zubrzycki says (and he may well be correct) then the immigrant may well be capable of adapting to our society sufficiently to ensure a productive and happy existence here. It will be difficult, but it will become easier as he progresses with the task. He will simultaneously no doubt enjoy the comforts of his original culture through contact with people who came from his native land. He can, in other words, have the best of both worlds: the decision is up to him – why not leave it to him to decide?

While we are on this issue: there have been British immigrants who have had great difficulty adapting, chiefly because their native land, while complementary to Australia, was so different, or they found Australians so different from the people they had known. There is surely as much difference between an Earl living in his castle in Hampshire and a toolmaker living in Wigan, Lancashire, as there is between an Aussie ocker in Brunswick and an Italian stonemason stepping off the airliner from Naples. The Earl and the toolmaker will never meet: ten years from now, the ocker and the stonemason, if neighbours, are likely to be sharing the same barbecue lunch in one another's backyards. We should not get excited about these differences or similarities: live and let live; and if it is government policy to encourage multiculturalism, let the government leave it at that – encouragement. If a government sees the need, it may also encourage Australians of Anglo-Celtic stock to understand and learn from peoples of other stock; about their cultures, apprehensions, perceptions. We do not need to encourage 'one hundred per cent Australianism' (the term has never existed, to my knowledge) in the way that Theodore Roosevelt, eighty years ago, exhorted his people to be 'one hundred per cent Americans'.

Tania Verstak, a White Russian by birth, elected Miss Australia in 1961.

We have matured since then, as have the Americans. But, similarly, is there really any need to foster hyphenated Australianism? We acknowledge and accept it in the first generation, we cannot do otherwise. We may tolerate it in the second and succeeding generations, provided we are always confident that the core culture is secure. Certainly we should not fear it. The culture, or cultures, of any country are what its people or peoples want that culture to be. We are the Australian peoples, but if immigration were brought to a halt tomorrow, in a generation or so from now, would Australia be multicultural, or one culture with many facets drawn from different countries? The latter, I think, is the more logical forecast.

Immigration will not halt tomorrow, we should all be grateful for that. As suspicion and mistrust of 'foreign' immigrants has diminished in recent decades, at least in relation to Continental Europeans, so we may expect that the chances of more or less complete tolerance of all immigrant peoples will increase. Thus, the need for assertive multicultural policies. beyond laws relating to discrimination, will diminish too.

That brings us, once more, to the Asians. The Asian component of immigration increased from 29.4 per cent in 1978-79 to 36.3 per cent in 1983-84, and so is almost double the intake from Britain and Ireland, which was 19.5 per cent in 1983-84 (Continental Europe rep-resented 15.5 per cent). These figures were the basis of a controversy, at the head of which was the Melbourne histo-rian, Professor Geoffrey Blainey. To any-body with a phobia about Asians, the Asian intake is cause for concern: those who see Asians as desirable will take the view that they will be accepted, just as Continental Europeans, who were at first a cause of suspicion, are now thoroughly accepted. San Francisco, a city similar to

Nestor San Jose and his family were among the first 100 Filipino skilled tradesmen to arrive in 1974 by assisted passage.

Colourful Minister for Immigration in the first Whitlam Labor Government and later Minister for Community Relations, Al Grassby at the Griffith Wine Festival in 1973. He was greeted in 20 different languages by members of his electorate. (Department of Immigration and Ethnic Affairs)

Sydney in style, has counted 22 per cent of its population as Asian. Blacks and Hispanics combined slightly outnumber the city's Asians. Nobody has seriously suggested that there is a race imbalance.

While we are at it, it is worth recalling that only 27 per cent of Americans are of British stock, 21 per cent are of German stock, and 17 per cent are of Irish stock. Almost 10 per cent are black. There are 13 million Hispanics and 3.4 million Asian newcomers. As Theodore H. White has noted, the United States has 'the texture of a nation unlike any before and unlike America even half a century ago'. Nobody seems too upset by the texture. And race relations have improved remarkably in the United States in the past two decades. It will be for Australia to welcome Asians, and ensure that we make them feel at home. They might be conspicuous in Chippendale or Canley Vale, but overall their numbers are small.

The recent debate over the Asian intake was gratifying in some respects, in spite of the heat it generated and the dark overtones of racism that attended it. The Minister for Immigration and Ethnic Affairs in 1984, Mr Stewart West, defended his Government's policies calmly and logically. He went on television frequently to state his case, and ended up a clear winner in the debate. By early 1985 the issue seemed to have been defused, giving Australians who oppose the present scale of Asian immigration an opportunity to reconsider their views. It was also notable that the Federal Opposition did not seek to make the issue a major one in the 1984 Federal election, which indicates that either the Opposition considered the issue did not have sufficient legs to win enough extra votes, or that there were more important items on the national agenda.

CHAPTER 14

The First Australians Now

THE DEBATE OVER MULTICULTURALISM is an abstract one, difficult to grasp for the average Anglo-Saxon Australian, who will no doubt continue to regard multiculturalism as pasta and vino on a lunch table on Sunday with loads of Italian relatives sitting around it, or a dish of lamb with Greeks in attendance, and so on ... The debate over the position of the original Australians – and especially over land rights – is much livelier. For one thing, land is tangible, and its value depends on many factors, including the minerals that lie beneath its surface. The arguments are intensified by emotional value judgments. The ocker-racist view has always been that the Aborigine was inferior to the white, did not make use of the land and thus did not deserve to hold

A protest march over Aboriginal land rights in Brisbane. The issue is hotly contended on both sides of the debate. (John Fairfax & Sons Ltd)

on to it after 1788: therefore, why should land be returned to the black now, and why should the black gain from valuable land with minimal or no effort, while the white has to slave over a lathe for wages? There are now a few well-educated white Australians who make the point, and they are no longer saying it behind their hands, that Australian blacks aren't owed anything except equal rights – that is, the right to public schools, public health facilities, and jobs for which they are qualified. Some will say that there are whites who have suffered in the past because they lost their land or livelihood to others who were bigger or stronger or smarter. There are, of course, large-scale examples of this right throughout history: the Romans pushed the Celts westward in Britain, the Angles, Saxons, Jutes, Danes and Normans barged in much later, and finally the Normans had their way. (And in some respects, they still hold sway.) It is surely not a mere academic

The meaning of these symbols, carved so deliberately, is not known. The photographer did not ask the Aborigines what they were doing or why. This lack of curiosity is typical of early twentieth century white Australia.

point, however, that each of these invasions had positive benefits for the country as a whole, and those who were initially disadvantaged reaped some benefit, or at least their descendants did. Britain too is a nation of immigrants.

But what of the lot of the Aborigines? The Celt in England or Ireland had his back to the wall from the time invaders shook his lifestyle and threatened his livelihood, but he co-existed with them, and much later his descendants could always sail over the seas to rich, virgin lands and occupy them, without much heed of the rights of the inhabitants, who often as not happened to have red skins.

Lebanese folk dancers perform with the Sydney Opera House as an appropriate backdrop and symbol of Australian multiculturalism. (Australian Picture Library)

The blessing of the fleet in process as part of the Carnivale '84 celebrations in Sydney. (Australian Picture Library)

In the United States, whites pushed the reds westward to land that, then, was least desirable in white eyes, and broke every treaty made for the security of reds. However, there were in the east reds who farmed and even had black slaves. So we could go round in circles trying to make sense out of this sort of analysis, and come up with a simple conclusion; the weak yield to the strong. But that would ignore at least two points: the Aboriginal race was not demonstrably better off as a result of white occupation, and in many respects the complete reverse was the case; and whatever theories of strong versus weak or survival of the fittest might be advanced in support of the way in which Western nations have developed and prospered, this is a nation which holds itself out as being civilised and humane. It is 1988, not 1938 or 1888.

The first comprehensive statistical report ever published on Aborigines was released in May 1985. It showed that proportionally, Aborigines are sicker and have poorer access to health care, poorer education in terms of achievements and opportunities, shorter life expectancies,

In this early 1970s photograph it is obvious that the powers-that-be take a dim view of land rights protests and fear violent outbursts. The presence of children bearing banners argues that their parents at least contemplate a peaceful protest. (John Fairfax & Sons Ltd)

more convictions at law and more gaol terms than other Australians. The report, by the Federal Department of Aboriginal Affairs, was very disturbing. Despite the fact that Federal Aboriginal-assistance programmes now amount to about $2500 per capita, life expectancy is a full 20 years lower than for whites, infant mortality is running at two-and-a-half times the rate for whites, unemployment is six times the rate for whites, and the proportion of blacks still in school after the age of 15 is one-sixth that of white pupils. (Given the white population's low regard for education, mentioned earlier, this is an appalling statistic – 95 per cent of black children have left school by the age of 15, which means that the vast majority are virtually condemned to manual or semi-skilled office labour.) Blacks go to prison 10 times more often than whites do. The average income of black families is less than one third that of white families. Federal Government assistance has more than doubled since 1982-83. What has assistance achieved? What still needs to be done? Can the plight of the Aborigines be solved with cash? If not, how can it be solved?

It is only in the past decade that the view has taken root in the minds of ordinary white Australians that perhaps the blacks are owed something. The basic problem that the black faces in trying to exist or co-exist with whites was largely ignored by the white multitude until recently. White Australians are typically conservative, believing that God looks after those who look after themselves and that you get out of anything what you put into it – or ought to get it – but that if all else fails, the government should look after the unfortunate and the weak. It is undeniable that in the past many blacks have lacked the will, means and expertise to join or even fully co-exist with whites in everyday life, and certainly they were never truly invited to try. Earlier generations of blacks were deprived of their land and subjugated; their numbers steadily dwindled because of the diseases they contracted, and they were shot and

An Aborigine arrested following disturbances in Sydney's Redfern area. (John Fairfax & Sons Ltd)

A demonstration showing Aboriginal resentment for land and civil rights violations by the white community. (John Fairfax & Sons Ltd)

poisoned by white men (though the extent of this genocide is now being questioned in some quarters). The net result has been an intense loss of pride and cultural awareness. There has been a recognition among sections of the white population of the intense relationship that blacks had with the land, of the fact that their culture had been developed, was intricate and subtle in its own way and thus was worthy of being accepted by whites as a culture. Some whites feel a sense of shame about collective neglect and abuse of the Aborigines; some feel that no existing generation can be held accountable for what happened in previous generations; and some feel that whether or not the Aborigine can, or should be invited to, assimilate, he is entitled to something, either in recompense or to help sustain him for the future. Just what he is entitled to is, of course, the subject of the hottest debates. Arguments about separatism aside, few whites will become aroused if blacks decide they

want a larger area of unproductive land in, say, the Great Sandy Desert. Banning a visiting camera crew from Ayers Rock may be a bit uppity, but the real question is the rights of blacks to land that is valuable to whites, and what portion of the proceeds from Aboriginal land exploited by whites should be given to the blacks (and in what way, and for what ends).

As matters stood after the re-election of the Hawke Government in December 1984, the Federal Government's policy, so far as it related to the mining industry, boiled down to three essentials. These were: the protection of Aboriginal sites; Aboriginal access to mining royalty equivalents; and Aboriginal control in relation to mining on Aboriginal land.

It has been accepted by Federal governments of both Liberal-National and Labor complexions that to deny Aborigines the right to prevent mining on their land was to deny the reality of land rights, but the Federal Government appeared to hedge this commitment

A graphic demonstration of the Aboriginal desire for land rights. (John Fairfax & Sons Ltd)

when it proposed an arbitration system to handle Aboriginal complaints about mining proposals. By mid-1985 the land rights picture was very blurred, and becoming hazier by the month. New South Wales and South Australia enacted land rights legislation as did the Northern Territory. Significantly, in Queensland and Western Australia, rural and mining States, there is great dispute about land rights. South Australia handed over 72 000 square kilometres of barren land on the edge of the Great Victoria Desert to the Pitjantjatjara tribe in late 1984, which was a triumph of sorts for ancestral rights. But in Western Australia major groups in the mining and petroleum industries were in direct conflict with the land aspirations of the Aborigines. Forty per cent of Western Australia's total surface was eligible for land rights claims under the Western Australian Government's land rights proposals.

The Burke Labor Government of Western Australia opposed the veto power that the Federal Labor Government had proposed to give to Aborigines in relation to all mining ventures on this land, and opposed provision of royalties as well. Even so, the WA Legislative Council (Upper House) rejected the legislation. This appeared to open the way for overriding Federal legislation, but that was opposed by black leaders in New South Wales, South Australia and the Northern Territory, who regarded their State and territorial laws as more to their liking.

Instead of the introduction of land rights bringing blacks and whites together, the issue seemed to be widening the gap between them. The Western Australian Government, in introducing its legislation, had sought to encourage mining companies, not deter them. A Perth lawyer appointed by the Government to investigate the situation had concluded that there was no compelling economic reason why Aboriginal communities should not have control over mining and petroleum activity on Aboriginal land. After the Legislative Council blocked the legislation, Sir Charles Court, the former Premier and elder statesman, pronounced: 'It is now time we brought the land rights nightmare to an end. There is neither personal advancement nor moral justification for imposing on Australia such festering racial inequality.'

On top of all this, relations had soured between the Federal Minister for Aboriginal Affairs, Mr Clyde Holding, and sections of the mining industry that he accused of using grossly distorted and exaggerated arguments against giving Aborigines some control over mining. At the same time, Aboriginal leaders from all over Australia met near Canberra and rejected out of hand the Government's

Aborigines gather on a street corner. Increased unemployment in the 1980s is probably partly to blame for the unrest that exists in many sections of the Aboriginal community. (John Fairfax & Sons Ltd)

land rights bill. The Australian Democrats were refusing to vote for any bill that did not have the endorsement of black groups, and Western Australian ministers opposed a national bill, so it looked as if federal legislation would be relegated to the backburner, there to simmer for who-knew-how-long?

Proposals for uniform national land rights legislation did languish thereafter. During the Western Australian election campaign in early 1986 the Federal Government agreed not to impose land rights legislation. Subsequently, the Federal Government agreed to a Western Australian plan to grant 99-year leases to Aborigines, but this fell short of land rights. Even Aborigines in Queensland had deeds of grants in trust to reserves that the Queensland Government had given them. Only in Tasmania were there no land rights whatsoever.

In the one hundred and ninety-ninth year of white settlement there were factors working to sharpen attention on Aborigines' grievances. One was a threat by activists to boycott, or even to disrupt, Bicentennial celebrations, in an attempt to embarrass white leaders and draw international attention to Aboriginal demands. Another factor was the disturbing number of Aboriginal deaths in gaol, some of which occurred within hours of incarceration. Officially, there have been 44 deaths in seven years, including at least 14 in the first eight months of 1987. However, the Committee to Defend Black Rights gives a figure of 90 deaths since 1980. Aboriginal leaders now pressed for a treaty, written into the Constitution, to incorporate Aboriginal sovereignty and subsuming the demand for land rights. What 'sovereignty' would entail was not clear, but prior ownership of the land seemed high on the list of definitions, which could imply not only land rights, but compensation for loss of land. Sovereignty could also include cultural rights, recognition of Aboriginal custom-

ary law, and even self-government (meaning perhaps even a nation within a nation).

The Federal Government offered instead a 'compact' and revived the issue of national land rights. It also acknowledged that the Australian community had an obligation to Aborigines, and it called for an understanding 'that in two hundred years of European settlement there have been many grave injustices done'.

That still leaves the question of the gulf between whites and blacks, how it can be overcome if it can be overcome, or whether an attempt ought to be made to overcome it. In terms of health and hygiene, certainly the effort has to be made. The same applies to job opportunities, schooling, and so on. It is, in some respects, a huge gulf, and wherever it is apparent, mutual resentment between blacks and whites is never far beneath the surface. The evidence is there, all the way from Redfern, the home of many Sydney blacks, to the Gulf of Carpentaria. There are still hotels in Australian cities and towns where it is unwise for white drinkers to tread, and many, many more where blacks are not welcome. Walk down Eveleigh Street, Redfern, and you can feel the tension and resentment. Violence has erupted sporadically in towns such as Moree, north-western New South Wales. Getting to the core of complaints is not always easy, and objectivity and calm, rational discussion are very often casualties of the situation.

Overcrowding of housing – which as often as not has been built with public funds – and inattention to basic rules of hygiene upsets white notions of correct form. There have been cases of social workers who simply could not convince black mothers of the necessity for their young children to clean their teeth. Things are changing, but only slowly. In remote mining areas whites have been known to flare with anger at the sight of a black driving down a dusty access road in a late-model second-hand car – the white worker, cut off from the mainstream of civilisation, is apt to resent the black who shares royalty or other payments from mining ventures, or derives benefits from government-funded housing projects, for example. The black, with ready access to cash, does not always stop to question the value of a vehicle he is being offered to purchase, and may pay thousands of dollars more than it is worth – so the price of all second-hand vehicles goes up, the white says. Then the black drives it around until it breaks down, and leaves it there. Things are changing, but not quickly enough.

Perhaps the solution lies in persistence, in holding out more of the white man's knowledge to the black, and perhaps in quietly insisting that, where necessary in individual cases, he make more effort to comprehend the white man's ways and to adopt those that make sense. It will take time. After two thousand generations, Australian Aborigines may claim that they are masters of time and change, but on an entirely different scale from that which whites are used to. The Aborigines are resilient, they have endured. The white man has not always been willing to learn from the black, and to his detriment and sometimes peril, has ignored the black man's history.

This is a nation whose immigrants have brought with them diverse histories and cultures. From 1788 the Anglo-Saxon culture dominated. In the years that followed the racial and cultural mix gradually broadened. It was not until the end of World War II that a concerted drive to populate Australia brought a wave of European migration and the dominance of the Anglo-Saxon culture was weakened. When these later migrants succeeded beyond all expectation the personal respect they won began to be extended to their cultures. Australian culture broadened. But the plight of the Aborigines, from that boarder perspective, shows that as a civilized nation we still have some way to go.

Aboriginal leaders complained that the Hawke Government lost its appetite for land rights in its first term in office. The Hawke Government responded that by 1988 Aborigines were sitting on 12.5 per cent of the continent excluding what State governments had handed over in the previous 20 years, and that more land had been given back to the Aborigines than to any minority indigenous people in the world.

Labor did 'water down' its land rights policies. When Aboriginal leaders demanded a treaty from the leaders of the descendants of the people who had occupied their continent, they were offered a compact instead. In 1988 black leaders made it plain that they regarded the accumulation of great wealth as their next step. At the same time, white leaders began to acknowledge sins and omissions more forcibly. The Federal Minister for Aboriginal Affairs, Mr Gerry Hand, said that 'We [the whites] have nearly wiped the Aboriginal people out ... [they are] some of the worst-off people in the world ...' and he proceeded to boycott the celebrations of the Bicentennial of white settlement. Prime Minister Hawke referred to the 'wrongs and crimes of the past'.

The new breed of Aboriginal leaders included people who were more reflective about the past, with a greater readiness to examine, unemotionally, the reasons for the vast gap in living standards between blacks and whites. But there were others who were more aggressive than leaders in previous decades, and whose demands implied that it was for whites to solve all problems relating to blacks. The debate continued, but with both sides showing more willingness to examine the core problems than had been the case in the past.

CHAPTER 15

Two Hundred Years After White Settlement

The four decades that followed World War II constitute a period as vital and as important as any in Australian history. The nation loosened its bond with Britain, moved closer to the United States in foreign policy, defence and lifestyle including popular culture, fostered immigration (especially non-British immigration) and enjoyed increased prosperity. There was a gradual dilution of some of the old insular attitudes, or at least a deep questioning of them, along with acknowledgement of and curiosity about less admirable Australian traits: among them, the so-called cultural cringe; them-and-us attitudes that begged the question of whether Australia was really a classless society; the great-level-

Part of the Interscan Microwave Handling System at testing stage. High-technology inventions such as this have enormous potential for earning much-needed export dollars. (Courtesy CSIRO, Department of Radiophysics.)

ler instinct and its handmaiden the Tall Poppy Syndrome. Each of these traits reflected the nation's origins; each betrayed a fear of inferiority, or of being seen as inferior to other, older white societies. And, for each, there was no longer any excuse: only explanations that should rightfully be used to point the way to a different future. These traits in turn were seen by sociologists and opinion-moulders as feeding a herd instinct, the instinct to level that ultimately gave primacy to the mood of the mob rather than fostering a more innovative, questing, questioning society that rewarded excellence and effort and shunned anti-intellectualism.

It is important to take stock of this after two hundred years of white settlement, and if the Bicentenary provided nothing else it was that it served its purpose in provoking a required measure of national reflection and reassessment of who Australians are, where the nation stands and, most important of all, where it needs to go. The late 1940s brought the beginnings of large-scale immigration, and that continues. In the cosseted 1950s Australia still rode on the sheep's back, still regarded England as the mother country, and relied for its international reputation on its sportsmen and sportswomen, and on its agricultural exports. Material affluence rolled over the land in the 1960s, when United States' investment surpassed Britain's, Japan's importance as a trading partner became unarguable and American entertainment and lifestyle predominated. Australia still had a marked tendency, however, to revert to old stereotypes in its thinking, particularly during crises such as the Vietnam War. Patriotism, reverence for the Anzacs (and thus any Australian soldier fighting on foreign soil) blinded Australians to the realities of the conflict that led to a profound political and social upheaval throughout Indo-China. By 1965 it was apparent to objective minds that the United States was very unlikely to succeed in Vietnam: as a sage succinctly put it: 'Doubling the effort to square the error'. Yet the Australian news media could not bring themselves to report the war as a modern Asian phenomenon, rather than through field glasses that had been trained on Gallipoli, Pozières, El Alamein and Kokoda Trail. American public sentiment swung against US participation, wrecking President Lyndon Baines Johnson's aspirations for re-election and causing a re-evaluation of national attitudes that continued for a decade or more. For many Australians, however, the war remained one that American forces had merely fought the wrong way or with insufficient force. They really meant that it was intolerable that the grandsons of Anzacs could be losers (any more than the Anzacs were). Every nation depends on myths, and they are valuable, but they can be deceiving.

In the post-1945 decades a flowering brought Australian painters, writers and other artists to international attention. Yet none of them achieved anything like the transitory fame overseas of Germaine Greer, one of the architects of modern feminism. Her work, *The Female Eunich*, was studied and praised and its tenets adopted in Britain, America and elsewhere while Australians still affected not to hear what they, and so many peoples, needed to hear most. The ocker tinge of beer-bellies, thongs and stubbies was difficult to eradicate; when that did begin to occur, some of the credit would go to the hilarious pop culture mockery of Barry Humphries and Paul Hogan, both of whom achieved international reputations, as did several Australian film-makers in the 1970s and 1980s.

Nonetheless, after two hundred years of white settlement far from Europe and America, the culture was still derivative. Harry Messel, an immigrant who became Professor of Physics at Sydney University, was referring to more than the education debate when he wrote, in August 1987, that Australia had an 'unerring way of following the bad from overseas and disregarding the good'. An examination of the nation's health and directions was underway, however. It was being forced on Australians because of a sharp reversal, in the 1980s, of the country's economic fortunes.

When wealth from extractive industries replaced agricultural products as the principal export earner Australians rejoiced, once again, in their good fortune to be born in, or to select or be brought to, the Lucky Country. There was nothing fragile about the industries that underpinned the nation's wealth. Egalitarianism ensured that a sufficient portion of that wealth would permeate the nation, even though relatively few Australians were actually directly involved in the production of that wealth. In 1961 the Menzies Government came within a few hundred votes of losing office because unemployment had reached two per cent. (A quarter of a century later unemployment would be eight per cent, but the government of the day would increase its majority in the House of Representatives in part because the public perception of political issues had grown infinitely more complex since 1961.) Liberal-Country Party national coalitions in the 1960s could rely on a healthy economy to balance federal budgets and soak up unemployment; manufacturing industries could be sheltered behind high tariff walls. An Australian dollar purchased $1.20 worth of American goods and services.

In 1987, eight indices affecting Australia were in decline. The factors were the national balance of payments deficit; the Federal Budget deficit; inflation (at two to three times that of our major trading partners); high interest rates; low prices overseas for our principal export commodities; high unemployment; uncompetitive wage rates; and, finally, a drastic devaluation of the Australian dollar ($1 purchased approximately 70c worth of American goods and services).

On Wednesday, 14 May 1986, just twenty months before the Bicentennial year, the Federal Treasurer, Mr Paul Keating, sounded alarm bells that rang all over the nation. The Australian trade deficit for the previous month had risen to $1.48 billion, threatening a total deficit for the 1985–86 financial year of $14 billion, or about $1000 a year for each man, woman and child. The Treasurer warned that if the Government failed to deal successfully with this worst balance of payments problem since the Great Depression of the 1930s, then 'Australia is basically done for; we will just end up being a third-rate economy.' If Australia was so undisciplined, so disinterested in its salvation and its economic well-being that it did not deal with these fundamental problems, he said, 'then you have gone: you are a banana republic'.

In the past, valuable export revenue was earned from agricultural products like wheat. (Courtesy Grain Handling Authority of NSW)

The official figures showed that Australia was digging itself an abyss of debt. The Federal Budget deficit had grown alarmingly, too: and 40 per cent of gross domestic product was being expended by the public sector, meaning governments (the proportion had risen over the years, just as taxes had risen drastically; but government expenditure had outraced all government receipts).

Nor did Australia's ills stop there. Other nations had endured the pain of wage restraint and national belt-tightening to bring down inflation, notably the United States, Japan and West Germany. Australians had deferred the tough decisions: the trade union movement had actually welcomed inflation as a cheap thrill because it made wage demands seem more logical. Neither of the major political groupings had addressed this problem adequately, and this in turn implied a gradual decline in competitiveness internationally, as well as signalling to our trading partners a weakness of national will. The devaluation of the Australian dollar once it was allowed to 'float' in international money markets increased the price of imports, and this should have helped the balance of payments by cutting imports and encouraging Australians to buy more local products. But by now local manufacturing was so uncompetitive that Australians continued to foot the bill for imports. Another dark sign; only half of the manufactured imports had competitors produced locally.

All these factors were known. The question was whether the public would understand or accept them as a precursor to remedial action. In the midst of the growing struggle of politicians of varying ideological persuasions to come to grips with the need to formulate remedies that would be acceptable to the electorate, it became obvious that for any prescription for economic ills to provide a cure there would have to be a very considerable change in some basic Australian attitudes; or rather, above and beyond that, in the attitudes of basic Australian power groups. If this reasoning was correct, then it followed that the stronger elements and power-brokers of the trade union movement were not covering themselves in glory. They continued to insist on their right to influence, or even govern, national policy on vital national issues, while refusing to accept economic reality. In the late 1980s Australia's mightiest export industry — coal — was threatened by declining profits and economic suicide. Even as the realities became apparent, trade unions baulked at ending restrictive work practices, successfully negotiated unrealistic wage increases, and then threatened coast-to-coast industrial action, which further impinged on the national reputation for ability to supply dwindling export markets on time, at cost. This in turn called into question the national will to alter attitudes that had once been employed to demonstrate egalitarianism but which now clearly signalled an ignorance of global economic realities. In short, was Australia going to be a full part of an increasingly global economy, or would it be content to slide further into a boondoggle economy of its own making? If it chose the former it would need to seek out new sources of wealth. One of these was the international finance industry itself; another, entrepreneurial development of Australian inventions for overseas markets; a third, tourism—to name but three. The success of the first two would not be at the threat of unrealistic attitudes in the blue-collar workforce in the way that basic extractive industries and agricultural products were in 1988. Australia, however, was not well placed to thrust itself into high-technology. After two hundred years of white settlement, Australians spent 9 per cent of their considerable federal taxes on insufficient defence, and just 9 per cent on education. On social security they spent 29 per cent. The next question thus became not whether priorities were wrong, but whether fundamental attitudes would change swiftly enough for the need for unproductive expenditures to reduce themselves and productive expenditures increase.

Norwich Park coal mine, Queensland. In the 1980s declining profits and restrictive work practices threaten the survival of our extractive industries. (Courtesy BHP–Utah Coal Limited)

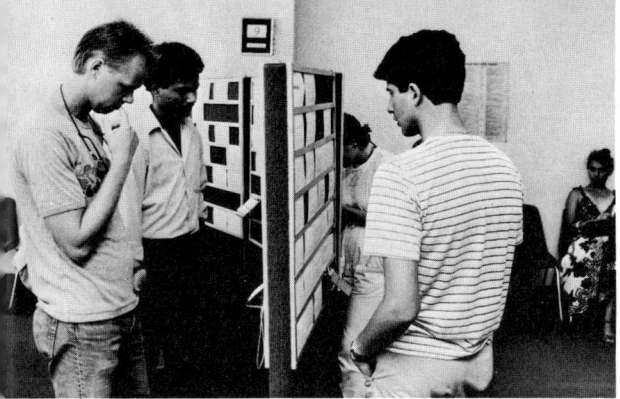

In the late 1980s the self-service board at the local CES is often the first port of call for unemployed school-leavers. (Courtesy Federal Department of Employment, Education and Training)

The fabric of Australia's most valuable institutions remained wholly intact: democratic, parliamentary institutions and the rule of the law. The essential economic and financial decisions would not tear the fabric of society. Nine decades ago, when the United States' immigration programme was at its peak and America was emerging as a powerhouse of production and human effort, Theodore Roosevelt said he wished to preach 'not the doctrine of ignoble ease, but the doctrine of the strenuous life'. After he became President he put it another way: 'The first requisite of a good citizen of this republic of ours is that he shall be able and willing to pull his weight.' Today, a former Australian Prime Minister, Malcolm Fraser, is remembered most of all in his public utterances for one which excited a great deal of derision from the mob: 'Life wasn't meant to be easy.' Professor Messel got it better when he quoted Henry Rosin. 'Decadence often looks better (in the short term) than what it is replacing. It takes the appearance of easing up which ends in giving up.'

As of the late 1980s, there was still time for Australia. But not a lot. As Messel said, 'When will Australians learn? Brawn stood this nation in good stead for its first two hundred years but it will be brains during next two hundred.'

Banana republics are not noted for their social cohesion.

It is to Australia's immense credit that throughout a period of declining economic fortunes and uncertainty for the future it has continued to encourage immigration, thus extending the population base. The natural increase in population fell to below zero in the 1980s, when the number of offspring produced by couples declined to about 1.8. Immigration would be needed not just to assist in the adjustment of native Australian attitudes, but also to keep the country from falling in on itself.

In the late 1980s there was considerable debate about not just the economy and what was perceived as a declining standard of living, but also about the quality of education (principally, the quality of schooling in State primary and secondary institutions) and about increasing poverty and a growing disparity in incomes between different social strata.

It will take some time before the quality of education debate is resolved. It is one of the most important in Australian history. For almost all of this century most Australians held scant regard for education, not much more for schooling — and did not know the difference, which is disturbing. If Professor Messel and many like him are correct, there will have to be profound changes in attitudes. 'She'll be right' and 'good enough' standards will have to yield to the pursuit of excellence: and that will go against the peculiar Australian definition of egalitarianism. A debate of nation-shaking proportions may therefore be in the offing if we are to avoid a slide of banana-like proportions. Some of the arguments mounted against change — and against excellence — at present suggest that cuckoos are flying over the wide brown land.

The debate about increasing poverty, and especially poverty as it affects children, also raises disturbing questions. At present the debate centres in part on wealth, particularly unearned wealth and tax evasion, which in turn leads to an animated debate about the need or otherwise for ordinary law-abiding citizens to carry an identity card when they know, and the Taxation Office knows, that they not only already pay their taxes, but pay more than they can afford, not least because of the need to prop up the shortfall in tax receipts caused by tax evaders. In the late 1980s there was a tangled debate about living standards that served only to confuse the fundamental issue, which was that for most Australians the material standard of living was falling. The confusion set in partly because of the number of unemployed in the lower-income groups. There is never a shortage of ideologues to harp on the disadvantages of these groups, especially when times are bad. The debate became heated, however, because of the vast increase in wealth of the richest people in the country, some of them with a net worth calculated in tens of millions of dollars, a few of whom paid less tax than an ordinary clerk. There was also a good deal of concern about corporate takeovers, some costing in excess of a billion dollars, that brought huge windfall profits to a few resourceful souls, but at what benefit to the community? These questions certainly needed to be answered. At the other end of the pay scale there were queries about when it would become obvious to more lower-income workers that their skills were inadequate for the times and their wages therefore incommensurate, too (driving employers to embrace the computer and other high-tech equipment with great speed). And it was not just the lot of lower-income earners that was precarious. For middle-income people, especially those attempting to establish a first home in the face of crippling interest rates, life was becoming intolerable in the big cities; initiative was being stultified by excessive income tax rates, and there was widespread feeling that at the national level political parties of all persuasions now paid only lip-service to qualities that had helped make Australia. The middle-

income earner, seeing surveys showing that at least a quarter of social security payments went to dole bludgers, double-dippers and people who were just plain indigent, felt that he was carrying more of the burden than he should have to bear.

The educated 'middles', for whom life was comfortable but never really secure, always put their children's future high on their list of priorities. Unless changes were forthcoming in Australian attitudes and economic performance, it seemed likely that some of these people would emigrate. Britain had suffered a brain drain in the 1960s in similar political and economic circumstances (when those leaving chose, in order of preference, the United States, Canada, New Zealand, and Australia).

The middle-income earners are usually the social cement in Western mixed economies. Australia had a difficult task attracting them in numbers. Ten years ago it would have been unthinkable that well-paid Australians would be talking of leaving. These are unhappy times.

For egalitarian-loving Australians, the current debates really come down to one debate: performance to meet the perceived needs of the third century of white settlement. There will be leaders and followers and those who are merely passive as the future unfolds. It is still an egalitarian country.

Australia, which a century ago was among the most affluent countries in the world, is, in 1988, barely in the top twenty. The incomes of Australian executives in 1988 are at precisely the same comparative level as workers: barely in the twenty top industrial nations. So in economic terms, the them-and-us argument should stop there. There may have to be a mild, hopefully not-too-prolonged prolonged hiccough while the country points higher, with tighter sails and strained sheets, and under a stricter, firmer helm. Better that than to beach. And the choice, after all, is still ours.

Further Reading

Blainey, Geoffrey, *The Tyranny of Distance*, rev.edn, MacMillan, Melbourne, 1982.

Borrie, W. D., and Packer D. R .G., *Italians and Germans in Australia: A Study of Assimilation*, Cheshire, Melbourne, 1954.

Berndt, R. M, and C. H., *The World of the First Australians*, Ure Smith, Sydney, 1977.

Bulletin, The Australian Family, Australian Consolidated Press, Sydney, 1976.

Calwell, A. A., *Be Just and Fear Not*, Rigby in association with Lloyd O'Neil, Adelaide, 1978.

Carboni, Raffaello, *The Eureka Stockade*, facsimile edition, Melbourne University Press, Melbourne, 1963.

Churchill, Winston S., *A History of the English-speaking Peoples*, Volume IV, *The Great Democracies*, Cassell, London, 1956.

Clark, C. M. H., *A History of Australia*, Volume IV, Melbourne University Press, Melbourne, 1978.

Cooke, Alistair, *Alistair Cooke's America*, Angus and Robertson, Sydney, 1974.

Crowley, Frank, ed., *A New History of Australia*, Heinemann, Melbourne, 1980.

Flood, Josephine, *Archaeology of the Dreamtime*, Collins, Sydney, 1983.

Game, Douglas M., *New South Wales and Victoria in 1885*

Hamilton, Pauline, *The Irish*, Thomas Nelson, Melbourne, 1978.

Hick, Arthur, *The Chinese in Australia*, Longmans, Melbourne, 1968.

Kearns, R. H. B., *Broken Hill, 1883-1893*, 2nd edn, Broken Hill Historical Society, Broken Hill, 1975.

Kiernan, Colin, *Calwell*, Thomas Nelson, Melbourne, 1977.

Lowenstein, Wendy, and Loh, Morag, *The Immigrants*, Penguin, Melbourne, 1978.

Manchester, William, *The Glory and the Dream*, Bantam Books, New York, 1975.

Manne, Robert, ed., *The New Conservatism in Australia*, Oxford University Press, Melbourne, 1982.

Place, Marian T., *Gold Down Under: The Story of the Australian Gold Rush*, Crowell-Collier Press.

Potts, E. Daniel, and Annette, *Young America and Australian Gold, Americans and the Gold Rush of the 1950s*, University of Queensland Press, St Lucia, 1974.

Price, Charles A., *German Settlers in South Australia*, Australian University Press, 1957.

Price, Charles A., *Greeks in Australia*, A.N.U. Press, Canberra, 1975.

Tay, Alice Erh-Soon, in collaboration with Connelly, Graeme, and Williams, Roger, *Teaching Human Rights*, Australian Government Publishing Service, Canberra, 1981.

Voight, Johannes H., ed., *New Beginnings: The Germans in New South Wales and Queensland*, Institute for Cultural Relations, Stuttgart, 1983.

Ward, Russel, *Australia*, Ure Smith, Sydney, 1975.

Index

Numbers in *italics* refer to an illustration

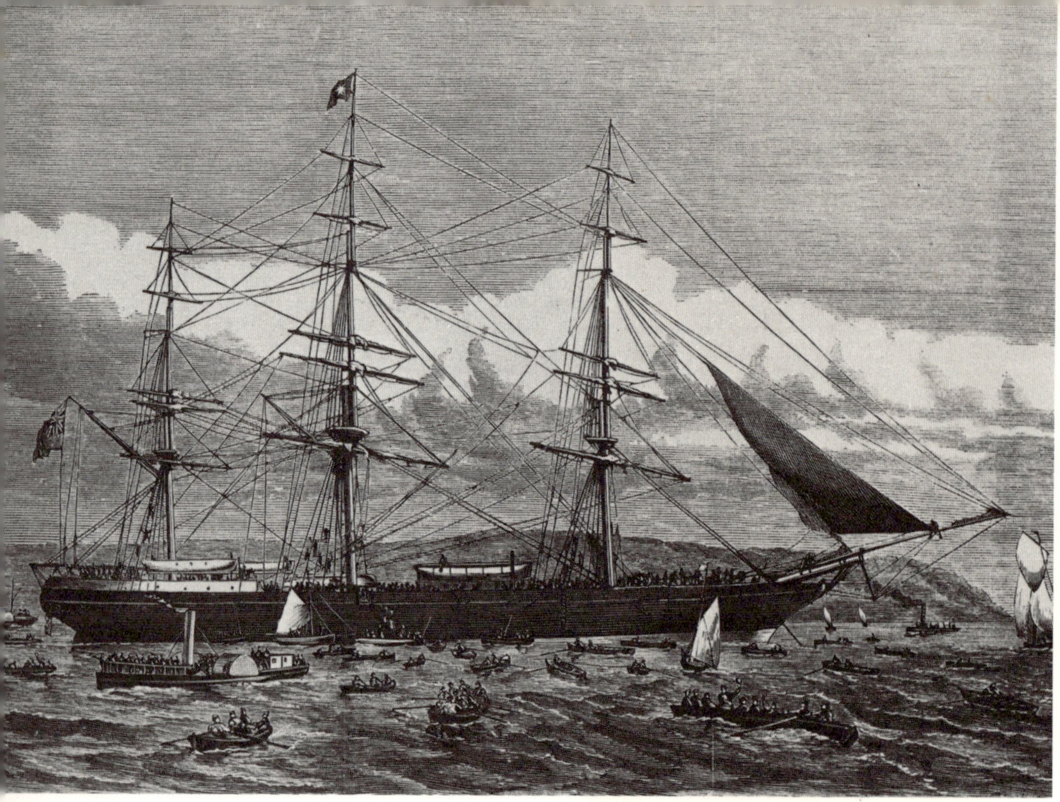

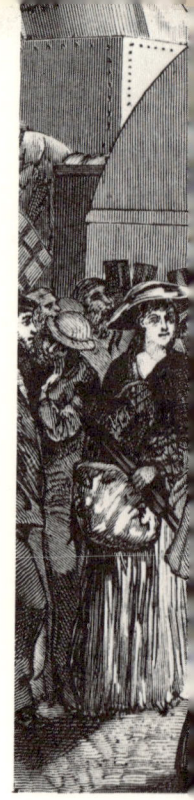

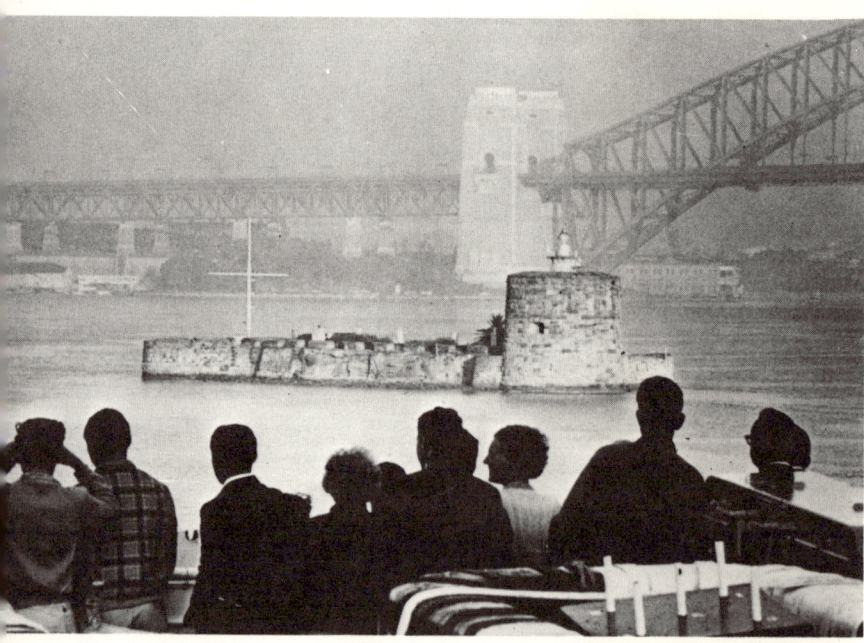

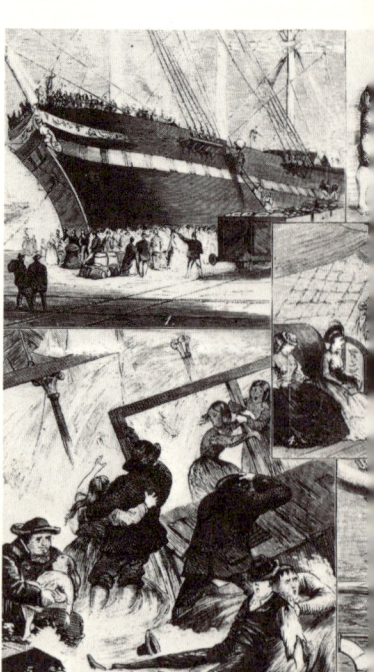

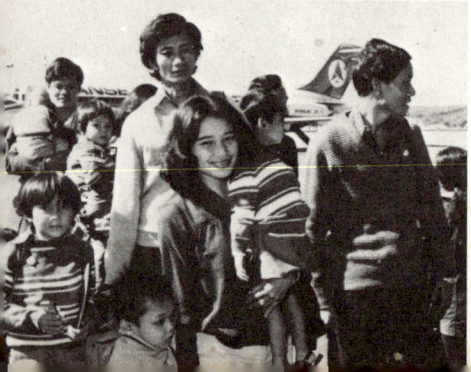

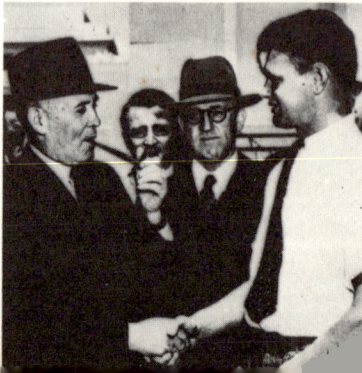

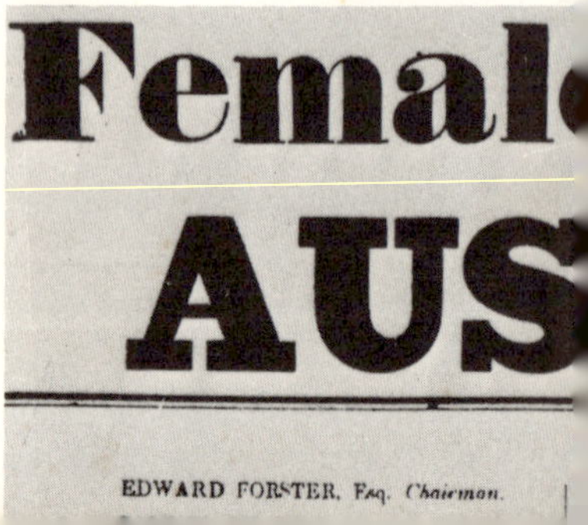

Femal

AUS

EDWARD FORSTER, Esq. Chairman.